Annotated Teacher's Edition

WRITE SOURCE

SkillsBook

EDITING AND PROOFREADING PRACTICE

a resource of student activities
to accompany
Write Source
Level 9

WRITE SOURCE.

GREAT SOURCE EDUCATION GROUP
a Houghton Mifflin Company
Wilmington, Massachusetts

A Few Words About the
Writers INC SkillsBook: Level 9

Before you begin . . .

The *SkillsBook* provides you with opportunities to practice the editing and proofreading skills presented in the *Write Source* text. The text contains guidelines, examples, and models to help you complete your work in the *SkillsBook*.

Each *SkillsBook* activity includes a brief introduction to the topic and refers you to the page numbers in the text for additional information and examples. The "Proofreading Activities" focus on punctuation and the mechanics of writing. The "Parts of Speech Activities" highlight each of the eight parts of speech. The "Sentences Activities" provide practice in sentence combining and in correcting common sentence problems.

The Extend

Most activities include an **Extend** at the end of the exercise. The purpose of the Extend is to provide ideas for follow-up work that will help you apply what you have learned to your own writing.

Authors: Pat Sebranek and Dave Kemper

Copyright © 2007 by Great Source Education Group, a division of Houghton Mifflin Company.
All rights reserved.

Permission is hereby granted to teachers who have purchased the **Write Source Teacher's Resource Package**, grade 9 (ISBN 978-0-669-53172-5), to photocopy in classroom quantities, for use by one teacher and his or her students only, the pages in this work that carry a copyright notice, provided each copy made shows the copyright notice. Such copies may not be sold, and further distribution is expressly prohibited. Teachers who have purchased only the *Write Source SkillsBook* (ISBN 978-0-669-53146-6) may not reproduce or transmit this work or portions thereof in any other form or by any other electronic or mechanical means, including any information storage or retrieval system, unless expressly permitted by federal copyright law or authorized in writing by Great Source Education Group. Address inquiries to Great Source Education Group, 181 Ballardvale Street, Wilmington, MA 01887.

Great Source and **Write Source** are registered trademarks of Houghton Mifflin Company.

Printed in the United States of America

International Standard Book Number: 978-0-669-53146-6 (student edition)
International Standard Book Number: 0-669-53146-4 (student edition)

1 2 3 4 5 6 7 8 9 10 POO 10 09 08 07 06

International Standard Book Number: 978-0-669-53150-3 (teacher's edition)
International Standard Book Number: 0-669-53150-2 (teacher's edition)

1 2 3 4 5 6 7 8 9 10 POO 10 09 08 07 06

CONTENTS

Proofreading Activities

Parts of Speech Activities

Nouns

Pronouns

Verbs

Adjectives & Adverbs

Prepositions, Conjunctions, & Interjections

Sentence Activities

Sentence Basics

Proofreading Activities

The activities in this section of your *SkillsBook* include sentences that need to be checked for punctuation, mechanics, or correct word choices. Most of the activities also include helpful textbook references. In addition, the **Extend** activities provide follow-up practice of certain skills.

Pretest: Punctuation

> **Place** periods, commas, and apostrophes where they are needed in the following paragraph.

1   I was new at school, but I wasn't alone. One-fourth of us were new

2   at school. We were ninth graders entering Betsy Ross High School for the

3   2005–2006 school year, but I was *really* new because I had just moved to

4   town from Portland, Oregon. I walked down the long, crowded hallways with

5   what I hoped looked like a calm expression, but my brain was turning a

6   million miles an hour. I was thinking to myself, "How am I going to fit

7   in?" I was thinking so hard that I somehow didn't see a huge, red-haired

8   guy with a buzz cut. He was a real mountain, and my head knocked into

9   his left shoulder.

> **Place** dashes, quotation marks, and underlining (for italics) in the following paragraphs.

1   "I—I'm sorry," I blurted. He rolled his eyes, shook his head, and strolled

2   down the hallway, completely ignoring me.

3   Well, maybe "fitting in" wasn't even possible among these giants; maybe

4   I should have just been praying that I wouldn't get crushed. Everyone

5   seemed to be at least four inches taller and sixty pounds heavier than I

6   was. "Man, oh man," I thought out loud. "How big do they grow kids

7   around here?" I felt like I was in the middle of a <u>Honey, I Shrunk the</u>

8   <u>Ninth Grader</u> movie.

Place semicolons, hyphens, and colons where they are needed in the following paragraphs.

1   To make myself feel better, I made a mental list of my talents; I

2   could touch my nose with the tip of my tongue; I could drink a glass of

3   water while standing on my head; and, as an encore, I could sing "The

4   Star-Spangled Banner" like Donald Duck. In the smarts department, I

5   knew I wasn't the dullest crayon in the box; (or) my grades were B's and C's.

6   Yikes! It was 7:44. I walked casually into the room; however, I

7   immediately looked at the front of the room. I didn't want to make eye

8   contact with any of the kids. I wasn't ready. I looked at the blackboard;

9   the teacher had written the following letter:

Add colons, commas, and quotation marks where they are needed in the following paragraphs.

1   Dear Students:

2   My name is Mrs. Bardurian. Look on your schedule, and if

3   you do not have "P1—English 9—Rm 195" printed on the first line,

4   you are in the wrong place.

5   If you are in the right place, get out a sheet of paper and

6   tell me about yourself. This is between you and me. Your goal is

7   very simple: Find your voice and use it.

8   Sincerely,

9   Mrs. Bardurian

10   I thought, "Find your voice and use it? Sure, if I can stop shaking long

11   enough to find my pen and paper, I'd be happy to look for my voice."

End Punctuation 1

The rules for end punctuation are very simple: (1) place a period at the end of a sentence that is a statement, (2) use a question mark if the sentence asks a question, and (3) use an exclamation point to express strong feelings. For more information about end punctuation, turn to 605.1, 605.4, and 606.1 in *Write Source*.

> **Place** periods, question marks, and exclamation points where they are needed in the following paragraphs. Also supply the necessary capital letters.

1   why do more and more Americans take vitamin supplements they

2   hope to stop cancer, heart disease, stress, hair loss, and other ailments

3   Americans spend $3.3 billion annually on megavitamins (large-dose

4   vitamins) examples include vitamin C with rose hips, an A-and-D combo,

5   vitamin B complex, selenium, beta-carotene, and zinc daily vitamin

6   supplements are not considered megavitamins

7   some people use a computer program to determine which megavitamins

8   to take they enter their age, sex, and other personal factors into the

9   computer program it calculates their vitamin needs other people follow

10 the guidelines listed in the government's figures for Recommended Dietary

11 Allowances (RDA)

12 what do the experts say about taking megadoses some say megadoses,

13 in certain cases, are beneficial others argue that the benefits of megadose

14 supplements remain largely unproven one thing that everyone agrees upon

15 is that people should try to meet as many of their vitamin and mineral

16 needs as they can by eating a healthful diet megavitamins are not

17 substitutes for good food

Extend: Choose a subject that interests you. Write a paragraph (or two) like the ones above. Leave out all end punctuation and capitalization. Exchange paragraphs with a classmate and add the necessary punctuation and capital letters. Check each other's work.

Writers INC 487.1, 488.1, and 488.4

End Punctuation 2

End punctuation marks—periods, question marks, and exclamation points—help readers move easily through your writing. For more information about end punctuation, turn to 605.1, 605.4, and 606.1 in *Write Source*.

> **Place** periods, question marks, and exclamation points where they are needed in the following paragraphs. Also put in capital letters where needed.

1   many people visit Nashville, Tennessee. the wooded, rolling hills and

2   the Cumberland River make Nashville a beautiful city. most people come

3   to hear country music, though, and to see their favorite musicians.

4   Nashville has long been known as the world's capital of country music.

5   can you believe it has more than 90 record labels, about 175 recording

6   studios, and 290 music publishing companies? some musicians have their

7   own labels. for example, John Prine started Oh Boy! Records, and Steve

8   Earle started E-Squared Records here.

9   Tourist attractions abound in Nashville. the Grand Ole Opry Museum

10   draws thousands of people. shrines dedicated to famous artists like Hank

11   Williams and Minnie Pearl are also popular tourist spots. tour buses cruise

12   past the current and former homes of stars.

13   visitors to Nashville keep their eyes open for a glimpse of a country

14   music star. one of the best places to bump into a star is Music Row. you

15   are also likely to see famous singers in an ordinary place like the post

16   office, a mall, or a grocery store. would you like to visit Nashville and

17   meet a superstar? what a thrill that would be!

Extend: Write a short piece about a place you have visited or a place you would like to visit. Include sentences that require periods, question marks, and exclamation points, but don't put in the end punctuation or beginning capitalization. Exchange papers with a classmate and add the correct punctuation and capital letters.

Review: End Punctuation

> **Place** periods, question marks, and exclamation points where they are needed in the following article. Also put in capital letters at the beginnings of sentences.

1   The Iditarod, Alaska's famous race for sled-dog teams, begins in

2   Anchorage and ends in Nome. *T*hat's a distance of 1,150 miles. *T*he first leg

3   of the race winds through birch forests, crosses frozen lakes, and follows

4   winding rivers. *S*oon the trail begins to rise, climbing into the mountains.

5   *T*he sleds cross over the range at Rainy Pass, almost 3,200 feet high. *T*o the

6   north of Rainy Pass, the mushers can see Mount McKinley. *D*id you know

7   that this is the tallest peak in North America? *I*t is a magnificent sight!

8   *O*nce out of the mountains, the trail drops into the Interior—a part of

9   Alaska that Jack London called "the land of icy silence." *T*emperatures in

10 the –30's are common there. *I*n fact, the mercury may drop to –50°F or

11 even –70°F. (or) *H*ow would you survive such cold temperatures? *S*ome of the

12 time, the trail follows the Kuskokwim River. *R*olling hills and a few spruce

13 trees alternate with tundra until the trail reaches the Yukon.

14 *I*n the Yukon, the icy silence gives way to howling winds. *T*hese north

15 winds can exceed 50 miles an hour. *N*ext the trail rises and crosses a low

16 pass in the Nulato Hills before dropping down to the coast. *M*any miles

17 of the Iditarod trail lie on the frozen Bering Sea. *T*he hard grains of snow

18 scrape the dogs' feet, and shifting ice can hide trail markers.

19 The early camaraderie of the race has given way to competition. *T*he

20 winner—from more than 70 teams—takes home nearly $100,000 in cash

21 and prizes. *C*an you believe these sled-dog teams spend as long as two

22 weeks on the trail in subzero weather?

Commas Between Independent Clauses

A comma precedes a coordinating conjunction that links two independent clauses. The coordinating conjunctions are *and, but, or, nor, for, so,* and *yet.* You can add variety to your writing by combining independent clauses with a coordinating conjunction and a comma to form compound sentences. Turn to 608.1 in *Write Source.*

> **Study** the sentences below. Place commas before the coordinating conjunctions that join two independent clauses.

1. The pretzel was probably invented in the seventh century by monks, and the children they taught loved the treat.

2. The first pretzels were soft and doughy, but today we also eat and enjoy the hard, crispy ones.

3. Hard pretzels may have been invented by a baker who fell asleep, so the pretzels he had in the oven baked to a crisp.

4. Water, flour, and yeast are the basic ingredients, and often a sprinkling of salt is added to the outside.

5. A long time ago, some brides and grooms used pretzels in their wedding ceremonies, for it was believed that pretzels brought good luck.

6. The most popular pretzel shape is the twist, but pretzels also come shaped as nuggets, sticks, and rings.

7. A one-ounce serving of pretzels contains approximately 110 calories, yet it contains almost no fat.

8. Pretzels continue to be a favorite snack for Americans, but potato chips and tortilla chips are still more popular.

9. Do you like pretzels, or do you prefer chips?

Extend: Take a closer look at the coordinating conjunctions that connect the independent clauses in the sentences above. Then, on your own paper, write a sentence for each of the seven coordinating conjunctions listed at the top of this page.

Commas in a Series &
Commas to Separate Adjectives 1

Commas separate words, phrases, or clauses in a series. A series must always contain at least three items. Turn to 610.2 in *Write Source* for more information.

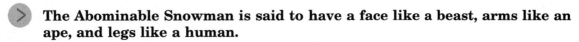 **The Abominable Snowman is said to have a face like a beast, arms like an ape, and legs like a human.**

Commas also separate two or more adjectives that equally modify a noun. Turn to 608.2 in *Write Source* for more information.

 **Legend has it that the Abominable Snowman is a sly, elusive beast that resembles a huge ape.**

> **Insert** commas where needed to separate items in a series in the sentences below. Also insert commas between adjectives that equally modify a noun.

1. This huge, hairy beast is said to walk upright like a human.

2. Reports say such creatures live on the high, frigid peaks of the Himalaya Mountains, as well as in remote parts of China, Russia, and Canada.

3. According to some stories, the Abominable Snowman comes down from the mountains to attack villagers, goats, and sheep.

4. Since the 1890s, explorers have discovered strange footprints in the cold, hard snow.

5. There is no direct, reliable evidence that the Abominable Snowman exists.

6. This creature is called a yeti, the Abominable Snowman, or Big Foot.

7. Eric Shipton—a respected, well-known explorer—took pictures of gigantic tracks in the snow near Mount Everest in 1951.

8. Many explorers went to Mount Everest to see for themselves, but none glimpsed the gigantic, hairy, apelike creature.

Extend: Write a paragraph about a beast from a book, movie, or your imagination. Use adjectives that equally describe some of your nouns. Use the two tests to determine if your adjectives are equal. (Turn to "A Closer Look" under 608.2 in *Write Source*.)

Commas in a Series &
Commas to Separate Adjectives 2

Commas separate words, phrases, or clauses in a series. A series must always contain at least three items. Turn to 610.2 in *Write Source* for more information.

> **Stock cars have special engines, doors, and windshields.**

Commas also separate two or more adjectives that equally modify a noun. Turn to 608.2.

> **Stock-car racing is a popular, well-respected spectator sport.**

Insert commas below where needed to separate items in a series. Also insert commas between equal adjectives. Two sentences do not need commas inserted.

1. Stock cars are altered to increase their speed, power, and endurance.

2. Only American-made, late-model sedans can be raced.

3. Stock cars start out as ordinary passenger cars, the kind that car dealers have in stock.

4. Drivers sit in the usual upright position, but they are strapped in with heavy, reinforced seat belts and shoulder harnesses.

5. Stock cars are heavier than formula-one cars, Indy cars, or drag-racing cars.

6. Stock cars have reinforced steel bodies and special fiberglass spoilers.

7. The well-tuned, high-power engine in a stock car pushes it to speeds of 190 miles per hour.

8. Race-car drivers prefer fast, smooth tracks.

9. Some races are held on super speedways that have wide, high-banked corners where cars can make the curves at nearly 175 miles per hour.

10. Racing flags signal drivers to drive with caution, to make a pit stop, to let a faster car pass, or to stop.

Extend: Compose four sentences about cars. In two of the sentences, use equal adjectives; in the other two, include a series of items. Use commas correctly.

Commas After Introductory Phrases and Clauses 1

A comma is used to separate an introductory word group from the rest of the sentence. Introductory word groups are usually clauses or phrases. Turn to 608.1 and 610.3 in *Write Source*. Read the examples carefully. By reading a sentence, you will sense when the introductory material ends and the main idea begins, but it is wise to learn to identify phrases and clauses. Turn to 742.1 and 744.

> **Read** each sentence below and insert commas where needed. Three sentences do not need commas.

1. During a long winter with lots of snow, there is no place on earth like the National Elk Refuge in Jackson Hole, Wyoming.

2. From November through April, the National Elk Refuge is home to about 7,500 elk.

3. When deep snow makes it hard to find food, elk come to this animal preserve.

4. The elk are fed alfalfa pellets to supplement their diet of natural grasses.

5. Prior to the establishment of the refuge, many elk starved.

6. Once the elk are safely within the refuge, they quickly learn to follow the feed wagon.

7. On their way to the National Elk Refuge, the elk face many hunters.

8. Each year hunters kill thousands of elk.

9. Some people feel that hunting is necessary because the ever-growing herd gets too large to be supported by the refuge throughout the winter.

10. Sitting in an open sleigh pulled by a Belgian draft horse, visitors can take a 45-minute ride among the elk herd.

11. At the visitor center, you can view a slide show, a film, and a number of exhibits about the National Elk Refuge.

Extend: Write three to five sentences using introductory word groups. Tell about visiting a relative's home or about a place you and your friends often visit. Underline your introductory word groups and add commas as needed.

Commas After Introductory Phrases and Clauses 2

Introductory word groups, which are usually phrases and clauses, are set off from the rest of the sentence with a comma. Read a sentence carefully. You will sense when the introductory material ends and the main sentence begins. Place a comma at that point. Turn to 608.1 and 610.3 in *Write Source*. Read the examples, pausing at the commas. For information about clauses and phrases, turn to 742.1 and 744.

Place commas after the introductory word groups in the following sentences.

1. Located at the Pacific Ocean's entrance to San Francisco Bay, the Golden Gate Bridge spans 4,600 feet of water.

2. Since the bridge spans the Golden Gate Strait, it is called the Golden Gate Bridge.

3. Expecting the bridge to be gold-colored, many visitors are surprised to see the bright red-orange color.

4. When selecting the orange color, Irving F. Morrow, consulting architect, said he thought the color would enhance the area's natural beauty.

5. As early as 1872, some people started talking about spanning the Golden Gate Strait, especially a railroad entrepreneur named Charles Crocker.

6. Nearly 50 years later, the idea of a bridge was revived by James Wilkins, newspaper editor for the *San Francisco Call Bulletin*.

7. Early in the summer of 1921, a cost estimate—$27 million—was presented by Joseph Strauss, an architect.

8. As is often the case when something new is proposed, many people, including other architects, criticized the plans.

9. Fortunately for the people of San Francisco, the bridge has been used with very few problems for 75 years.

Extend: Write three sentences about another famous structure in the United States. Introduce each sentence with a clause or a phrase and, of course, a comma.

Review: Commas 1

> **Place** commas in each sentence. Write the rule that explains the use of each comma.

1. Abstract art is a kind of painting‸drawing‸and sculpture that flourished in the twentieth century.

RULE: *Use commas to separate items in a series.*

2. While traditional painters filled their canvases with objects that a viewer could easily identify‸abstract artists were likely to fill their canvases with shapes, swirls, and thick paint.

RULE: *Use a comma to separate introductory information.*

3. Pablo Picasso‸Alexander Calder‸and Henry Moore all created abstract art.

RULE: *Use commas to separate items in a series.*

4. These bold‸innovative artists rejected many of the rules and customs of earlier art.

RULE: *Use a comma to separate adjectives that equally modify a noun.*

5. To provide contrast in their art‸some abstract painters left portions of their canvases unpainted.

RULE: *Use a comma to separate introductory information.*

6. Jackson Pollock—a free-thinking‸energetic painter—dripped and splattered paint onto a canvas spread on the floor.

RULE: *Use a comma to separate adjectives that equally modify a noun.*

7. This seemingly carefree‸undisciplined painting bewildered critics‸viewers‸ and some artists.

RULE: *Use a comma to separate adjectives that equally modify a noun.*

RULE: *Use a comma to separate items in a series.*

8. The critics began to call Pollock and others like him "action painters"‸ but most people today simply refer to them as abstract painters.

RULE: *Use a comma before a coordinating conjunction to separate two independent clauses.*

Commas to Set Off Explanatory Words & Appositives

Commas are used to enclose an explanatory word or phrase. Turn to 612.2 in *Write Source*.

> **The Dixie Chicks, a crossover musical group, attracts both country and pop music fans.**

A specific kind of explanatory word or phrase called an *appositive* identifies or renames a preceding noun or pronoun. Turn to 610.1 in *Write Source*.

> **This group has two backup singers to support the lead vocalist, Natalie Maines.**

Place commas where they are needed below.

1. Two sisters, Emily (Erwin) Robison and Martie (Erwin) Seidel, started The Dixie Chicks.

2. They joined with Natalie Maines, a pop vocalist, in 1995.

3. The sisters, Emily and Martie, grew up studying classical music.

4. They also played two stringed instruments, the fiddle and the banjo.

5. Two political candidates, Ross Perot and George W. Bush, asked them to play at fund-raisers.

6. These two men, Perot and Bush, were fans of The Dixie Chicks when they were still a little-known group.

7. Emily Robison and Martie Seidel, the two sisters, recorded three independent albums before forming the current group.

8. The two young musicians, well trained in the basics of music, once sang on street corners.

9. The Dixie Chicks, a crossover trio, have won two Country Music Awards, an American Music Award, and three Grammy nominations.

10. This group, headquartered in Nashville, attracts both country and pop music fans.

Extend: Write three to five sentences about a music group you like. Use explanatory phrases and appositives. Be sure to punctuate your sentences correctly.

Commas with Nonrestrictive Phrases and Clauses 1

Nonrestrictive phrases and clauses, sometimes called unnecessary or nonessential word groups, can be removed from a sentence without changing its basic meaning. Always place commas around nonrestrictive phrases and clauses. Study the examples below and compare nonrestrictive clauses with restrictive clauses. Turn to 612.2 in *Write Source* for more information.

> **Auroras, *which are displays of light in the sky*, can be seen only at night.**
> (nonrestrictive clause)

> **Lights that dance in the night sky are called auroras.**
> (restrictive clause.)

> **Auroras, *flickering lights in the evening sky*, inspire poets.**
> (nonrestrictive phrase)

> **People wanting to see auroras must wait patiently since auroras do not occur every night.** (restrictive phrase)

Place commas around the nonrestrictive phrases and clauses in the sentences below. (Some sentences have no nonrestrictive phrases or clauses.)

1. Auroras, electrically charged particles from the sun, illuminate the sky.

2. The electrically charged particles that travel toward the earth's magnetic field collide with atoms and molecules in our atmosphere.

3. Auroras, which are called *aurora borealis* in the northern hemisphere and *aurora australis* in the southern hemisphere, move and flicker.

4. People in far northern or southern regions often see the auroras.

5. The colors that are most often seen in auroras are green, red, and purple.

6. Auroras, which sometimes extend for thousands of miles across the sky, occur from 60 to 620 miles above the earth.

7. The solar wind, which carries a continuous stream of electrically charged particles from the sun, is the source of auroras.

8. Violent eruptions on the sun increase the number of electrically charged particles that travel into the earth's atmosphere on the solar wind.

Extend: Write four sentences about the sun and the stars. In the first two, include a nonrestrictive phrase or clause. In the other two, include a restrictive phrase or clause.

Commas with Nonrestrictive Phrases and Clauses 2

Nonrestrictive phrases and clauses, also called nonessential or unnecessary word groups, can be removed from a sentence without changing the basic meaning of the sentence. Nonrestrictive phrases and clauses are set off with commas. Turn to 612.2 in *Write Source*.

> **Place** commas around the nonrestrictive phrases and nonrestrictive clauses in the following sentences.

1. New York City subways, which run both above and below ground, are ridden by more than a million people each day.

2. Subway commuters, riding back and forth on the subways daily, become accustomed to many inconveniences.

3. Standing room only, which is a major inconvenience, occurs regularly during rush hours.

4. Pushing and shoving to board the train is an everyday happening.

5. Dank stations, whose walls drip dirty water, are common sights.

6. Blaring stereos, which are played at brain-piercing volumes, provide background traveling music.

7. Some unhappy commuters, who are trying to make using the subway system more pleasant, have convinced officials to put poems where there would normally be advertising.

8. Buses, which are the alternative to subways, lack some of the negatives associated with train travel.

9. Bus riders, who don't seem to be as aggressive as train riders, may be more mellow than train passengers because bus travel is less stressful.

Extend: Write three to five sentences about public transportation that contain an unnecessary phrase or clause (nonrestrictive). Make sure to set off the nonessential material with commas.

Commas with Nonrestrictive Phrases and Clauses 3

Commas are used to set off nonrestrictive phrases and clauses from the rest of a sentence. Nonrestrictive phrases and clauses can be removed from a sentence without changing the basic meaning. Turn to 612.2 in *Write Source* for more information.

> **Place commas around the nonrestrictive phrases and clauses in the sentences below.**

1. Nolan Ryan, who could throw a fastball close to 100 mph, says many of his 5,714 strikeouts came on the curveball.

2. Ryan's coach said, "The hitter would see the curveball that was coming at his head and freeze."

3. The curveball, which is also called the "hook," the "snapdragon," or "Uncle Charlie," has long been a part of American baseball.

4. Little League pitchers who dream about throwing their first curveball may never get the chance.

5. The curveball, that famous all-American pitch, has helped pitchers become heroes, but the curveball is going out of style.

6. The curveball is being replaced by other breaking pitches, which have names like "slider," "sinker," "split-finger fastball," and "knuckleball."

7. Today most pitching staffs in the major leagues have only one pitcher who throws a curveball.

8. The slider, which is easier to learn and easier to control, has become the preferred breaking pitch.

9. Pitchers who learn to throw a slider lose their ability to throw a curveball because each pitch uses a different set of muscles.

10. Steve Stone, who won 25 games and a Cy Young Award in 1980, admits he overused the curveball and never pitched as well again.

11. When pitchers throw a curveball, which sometimes starts high and drops low, they must control both the direction and the distance.

12. If young people, whose muscles and bones aren't fully developed, throw breaking balls, they risk forming certain types of calcium deposits.

13. Young people who practice pitching should wait until they are older before throwing curveballs and other breaking balls.

14. The advice that comes from professional pitchers is to wait until age 15 or 16.

Write answers to the following questions.

---

1. Which words introduce the nonrestrictive and restrictive clauses in sentences 11–14 above? (List them.) _which, whose, who, that_

2. What are these words called? Turn to 535.2 and the chart on page 535 in *Write Source*. _relative pronouns_

3. Why is this name a good choice? _These words "relate" a phrase or clause to a noun. They either add an aside about that noun (nonrestrictive) or narrow the definition of the noun (restrictive)._

Extend: Explore the sentences in this exercise. (You may wish to work with a partner.) Find and underline with one line the nouns that the nonrestrictive and restrictive clauses modify. Then find the special pronouns at the beginning of each clause and underline them with two lines. Turn to page 701 for information about nouns and 704.1 and 706.2 in *Write Source* for information about relative pronouns.

Other Uses for Commas

Commas are used to set off dates (turn to 614.1 in *Write Source*); to set off items in addresses (turn to 614.2); to show hundreds, thousands, millions, and so forth in numbers (turn to 614.3); to set off the exact words of a speaker (turn to 616.1); and to separate a noun of direct address from the rest of the sentence (turn to 616.4).

> **Place** commas where they are needed in the following sentences.

1   Oprah Winfrey said, "Lots of people want to ride with you in the limo,

2   but what you want is someone who will take the bus with you when the

3   limo breaks down."

4   "I think," Bill said, "that Oprah Winfrey made a wise statement."

5   "Yes," Sarah replied, "and when I'm famous, you can ride in my limo."

6   "How are you going to become famous, Sarah?" Bill asked.

7   "When I live at 1600 Pennsylvania Avenue NW, Washington, D.C.

8   20006, I'll be famous," Sarah said.

9   "So you plan to marry the president of the United States," said Bill.

10 "No," Sarah said, "I plan to be the president of the United States.

11 Or maybe I'll be a pilot and fly an SR-71 reconnaissance plane for 3,000

12 miles at an altitude of 80,000 feet," Sarah replied.

13 Bill said, "Maybe you can become famous by making people laugh."

14 "Good idea," Sarah replied. "I'll be a famous emcee on a game show.

15 How's this: Do you know which state produces more than 784,000 tons of

16 alfalfa annually?"

17 "No, Sarah, and no normal person would," Bill answered.

18 "Well, Bill, if you want to be a contestant on my game show, you'll

19 have to know things like that."

Extend: Write a dialogue between yourself and someone you know about being famous. Use quotation marks and commas correctly. Exchange papers with a classmate and check each other's work.

Writers INC 492.1, 492.2, 493.1, 492.3, and 493.2

Review: Commas 2

> Place **commas where they are needed in the sentences below.**

1   The story of Paricutin, a volcano formed recently in Mexico, is an

2   interesting one. On February 20, 1943, a local farmer, who had stopped to

3   rest while plowing, was startled by a column of smoke rising from the

4   middle of his cornfield. Assuming that he must have somehow started a

5   fire, he rushed to put it out. He thought the smoke was coming from an

6   open fire, but he found that the smoke was coming from a small hole in

7   the ground. The farmer thought for a moment about how to put out this

8   underground fire, and then he put a stone over the hole. He checked the

9   hole later and was alarmed by the increase of dense black smoke. The

10   farmer recalled feeling the ground tremble, and he noted that the soil

11   felt hotter than ever under his bare feet. He hurried to town to tell the

12   mayor and to bring some people back with him.

13   When they arrived some time later, they saw black smoke billowing

14   from a hole 30 feet deep. The first explosion came that very night, when

15   a thick column of smoke, cinders, and ash shot upward for more than a

16   mile. Explosions followed every few seconds; rocks, which varied in size

17   from that of a walnut to that of a house, were hurled into the air. Lava

18   began to flow two days later, and the volcano continued to erupt for many

19   months. The lava flows and ash showers obliterated surrounding farms,

20   forests, and villages. Paricutin, the first town destroyed by the eruption,

21   gave up its very name to the new "mountain of fire."

Semicolons to Join Independent Clauses

Semicolons can join independent clauses in two ways, as shown in the examples below. Look for more information at 618.1 and 618.2 in *Write Source*.

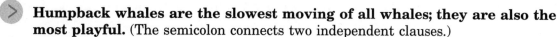 **Humpback whales are the slowest moving of all whales; they are also the most playful.** (The semicolon connects two independent clauses.)

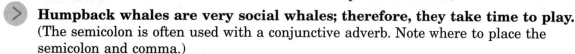 **Humpback whales are very social whales; therefore, they take time to play.** (The semicolon is often used with a conjunctive adverb. Note where to place the semicolon and comma.)

> **Place** semicolons where needed in the following sentences. Add commas where necessary.

1. Humpback whales migrate every year; they spend the summers in cool northern waters.

2. These whales can't smell, taste, or see well; however, they have excellent hearing.

3. The calves drink up to two gallons of milk per feeding; they may feed 48 times per day.

4. At this rate they gain up to 200 pounds a day; moreover, they grow nearly a foot a week.

5. Humpback whales are disappearing at an alarming rate; their population has dwindled from 102,000 to 8,700.

6. Humpbacks lift their bodies almost completely out of the water; this is called "breaching."

7. Humpbacks also point their heads down toward the ocean's floor and make sounds; this is called "singing."

8. No one knows why whales sing; perhaps it is one of the ways they communicate.

9. Many whale species "sing"; still, the best singers are the humpbacks.

10. Humpbacks are called "floaters"; they float when they die.

11. Humpbacks breathe in through two nostrils called blowholes, then, they exhale a spout of water vapor.

12. Humpbacks hit the water with their huge flippers, the sound can be heard for miles and miles.

13. Humpbacks breach and slap water, therefore, people love to watch them.

14. Adult humpbacks weigh about 40 tons, however, they can leap about 50 feet into the air.

Write sentences according to the directions listed below.

Answers will vary.

1. Join two clauses with a conjunctive adverb. Use a semicolon and a comma correctly.

   Janie and Cleo went to a movie; meanwhile, Luis stayed home to

   work on his history paper.

2. Join two independent clauses. Use a semicolon.

   Reading the assignment is easy; writing answers to the questions

   is difficult.

3. Join two clauses with the conjunctive adverb *however.* Use a semicolon and a comma correctly.

   I like to play word games; however, I play "Go Fish" with my little

   sister.

4. Join two independent clauses using a semicolon correctly.

   Summer is too short; winter is too long.

5. Join two clauses with the conjunctive adverb *instead.* Use a semicolon and a comma correctly.

   Don't wait for me to finish eating; instead, go pick up your sister

   from soccer practice.

Colons

Colons introduce lists, follow business letter salutations, and more. Turn to 620.1–620.6 in *Write Source* for more details and examples.

> **Place** colons where they are needed in the following letter written by students to the school's nutritionist.

1 Dear Mrs. Myers:

2 We eat lunch between 11:25 and 12:05 and have a number of problems

3 during our lunch period. We would certainly appreciate it if someone would

4 refill the ketchup bottles or at least ask the people who eat from 10:45 to

5 11:25 to use less ketchup. Also, we feel there are too many rules: take only

6 what you can eat, eat fast, bus your tray, recycle, keep your voice down,

7 and do not run.

8 A real problem occurred one day last week: we ran out of lowfat milk.

9 We would like to recommend the following: have plenty of lowfat milk, put

10 salad on the menu every day, and check the ketchup supply.

11 We have four dislikes: tuna casserole, peanut-butter pancakes, rye bread,

12 and prune bars. Thank you for encouraging us to eat less of those

13 ingredients, salt and sugar. However, we would like to make one

14 suggestion: more frozen yogurt!

15 Sincerely,

16 Jake Barnes, Ward McClain, and Stan Torres

Extend: Practice using colons. Write a letter to the person who plans the lunch menu in your school or to someone who does something for you. If you include complaints, you should also include compliments.

Review: Semicolons & Colons

> **Circle** the correct punctuation mark for each of the following rules. Then complete the examples to illustrate each rule.

Answers will vary.

1. RULE: Use a *semicolon /* (colon) to introduce a list.

 I love the following fruits: apricots, apples, cherries, and raspberries.

2. RULE: Use a *semicolon /* (colon) to emphasize an idea or a word.

 If there is one food I don't want to eat, it's this: okra.

3. RULE: Use a (semicolon) */ colon* to join two independent clauses when no linking word is present.

 Some people don't eat enough potassium; they could increase their intake by eating bananas.

4. RULE: Use a (semicolon) */ colon* before a conjunctive adverb when it joins two independent clauses.

 I enjoy going to the movies; however, I wish the tickets were less expensive.

5. RULE: Use a *semicolon /* (colon) after the salutation of a business letter.

 Dear Justice Ginsberg:

 Please explain the court's latest decision for me.

6. RULE: Use a *semicolon /* (colon) between the parts of a number indicating time.

 At 8:30 p.m.

7. RULE: Use a (semicolon) */ colon* to separate groups of words that already contain commas.

 I packed a toothbrush, deodorant, and shampoo; blue jeans, hiking boots, and jacket; fishhooks, poles, and a net.

Hyphens 1

Use hyphens in the following situations: to form compound words, to join a capital letter to a noun or participle, to write out numbers from twenty-one to ninety-nine, and to join two or more words that serve as a single adjective.

> **My great-grandmother wrote a diary.**
> (*Great-grandmother* is a compound word. Turn to 624.1.)

> **She never wore a T-shirt!**
> (*T-shirt* is a word made by joining a capital letter to a noun. Turn to 624.4.)

> **She was twenty-two when she came to America.**
> (*Twenty-two* is a compound number. Turn to 626.1.)

> **She and Grandpa, both Swedish-speaking immigrants, opened a bakery.**
> (*Swedish-speaking* serves as a single adjective. Turn to 624.3.)

Insert hyphens where needed in the following sentences.

1. I was a smart six-year-old when I first met my great-grandmother.

2. I remember it was a not-so-pleasant day, even though she had made some delicious orange juice.

3. My forty-two-year-old father had lost his job the day before.

4. He was working in a fast-growing business.

5. He said, "I don't have state-of-the-art computer skills, and I need them."

6. My great-grandmother said, "You can make a U-turn in your career and go back and learn them."

7. "I'm too old. I'm an over-the-hill student," he said.

8. My great-grandmother laughed and said, "Yesterday I replaced my out-of-date printer with a laserjet model."

9. My great-uncles and great-aunts laughed.

10. My father smiled and said, "Well, maybe forty-two isn't over the hill."

Extend: Write four sentences about one or two of your relatives. In each sentence, include a different type of hyphenated word as explained in the previous exercise.

Writers INC 495.4, 495.5, 496.1, and 497.3

Hyphens 2

A hyphen is often used to make new words beginning with the prefixes *self-*, *ex-*, *all-*, *great-*, and *half-*. A hyphen is used to join numbers indicating the life span of a person and the score in a contest or vote. A hyphen is also used to separate a word at the end of a line of print.

> **Self-respect is necessary before you can respect others.**
> (A hyphen is usually used to form a word with the prefix *self-*. Turn to 624.2.)

> **Eleanor Roosevelt (1884–1962) was a writer and U.N. delegate.**
> (A hyphen is used to join numbers indicating a life span. Turn to 626.3.)

> **The city council voted 34–8 for a new public library.**
> (A hyphen is used to join numbers in a vote or a game score. Turn to 626.3.)

Use hyphens to show where the following words can be divided at the end of a line. Note that some should *not* be divided. Refer to 626.5 in *Write Source* and use a dictionary.

1. winning **win-ning**
2. sometimes **some-times**
3. wouldn't **wouldn't**
4. central **cen-tral**
5. drama **drama**

6. brother-in-law **brother-in-law**
7. loosen **loos-en**
8. delicate **deli-cate**
9. equal **equal**
10. among **among**

Place hyphens where needed in the following sentences.

1. Franklin Delano Roosevelt (1882-1945) was our thirty-second president.
2. During his presidential terms (1933-1945), World War II began.
3. In Roosevelt's first election, he was elected by an electoral vote of 472-59.
4. Who was president during the post-depression years?
5. Franklin Delano Roosevelt was an ex-governor of which state?
6. His cousin Theodore Roosevelt (1858-1919) was the twenty-sixth president.
7. Congress voted unanimously 82-0 to enter World War II.
8. The support was anything but half-hearted.

Dashes

Turn to 640.1–640.5 in *Write Source* for five ways that dashes are used. Read the explanations and study the examples.

> **Insert** dashes where they can be used in the following sentences.

1. Ernest Shackleton had one goal and one goal only to travel all the way across Antarctica.

2. Shackleton's ship, *Endurance* an appropriate name as it turned out was caught in heavy ice and crushed in October 1915.

3. Fleeing their crushed ship, drifting on an ice floe for five months, surviving on penguin meat and seal blubber this is what Shackleton and his crew endured.

4. Eventually they found Elephant Island a tiny, windswept place hundreds of miles from civilization.

5. Ernest Shackleton amazed the world in fact, stunned the world when he and his entire crew survived.

6. "You aren't you can't be Ernest Shackleton," said the man at the whaling station on the island of South Georgia when Shackleton arrived.

7. "I am Ernest Shackleton. You thought me doomed? You thought me and my men" He could say no more.

8. Not one member of the crew died not in the entire 22-month ordeal of cold, hunger, and danger.

9. Six years later, in 1922, Shackleton died of a heart attack on South Georgia Island en route to where else? Antarctica.

Extend: Imagine you are Shackleton or one of his crew. Write about your ordeal. Use dashes in as many ways as you can—enclose a sudden break, show faltering speech, emphasize a word or phrase or clause, show missing words or letters, or set off an introductory series.

Review: Hyphens & Dashes

Place hyphens where needed in the following words and phrases.

1. great-great-grandfather
2. cheese-filled celery sticks
3. four-tenths
4. four-, six-, and eight-inch widths
5. score of 11-9
6. ex-mayor
7. big-boned athlete
8. twelve-year-old boy
9. great-aunt
10. all-conference team
11. six-year-old girl
12. U-turn
13. 1908-2000 C.E.
14. T-shirt
15. vote of 321-642
16. mid-May
17. state-of-the-art technology
18. self-respect
19. nine-tenths
20. all-out effort

Place dashes in the following sentences.

1. In 1941, when the United States entered World War II, the U.S. Army Air Corps—later the United States Air Force—needed pilots desperately.

2. Chuck Yeager—only 19 years old—joined the corps.

3. His talent for flying seemed to be a natural gift—a gift that made him an incredible pilot and true ace.

4. Then, on his ninth mission, tragedy struck—the American ace was shot down.

5. He parachuted to the ground—wounded, bleeding, no feeling in his legs—somewhere in German-occupied France.

6. Incredibly, he escaped all the way across the Pyrenees Mountains into Spain—he even helped the French Underground along the way!

28

Apostrophes in Contractions & to Show Omitted Letters or Numbers

An apostrophe is used to make a contraction *(can't)*. An apostrophe is also used to show that letters have been omitted in words or numbers that are spelled as they are actually spoken *(good mornin'* and *class of '99)*. Turn to 628.1 in *Write Source.*

> **Place** apostrophes where needed in the following sentences.

1. "Don't you like asparagus?" Mom asked.

2. "I can't eat that green stuff," my little brother grumbled.

3. "Well, then I'll serve you purple vegetables," said Mom.

4. "You can't find any purple vegetables," said my little brother.

5. "Isn't eggplant purple?" my mother said to me.

6. "I'm not sure. Maybe it is, but he won't eat it," I responded.

7. "No, I suppose you're right," Mom sighed.

8. She added, "I've tried everything to get him to eat vegetables."

9. "I'll see if I can influence him," said Dad.

10. "If you eat your vegetables, I'll take you for a ride in the '57 Chevy convertible," said Dad.

11. Dad had restored this classic car during the summer of '04.

12. It wasn't his first car, but it was his favorite.

13. He'd always driven it in the homecoming parade with a banner that said "Class of '80" on it.

14. "I sure don't like vegetables, but I sure like ridin' in that car," said my little brother.

15. "Well then, we'll go right after you eat your vegetables," said Dad.

Extend: Write a conversation between yourself and a cousin (or friend) about something you did together when you were little. Include some contractions in the conversation, and challenge yourself by including some numbers and words that need apostrophes because they are spelled as they are actually spoken.

Apostrophes to Form Possessives 1

Use apostrophes to show possession. Turn to 628.2–630.2 in *Write Source*.

> **Grandpa's hair, Chicago's wind, men's room, woman's office**
> (When a word—either singular or plural—does not end in *s*, add an apostrophe and *s* to form the possessive.)

> **players' uniforms, lawyers' arguments, dogs' collars**
> (When the plural of a word ends in *s*, add only an apostrophe.)

> **great-grandma's diary, somebody's house, son-in-law's job**
> (In compound words, make only the last word possessive.)

Place apostrophes in each of the following phrases to show possession.

1. Jane's prom dress **2.** the town's climate **3.** men's clothes **4.** daughter-in-law's teeth (singular) **5.** the women's exercises **6.** that girl's opinions **7.** all the girls' clothes (plural) **8.** children's rooms **9.** love's blessings **10.** someone's beauty **11.** the cows' path (plural) **12.** baby's crib **13.** babies' rattles **14.** a month's work **15.** the journey's itinerary **16.** stairs' carpeting (plural) **17.** a year's passage **18.** a headlight's beam **19.** the headlights' beams **20.** people's judgments

Write sentences containing possessives using the instructions below.

1. Show that one boy owns two dogs, and both dogs need a bath.

Jack's dogs, Sam and Beauty, need a bath.

2. Show that both of your great-grandmothers kept diaries.

I have my great-grandmothers' diaries.

3. Show that a hat, a pair of shoes, and a coat left on the porch belong to John.

John's hat, pair of shoes, and coat were left on the porch.

4. Show that apples and chicken are favorite foods for both Ceema and Anna.

Ceema's and Anna's favorite foods are apples and chicken.

Extend: Write instructions for three sentences that contain possessives (as in the exercise above). Exchange instructions with a classmate and complete each other's exercise.

Apostrophes to Form Possessives 2

> **Brown, Jenkins, and Smith's law firm**
> (When possession is shared by more than one noun, use the possessive form for the last noun in the series. Turn to 628.4.)

> **Brown's, Jenkins', and Smith's law firms**
> (When possession is individual, make each noun possessive. Turn to 628.2.)

> **boss's salary, Kiss's album** (When a singular noun ends in *s*, there are two ways to form the possessive. If the word has one syllable and can be pronounced easily, add an apostrophe and *s*. Turn to 628.3.)

> **Ramses' tomb** (The other way is to add only an apostrophe. This is recommended when adding an *s* to the word would make the pronunciation difficult—*Moses's staff* or *Sophocles's plays*. Adding only an apostrophe is preferred for words of more than one syllable. Turn to 628.3.)

Place an apostrophe and s where needed to form possessives in the following phrases.

1. Dad and Mom's horse **2.** Molly, Polly, and Mom's vacation **3.** George's and Sam's lunches **4.** the lion's and the horse's manes **5.** our town's and their town's festivals **6.** Jane and Sal's dog **7.** the car's and the truck's headlights **8.** the boy's and the girl's chairs **9.** Moss's elephants **10.** Adam and Lois's address

Write the plural, as well as the singular and plural possessives, for the words below.

	Plural	Possessive Singular	Possessive Plural
1. child	children	child's	children's
2. man	men	man's	men's
3. mother-in-law	mothers-in-law	mother-in-law's	mothers-in-law's
4. lady	ladies	lady's	ladies'
5. woman	women	woman's	women's

Extend: Write sentences for the five words listed above. Practice forming both singular and plural possessives.

Writers INC 499.4 and 498.3

Review: Apostrophes

> **Write** the possessive form or the contraction for the underlined word or words.

Tena/Dorothy's	**1.** Tena and Dorothy grandfather is 82 years old.
Dean's/Marvin's	**2.** Dean and Marvin sleeping bags got wet in the rain.
commander in chief's	**3.** The commander in chief desk was always neat.
players'	**4.** The basketball players uniforms were scattered over the floor. (*Players* is plural.)
Haven't	**5.** Havent you finished the test?
sister-in-law's	**6.** My sister-in-law hobby is swimming.
children's	**7.** The children band is playing at 7 P.M.
cities'	**8.** The cities mayors all met in Washington.
Isn't	**9.** Isnt there a better answer to the problem?
Felipe's	**10.** Felipe textbooks are lying in the cafeteria.
principal's	**11.** The principal disciplinary actions were fair.
girl's	**12.** Both of the girls baseball uniforms are hanging up in the bus. (One girl owns both uniforms.)
Harlen/Charlie/Ron's	**13.** Harlen, Charlie, and Ron raft floated away.
Laura's/Linda's/Latonya's	**14.** Laura, Linda, and Latonya fathers will help them.
class's	**15.** The class future is uncertain.
coach's	**16.** The coach whistle was plugged.
men's	**17.** The mens meeting is finished.
can't	**18.** He mumbled, "I cant remember."
don't	**19.** Why dont you write some more sentences?
can't	**20.** I cant think of anything more to write.

Quotation Marks with Titles & Special Words

Quotation marks are used to punctuate titles of songs, short poems, short stories, lectures, episodes from radio and television programs, chapters of books, unpublished works, and articles from newspapers, magazines, and encyclopedias. Quotation marks are also used to point out a word that is being used in a special way or to indicate that a word is slang. Turn to 634.2–634.3 in *Write Source*.

> **I heard Samuel Barber's "Knoxville: Summer of 1915" last night.**
> (Use quotation marks around the name of a song.)

> **I think it could be called a musical "essay."**
> (Quotation marks point out a word used in a special way.)

> **It's a "cool" piece of music about a hot summer night.**
> (Quotation marks indicate that a word is slang.)

Write sentences below using quotation marks correctly.

Answers will vary.

1. Include the title of your favorite song in a sentence.

"Row, Row, Row Your Boat" is my favorite camp song.

2. Use a short story title in a sentence.

Have you read O'Henry's story "The Gift of the Magi"?

3. Use the title of a nursery rhyme in a sentence.

"Baa Baa Black Sheep" is a nursery rhyme I know.

4. Use one of your favorite slang words in a sentence.

All I can say about my burnt toast is, "Rats!"

5. Make up the title of a magazine article and use it in a sentence.

Read the magazine article "Common Sense Is on the Rise."

6. Write a sentence using one of these words—*guide, green, honesty*— in a special way.

I couldn't see any "green" around her gills; in fact, I didn't know she even had gills.

Extend: List five titles that would require quotation marks. Ask a classmate to write sentences using the titles and to use quotation marks correctly. Check each other's work.

Quotation Marks with Dialogue

Use quotation marks to punctuate dialogue. Study the examples below to see where other punctuation marks are placed. Turn to 632.1, 632.2, and 634.1 in *Write Source*.

> **"Today we are going down into the Grand Canyon," said Mr. Thomas. "It will be a grand journey."** (A period follows *Thomas* because the preceding quotation is a complete sentence. Notice where the quotation marks are placed.)

> **"Well," said Jane, "that's impossible!"**
> (A comma follows *Jane* because what follows completes the sentence.)

> **"How can we go down into the Grand Canyon while sitting in our desks?" Tony asked.** (The question mark is placed inside the quotation marks because the quotation is a question.)

Punctuate the following sentences with quotation marks, commas, and end marks.

1. "We will pretend," said Mr. Thomas. "When I put a slide on the screen, you ask questions and make comments as if you are really there."

2. "I recognize that place," whispered Colleen.

3. "What river is that?" asked Mark.

4. "I know," said Jack. "It's the Colorado River. It has carved its way down through all that rock making the Grand Canyon."

5. "I don't believe it," said Miesha. "How long has it been carving the rocks?"

6. "Well, you'll find this hard to believe, too, Miesha, but the Colorado River has been carving the Grand Canyon for about 6 million years," replied Mr. Thomas.

7. "How wide is the canyon?" asked Roger.

8. Mr. Thomas replied, "It's at least 10 miles across."

9. "How deep is the Grand Canyon?" asked Roger. "I'm getting dizzy up here."

10. "I know! It's a mile deep!" laughed Jane.

Extend: Imagine you are visiting a famous place with your friends or family. Write a dialogue about it, punctuating it carefully. If you choose a place you have actually seen, it will be easier to include interesting facts. Otherwise, use an encyclopedia to learn more about a place you would like to visit someday.

Quotation Marks & Diagonals

Place quotation marks where needed in the following student essay, "Poets Are Different." When placing diagonals (slash marks) in the poem, which is included in the essay, remember that each new line of poetry begins with a capital letter. Turn to 632.1–634.2 and 638.4 in *Write Source*.

1   One of my teachers said, "All I can say is that poets are different from

2   the people I live with and different from me. And, yet, I honor them in

3   some way . . . some way that I can't quite label." That's how I feel, too.

4   Sometimes my mind says *yes* when I read a poet's words. This

5   happens when I read these lines by Thoreau: "A lake is the landscape's

6   most beautiful and expressive feature. It is earth's eye . . . ."

7   Sometimes my mind says *no!* For instance, whenever I read this line

8   by Walt Whitman, the "no" happens: "the delicious singing of the mother."

9   How can singing be delicious? Grilled steak and a baked potato (loaded)

10 are delicious.

11   Have you ever read "Victory in the Eye of the Beholder"? It's about a

12 baseball game. The poet writes the lines like this:

13   Their hero swings/And the ball rockets away./Fielders run/Calling,

14   "I've got it, I've got it!"/But the fans know better/And the ball sails

15   on./Like a giant wave,/They stand to their feet once more/Yelling his

16   name/As he stomps on homeplate/And bows deeply to the crowd./The

17   game is theirs.

Extend: Create three to five sentences about song lyrics that demonstrate the rules for using quotation marks. Turn to 632.1–634.2 in *Write Source*.

Italics (Underlining) & Quotation Marks

Italics is a printer's term for a style of type that is slightly slanted. In material that is handwritten or typed on a machine that cannot print in italics, each word or letter that should be in italics is underlined.

Italics (underlining) is used to indicate the titles of magazines, newspapers, pamphlets, books, plays, films, radio and television programs, book-length poems, ballets, operas, lengthy musical compositions, record albums, CD's, legal cases, the names of ships and aircraft, scientific names, and foreign words. Turn to 636.1–636.4 in *Write Source*.

Quotation marks are also used to indicate some titles. Turn to 634.3 and 636.1–636.2 in *Write Source* to help you decide when to use quotation marks and when to underline or use italics.

> **Write** a **Q** in the blank if quotation marks should be used or a **U** if underlining should be used.

U	**1.** Titanic *(ship)*		U	**13.** Los Angeles Times *(newspaper)*
Q	**2.** America the Beautiful *(song)*		Q	**14.** short story
U	**3.** an opera		Q	**15.** radio episode
U	**4.** Reader's Digest *(magazine)*		Q	**16.** The Raven *(poem)*
U	**5.** radio program		U	**17.** yucca brevifolia *(Joshua tree)*
U	**6.** Jurassic Park *(novel)*		U	**18.** pamphlet
Q	**7.** magazine article		Q	**19.** Jack and Jill *(nursery rhyme)*
Q	**8.** television episode		U	**20.** Macbeth *(play)*
U	**9.** television program		U	**21.** movie
U	**10.** Brown vs. Brown *(legal case)*		U	**22.** CD
U	**11.** bonjour *(French)*		Q	**23.** chapter in a book
U	**12.** Writers INC *(book)*		Q	**24.** speech or lecture title

Extend: Write a paragraph that includes the titles of your favorite movie, TV show, song, CD, magazine, novel, and short story. Try to include at least seven titles. Use quotation marks and italics (underlining) correctly.

Review: Quotation Marks & Italics (Underlining)

> **Add** quotation marks where they are needed. Underline words that should be in italics.

1. "Please pass the toast," she said.

2. "The Conqueror Worm" is a poem written by Edgar Allan Poe.

3. A Literary History of the United States is a fine resource book.

4. "Why did you play my Rock 'n' Roll Racing?" Justin asked.

5. "I had to," said Benji, "because mine was broken."

6. He likes "clunky" because the word is onomatopoeic.

7. Formal writing does not use phrases like "that's really decent" or "far out."

8. Gone with the Wind is an exciting film that is still respected today.

9. The Greek word Kalimera means the same as the German words guten tag.

10. The city paper Daily Tribune carried an article entitled "Foot Lake Will Be Cleaned."

11. "Did you study Faulkner's short story 'Two Soldiers'?" she asked.

12. "No," he replied, "we read Thurber's short story 'Catbird Seat' last week."

13. "Does your group sing 'America the Beautiful'?" she asked.

14. Aunt Midge calls Billy her Kleines Kind.

15. I'm glad I didn't sail on the Titanic.

16. The Great Gatsby is F. Scott Fitzgerald's most popular novel.

17. Dave Matthews has recorded many CD's, but Crash is probably his best.

18. "That's fine," she said, "but who wants to read his essay 'The Incredible Journey'?"

19. "I do," Jordan replied.

38

Punctuation in Math

Look at the following examples of how to use punctuation in math.

> **There are more than 200 billion stars in the known universe—that's more than 200,000,000,000.** (The commas separate a series of numbers in order to distinguish hundreds, thousands, millions, and so on. Turn to 614.3.)

> **The sun, also a star, is only one-thousandth the diameter of the largest stars.** (The hyphen is used between elements of a fraction. Turn to 626.1.)

> **Astronomers measure the distance to stars in light-years. One light-year is 5.88 trillion miles.** (The period is used as a decimal point. Turn to 605.3.)

> **Other than the sun, the nearest star is 4.3 light-years (25 trillion miles) away.** (Parentheses are used to enclose supplementary information. See 638.1.)

> **Stars are 3/4 hydrogen and almost 1/4 helium.** (The diagonal forms a fraction.)

Insert the correct punctuation in the following sentences.

1. Red stars are about 5,000° F (2,800° C), but blue stars can be up to 50,000° F (28,000° C).

2. A yellowish star, like our sun, is only one-fifth the temperature of a blue star.

3. Supergiants, the largest of the stars, have diameters that are more than 1,000 times larger than the sun's diameter.

4. White dwarfs are only 1/100 the size of the sun.

5. Some white dwarfs are only 5,200 miles (8,700 kilometers) in diameter.

6. Star clusters are groups of 10,000 to 1,000,000 densely packed stars.

7. In some clusters, stars can be less than one-hundredth of a light-year (5,880,000,000 miles) away from each other.

8. Absolute magnitude is a star's brightness if the star were 32.6 (32 and six-tenths) light-years from the earth.

Extend: Write several sentences about what you are studying in math, science, accounting, or some other course in which numbers are often used. Use as many math punctuation marks as you can.

Other Forms of Punctuation 1

> **Review** the following uses of punctuation. Then write another example that uses the punctuation correctly.

Answers will vary.

1. I had just come home from school and reached into the mailbox . . . but there was nothing there. (The ellipsis indicates a pause. Turn to 642.3.)

Panic hit as Gary realized he could be totally lost . . . then he

heard someone walking up behind him.

2. I went home at four o'clock (?) before going to practice. (The question mark shows uncertainty. Turn to 606.2.)

I think my dental appointment is at 3:30 P.M. (?) on Thursday

afternoon.

3. It must have been my little brother (who else could it be?) who took my coat. (This question mark is used for a short question within parentheses. See 606.3.)

Maria claimed to have the flu (was I suspicious?) on the day of

the exam.

4. Cal Ripken, Jr., is one of the best baseball players in the world. (Commas enclose the title "Jr." following the surname. See 614.4.)

Martin Luther King, Jr., has a national day that honors his life.

5. Yeah, I think there's room for another person to come to the concert. (This comma sets off an interjection. Turn to 616.2.)

Wow, I got the last ticket!

Extend: Write a conversation between yourself and a friend about going to a party. Try to use as many of the different punctuation marks in this exercise as you can.

Other Forms of Punctuation 2

> **Review** the following examples of punctuation. Then write another example that uses the punctuation correctly.

Answers will vary.

1. Mr. Smith, I need another day to finish the assignment because my computer crashed last night. (The comma separates the noun of address, *Mr. Smith*. See 616.4.)

Dad, I'm sorry I forgot to carry out the recycling bins this

morning.

2. We call him Dr. Hendrick because he has a Ph.D. in English literature (*Dr.* and *Ph.D.* require periods because they are abbreviations. See 614.4.)

My aunt got her Ph.D. in counseling from Texas A & M, so now

we call her Dr. Denise.

3. Would you please hand me the five-, seven-, and nine-sixteenths sockets. (The hyphen is used in a series of two or more words that have a common element that is omitted until the last term. See 626.2.)

I couldn't decide if I wanted three-, four-, or five-by-six-inch note

cards.

4. I opened the door slowly and saw who it was waiting in my room—my best friend, Jaime. (The dash is used to emphasize *my best friend, Jaime*. Turn to 640.5.)

Heather really didn't expect to get what she wanted for her

birthday, but she did—a horse.

5. Our basketball team is the crème de la crème. No one is going to beat us this year. (The underlining indicates a phrase of foreign words. See 636.4.)

My mom always says C'est la vie instead of "That's life."

Extend: Write five sentences requiring each of the types of punctuation above; however, don't punctuate your sentences. Exchange papers. Check each other's work.

Pretest: Capitalization

> **Cross** out incorrect capitalization. If the word should be capitalized, write the letter above it. If the word should not be capitalized, do not write anything.

1. When the winds come rolling in over the ~~b~~lack ~~r~~ock ~~d~~esert near ~~r~~eno, ~~n~~evada,
   (B R D R N)

   land "sailors" jump on their three-wheeled "boats" and catch a wild ride.

2. Until recently, ~~b~~lack ~~r~~ock's playa, or salt flats, was a place where few have
   (B R)

   visited. It's been called the "vacant heart of the ~~w~~est."
   (W)

3. ~~b~~ack in the 1800s, ~~m~~ormons and other ~~R~~eligious ~~G~~roups crossed this dangerous
   (B   M)

   wasteland looking for a place to worship ~~g~~od.
   (G)

4. ~~i~~n 1849, they were followed by the forty-niners—the gold seekers, not the ~~s~~an
   (I)   (S)

   ~~f~~rancisco ~~F~~ootball ~~T~~eam.
   (F)

5. Shortly after the ~~c~~alifornia gold rush, the ~~w~~estern Pacific ~~r~~ailroad built a track
   (C)   (W)   (R)

   across the playa, making it easier for others to follow.

6. It was mainly ~~c~~hinese, ~~i~~rish, and ~~a~~frican ~~a~~merican labor that built the railroad.
   (C   I   A   A)

7. However, when the laborers did not put down roots in the area, their ~~m~~andarin,
   (M)

   ~~g~~aelic, and ~~s~~wahili languages disappeared.
   (G   S)

8. Several ~~D~~ecades went by before someone discovered that the ~~D~~esert was a

   perfect training ground for World ~~w~~ar II aviators.
   (W)

9. Because of its remote location and vast, flat expanses, the playa was chosen as

   the site of the first ~~S~~upersonic ~~L~~and speed record.

10. On ~~w~~ednesday, ~~o~~ctober 15, 1997, ~~a~~ndy ~~g~~reen and his ~~b~~ritish jet-propelled car,
    (W   O   A   G   B)

    the ~~t~~hrust ~~ssc~~, broke the ~~S~~ound ~~B~~arrier.
    (T   SSC)

11. ~~l~~ight fixtures were knocked off the ceilings in the town of ~~g~~erlach, five miles
    (L)   (G)

    away.

12. Rocket clubs, such as *A*ero-*P*ac, like the wide-open spaces to launch their hand-built rockets.

13. The *FAA* (*F*ederal *A*viation *A*dministration) granted the clubs launch clearance to 100,000 feet.

14. The *U*tah *R*ocket *C*lub launches rockets in this desert.

15. The cost of launching rockets is shared by the ¢lub.

16. The local justice of the peace, *P*hil *T*homas, said festivals and speed records do not reflect the true rural *N*evada.

17. The desert there is an environment where hardworking people call their ¢hevy, *F*ord, or *D*odge pickups "*A*unt Betsy" or "*F*ather *M*ulligan."

18. It is a place where *D*emocrats and *R*epublicans gather on dusty ¢treet corners to argue ₽olitics alongside ₤nvironmentalists and ₣armers.

19. With all the recent activity, the *U.S.* *B*ureau of *L*and *M*anagement has been working hard to manage the fragile ecology of the playa area.

Capitalization 1

One of the keys to correct capitalization is remembering to capitalize all proper nouns and proper adjectives. Review 648.1 in *Write Source*.

> **Cross out** incorrect capitalization and write the correct letter above it.

1. T
   ~~t~~he legendary track star J~~j~~esse O~~o~~wens was born on S~~s~~eptember 12, 1913, in the
   O   A
   rural town of ~~o~~akville, ~~a~~labama.

2. B
   ~~b~~oils, fevers, chest colds, and pneumonia plagued his childhood, but with hard
   C   R   J
   work and help from friends like ~~c~~oach ~~r~~iley, ~~j~~esse blossomed.

3. T O
   ~~t~~he ~~o~~wens family was poor; J~~j~~esse's father was a sharecropper and his granddad
   was a former slave.

4. M   C   E
   ~~m~~eat was served only on special occasions or holidays like ~~c~~hristmas and ~~e~~aster.

5. J   G   A   B
   ~~j~~esse's parents held a powerful belief in ~~g~~od. ~~a~~s devout ~~b~~aptists, they helped
   B   S
   their children memorize a different ~~b~~ible verse each ~~s~~unday.

6. I   A   A   N
   ~~i~~n 1922, the entire family, including ~~a~~unt ~~a~~ddie, moved to the ~~n~~orth so that
   J   H
   ~~j~~esse's father, ~~h~~enry, could get a job in the steel mills.

7. J   E   M   D   L
   ~~j~~esse's mother, ~~e~~mma, thought that living north of the ~~m~~ason-~~d~~ixon ~~l~~ine would
   help the children get a better education.

8. I   S   J C   A
   ~~i~~n the ~~s~~outh, ~~j~~im ~~c~~row laws created separate schools that segregated ~~a~~frican
   A
   ~~a~~merican children from white children.

9. O   B   E   S   O   J   C   O
   ~~o~~n his first day at ~~b~~olton ~~e~~lementary ~~s~~chool in ~~o~~hio, ~~j~~ames ~~c~~leveland ~~o~~wens
   received the nickname that stuck with him for the rest of his life.

10. A
    ~~a~~ teacher thought the young boy said his name was "J~~j~~esse" when he had, in fact,
    J C
    shyly answered "~~j~~.~~c~~."

Extend: Write three to five sentences about a famous athlete, but don't capitalize the **proper nouns or proper adjectives.** Exchange your paper with a classmate and correct each other's capitalization.

Capitalization 2

Continue to explore specific uses of capitalization. Turn to *Write Source* 648.1–652.5.

> **Cross out** incorrect capitalization and write the correct letter above it.

1. J̶esse O̶wens always struggled with school, especially with E̶nglish and social studies, because of his illnesses and lack of early education.

2. J̶esse's winning personality and friendly nature helped him become student council president and captain of the basketball team at F̶airmount J̶unior H̶igh.

3. I̶n college, J̶esse O̶wens was called the "B̶uckeye B̶ullet" from O̶hio S̶tate U̶niversity.

4. I̶t took only 45 minutes for J̶esse to smash three world records and tie a fourth during a track and field meet in A̶nn A̶rbor, M̶ichigan.

5. I̶n 1936, J̶esse and the U̶.S̶. O̶lympic track team sailed to E̶urope from N̶ew Y̶ork on a luxury steamship, the S̶.S̶. M̶anhattan.

6. J̶esse won four gold medals in the O̶lympic G̶ames in B̶erlin, G̶ermany.

7. A̶merica was in the midst of the G̶reat D̶epression, and A̶mericans were looking for a hero.

8. T̶hey found one in the N̶ational C̶ollegiate A̶thletic A̶ssociation (N̶C̶A̶A̶) track star, J̶esse O̶wens.

9. L̶ater he received the C̶ongressional M̶edal of F̶reedom for his work with underprivileged youth.

10. J̶esse O̶wens is remembered today for his O̶lympic medals, his N̶C̶A̶A̶ records, and his dedication to youth.

Extend: Write five sentences that illustrate capitalization rules 650.2 through 650.6 in *Write Source.*

Capitalization 3

Explore specific uses of capitalization. Turn to 648.1–652.5 in *Write Source*.

> **Cross out** incorrect capitalization and write the correct letter above it.

1. The great artist ~~n~~orman ~~r~~ockwell was born in ~~n~~ew ~~y~~ork ~~c~~ity in 1894.

2. ~~a~~t age 15, ~~r~~ockwell enrolled at the ~~n~~ational ~~a~~cademy ~~s~~chool.

3. ~~l~~ater that year, he was asked to design his first works of art—~~c~~hristmas cards.

4. By the age of 20, ~~r~~ockwell had become art editor for *~~b~~oys' ~~l~~ife* magazine.

5. During ~~w~~orld ~~w~~ar I, ~~r~~ockwell was stationed in ~~c~~harleston, ~~s~~outh ~~c~~arolina, but he

    continued to draw.

6. Much of his art dealt with his ideal of ~~a~~merican patriotism and his love of

    small town ~~a~~merica.

7. One of his pictures, called "~~a~~ ~~f~~amily ~~t~~ree," appeared on the cover of *~~t~~he ~~s~~aturday

    ~~e~~vening ~~p~~ost* in ~~o~~ctober 1959.

8. It humorously traces the ancestors of the "typical" ~~u~~.~~s~~. family.

9. The picture shows how most ~~a~~mericans represent not one but many

    nationalities and religions.

10. The limbs on the tree branch backward from the 1950s through the ~~r~~oaring

    ~~t~~wenties.

11. Ironically, the 1920s flapper has a ~~p~~rotestant minister for a father.

12. The branches continue downward through the ~~w~~ild ~~w~~est of the late 1800s.

13. A cowboy's parents are a grizzled prospector and a beautiful ~~n~~avajo princess.

14. The grandparents are ~~y~~ankee and ~~c~~onfederate soldiers, split during the ~~c~~ivil

    ~~w~~ar.

Extend: Write five sentences that illustrate capitalization rules 508.6 through 509.4 in *Write Source*.

Review: Capitalization

> **Cross out** incorrect capitalization and write the correct letter above it.

1. ~~i~~In the movie ~~s~~*sister* ~~a~~*act 2*, ~~w~~whoopi ~~g~~goldberg plays ~~d~~deloris, a ~~l~~las ~~v~~vegas lounge singer.

2. ~~s~~she is brought to the ~~w~~west ~~c~~coast by friends who are nuns.

3. ~~d~~deloris is asked to once again become ~~s~~sister ~~m~~mary ~~c~~clarence, the school's music teacher, and help keep their ~~c~~catholic school open.

4. ~~i~~if the school closes, the racially mixed neighborhood of ~~l~~latino, ~~a~~african ~~a~~american, and ~~a~~anglo residents will be without a school.

5. ~~t~~the sisters are upset because there will never be another ~~c~~christmas pageant, ~~m~~may crowning, or ~~j~~june graduation at ~~s~~st. ~~f~~francis ~~h~~high ~~s~~school.

6. ~~t~~the film's bad guy is the principal, ~~m~~mr. ~~c~~crisp, who wants to take an early retirement.

7. ~~f~~father ~~w~~wolfgang is the school chef whose "wurst" meal is his best. (~~h~~he can cook only ~~g~~german sausage.)

8. ~~t~~the ~~l~~latin teacher, ~~f~~father ~~t~~thomas, is concerned; the mathematics teacher, ~~f~~father ~~i~~ignatius, is hopeful. ~~o~~or is it the other way around?

9. ~~s~~sister ~~m~~mary ~~c~~clarence knows the value of the old saying: "~~g~~god helps those who help themselves."

10. ~~s~~sister ~~m~~mary ~~c~~clarence and her newly inspired students win a contest by performing a combination of gospel and rap music while using ~~a~~american sign language. (~~i~~in the process, they save the school.)

Pretest: Numbers & Abbreviations

> **Write** the correct form (numerals, words, or letters) above the underlined numbers and abbreviations below. If the form is correct, write **C** above it.

1. *Two* **C**
2 of the <u>seven</u> contestants won a ribbon.

2. *1,079*
All <u>one thousand seventy nine</u> of the students took the ACT test today.

3. *250*
The population of that little village is <u>two hundred and fifty</u>.

4. *90*
The average temperature is <u>ninety</u> °F.

5. *3*
Did you put in <u>three</u> tbsp. of butter?

6. *23 to 4*
He was elected by a vote of <u>twenty-three to four</u>.

7. *C*
Remember your appointment is at <u>4:00 p.m.</u>

8. *four*
Did you say my appointment was at <u>4</u> o'clock?

9. *5* *7*
I am <u>five</u>' and <u>seven</u>" tall.

10. *C*
He kept <u>8 percent</u> of the funds for himself.

11. *ten 12-foot*
Did you order <u>10 12-foot</u> subs for the party?

12. *35 mph* *25 mph*
He was driving <u>thirty-five mph</u> in a <u>25 miles per hour</u> zone.

> **Write** abbreviations for the following words.

1. California _____*CA*_____ or _____*Calif.*_____

8. and so forth _____*etc.*_____

2. Washington _____*WA*_____ or _____*Wash.*_____

9. apartment _____*apt.*_____

3. Street _____*St.*_____

10. teaspoon _____*tsp*_____

4. quart _____*qt*_____

11. gallon _____*gal.*_____

5. as soon as possible _____*ASAP*_____

12. gross national product _____*GNP*_____

6. liter _____*l*_____

13. kilogram _____*kg*_____

7. Incorporated _____*Inc.*_____

14. public relations _____*PR*_____

Numbers

In most contemporary writing, numbers below 10 are *usually* spelled out. Review 658.1–658.4 in *Write Source* before you do this exercise.

> **Underline** the misused numbers and write the correct versions above them.

1. *One-half* *one-half* 1/2 salsa and 1/2 fusion, Latin music draws from many different Hispanic and Caribbean cultures.

2. Latinos currently make up more than fourteen *14* percent of the United States population, and that number will increase to 15% *percent* by the year twenty twenty *2020*.

3. With several million listeners, *La Mega* ninety-seven point nine *97.9*, a New York radio station, is one of the most popular Hispanic stations in the United States.

4. Despite such a large local audience, the Hispanic stations reach only about five *5* % *percent* of the radio listeners.

5. This means Latin pop groups often cross over into English. One of these groups, Santana, has been crossing over for thirty *30* years.

6. Ricky Martin has had a number-one Spanish hit in 22 countries, including the United States.

7. Singing with the pop group Menudo made Martin famous, but singing the World Cup soccer anthem, *La Copa de la Vida,* at the nineteen-ninety-nine *1999* Grammy Awards made him an international superstar.

8. Another crossover singer, Cuban-born Gloria Estefan, and her husband, Emilio, head a two hundred million *$200 million* dollar music empire.

9. The 2 *two* Estefans are also ranked on the *Forbes* list of the five hundred *500* wealthiest entertainers.

Extend: Write three to five sentences using lots of numbers. Exchange your sentences with a classmate. After completing each other's worksheets, check your answers.

Abbreviations, Acronyms, & Initialisms

In formal writing, most abbreviations are spelled out. Turn to 660.1–662.3 in *Write Source*.

> **Write** the full word(s) above each underlined abbreviation. Use your handbook.

             information

1. The following statements are based on <u>info</u> found in *The Guinness Book of*

    World Records.

            Farmers Home Administration

2. According to a spokesperson for the <u>FmHA</u>, Charles Houghton of New Boston,
New Hampshire   *pound*
    <u>NH</u>, grew a record 1,337-<u>lb.</u> pumpkin.

3. The youngest person to ever enter college was Michael Kearney, who entered
         Junior   *years*   *months*
    Santa Rosa <u>Jr.</u> College at the age of six <u>yrs.</u>, seven <u>mos.</u>

                                     miles per hour

4. The fastest land bird on record was an ostrich clocked at 72 <u>mph.</u>
           Georgia

5. Willie Jones of Atlanta, <u>GA</u>, survived heatstroke despite a body temperature of
      Fahrenheit
    115 degrees <u>F.</u>
    Federal Communications Commission

6. The <u>FCC</u> estimates that Paul Harvey's news program was the top radio show in

    1996.
    Federal Deposit Insurance Corporation   *Limited*

7. According to the <u>FDIC</u>, the Bank of East Asia, <u>Ltd.</u>, has assets of $144 million.
                         miles   *yards*

8. The longest sausage ever made was 36 <u>mi.</u> and 1,320 <u>yds.</u> long.
            South Carolina. United States of America

9. Tim Montgomery of Gaffney, <u>SC</u>, <u>USA</u>, is the 2002 world record holder of the
      meter
    100-<u>m.</u> dash, making him the "Fastest Man Alive."
            gross national product   *United States*

10. Valued at 10 trillion dollars, the <u>GNP</u> for the <u>U.S.</u> is the largest in the world.

Extend: Imagine that you and some friends are forming a new club. Come up with three or four acronyms (and what they mean, of course) for the name of your club.

Review: Numbers & Abbreviations

> **Underline** the incorrect usage of numbers and abbreviations in the following sentences. **Write the corrections above.**

1. The Panama Canal, located in what is now the Rep. *(Republic)* of Panama, has been called the "8th *(eighth)* wonder of the world."

2. Located at approximately 80 deg. W. lat. *(degrees west latitude)* and 10 deg. N. long. *(degrees north longitude)*, it has cut more than 7,800 mi. *(miles)* off the journey from one side of N. *(North)* America to the other.

3. The canal saves wks. *(weeks)*—if not mths. *(months)*—of travel around Cape Horn.

4. A railroad across Panama was built 1st *(first)* in 1855, but that construction claimed the lives of more than six thousand *(6,000)* workers, mostly from disease.

5. After France failed to complete the Pan. *(Panama)* Canal in 1904, Pres. *(President)* Teddy Roosevelt proposed that the U.S. *(United States)* take over the project.

6. Before the canal could be built, the worker pop. *(population)* had to be protected from yellow fever, malaria, and smallpox.

7. Col. Wm. *(Colonel William)* Gorgas solved the problem with gals. *(gallons)* of kerosene, lbs. *(pounds)* of soap, and tons of pyrethrum powder.

8. On Aug. *(August)* 15, 1914, a cement boat called the *Ancon* was the 1st *(first)* ship to use the Panama Canal.

9. The canal's locks are 110 ft. *(feet)* wide by 1,000 ft. *(feet)* long by 23 yds. *(yards)* deep.

10. The total cost was $380,000,000 *(million)*, which would be more than the entire La. *(Louisiana)* Purchase.

11. The canal is still used today, 91 yrs. *(years)* after opening.

12. Cargo ships cut 100's *(hundreds)* of hrs. *(hours)* from their sailing time by using the Pan. *(Panama)* Canal.

Pretest: Plurals & Spelling

> **Write** the correct plural form above all the underlined words.

1. The canyon echoed with the thunder from the <u>hoof</u> of the stampeding mustangs.
   hoofs (or) hooves

2. Most of my <u>hunch</u> turn out to be correct.
   hunches

3. Both <u>bakery</u> had many <u>loaf</u> of bread on display.
   bakeries ... *loaves*

4. <u>Pizza</u> in Italy are often made with sun-dried <u>tomato</u>.
   Pizzas ... *tomatoes*

5. The <u>radius</u> of the circles were equal.
   radii

6. The stray dog ate three <u>bowlful</u> of food.
   bowlfuls

7. How many <u>wife</u> did King Henry VIII have altogether?
   wives

8. The <u>alto</u> needed to sing louder, or they would not have been heard above the <u>soprano</u>.
   altos ... *sopranos*

9. Both disc <u>jockey</u> had huge collections of <u>CD</u>.
   jockeys ... *CD's (or) CDs*

> **Write** the correct spelling above each misspelled word in the following sentences.

1. A driver's lisence lists the person's hieght and waight.
   license ... *height* ... *weight*

2. The preliminery vote in Britain's Parlament was in favor of the Labour Party.
   preliminary ... *Parliament*

3. The writting under the photograph was almost illegable.
   writing ... *illegible*

4. It is quiet likeley that the liutent told the sargent to ship the missales.
   quite likely ... *lieutenant* ... *sergeant* ... *missiles*

5. The libary has the origenal copy of the manuscrip.
   library ... *original* ... *manuscript*

6. There was not enough spaggetti to feed the majorety of the students.
   spaghetti ... *majority*

7. Insidently, I hope you have desided to enter the compitition.
   Incidentally ... *decided* ... *competition*

8. It is probebly uneccesary to write the messege in more than two parragraphs.
   probably unnecessary ... *message* ... *paragraphs*

9. The atheletes left their street close in the gymnaseum's locker room.
   athletes ... *clothes* ... *gymnasium's*

10. Her incredeble courage was accknowleged and apreciated.
    incredible ... *acknowledged appreciated*

Plurals 1

Learning the rules for forming plurals helps you become a good speller. Turn to 654.1–656.4 in *Write Source*.

> **Write** the correct plural form above each underlined noun. Put a *C* above any underlined word that is correct.

1. My relatives are Montana <u>cowboy</u> *(cowboys)* who work the <u>ranch</u> *(ranches)* where the deer and the <u>antelope</u> *(C)* play.

2. Uncle Clem uses <u>bagful</u> *(bagfuls)* of colorful western slang.

3. He brags that his boots are so fine, you can see the <u>callus</u> *(calluses)* on his <u>toes</u> *(C)*.

4. And he insists that his <u>sneeze</u> *(sneezes)* are louder than two <u>bullfrog</u> *(bullfrogs)* with a bullhorn.

5. Aunt Maggie says he couldn't carry a tune even if the <u>banjo</u> *(banjos)* had two <u>handle</u> *(handles)*.

6. When he sings "<u>Penny</u> *(Pennies)* from Heaven," it sounds more like howling.

7. Clem likes to say that his <u>brother-in-law</u> *(brothers-in-law)*, Jake and Randy, are as quiet as <u>sheep</u> *(C)* with their <u>mouth</u> *(mouths)* full.

8. He says it was once so hot, the <u>cactus</u> *(cacti (or) cactuses)* melted.

9. One time, when I asked why bandits wore <u>handkerchief</u> *(handkerchiefs (or) handkerchieves)* over their noses, he replied, "Because bandits don't take baths, that's why."

10. Uncle Clem claims his favorite meal is <u>potato</u> *(potatoes)* and <u>quail</u> *(C)*.

11. He has been known to eat five <u>plateful</u> *(platefuls)* of <u>potato</u> *(potatoes)* and two <u>loaf</u> *(loaves)* of bread at a single meal.

12. Once, when I used one of his best <u>knife</u> *(knives)* to whittle, I could hear him screeching louder than three <u>coyote</u> *(coyotes)* in a gunnysack.

Extend: Write four to six sentences about a one-of-a-kind person you know. Include at least one plural in each sentence, and check your spelling.

Plurals 2

Here are more plurals for you to practice with. Review 654.1–656.4 in *Write Source*.

> **Write** the correct plural form above each underlined word.

1. Last summer I visited St. Petersburg, one of the great, ancient <u>city</u> *cities* of Russia.

2. The day I remember best was when I went to the city park and watched as men of all <u>age</u> *ages* swapped <u>story</u> *stories* and played board games.

3. I was surprised that I did not see any <u>female</u> *females*, so I asked why there were no <u>woman</u> *women* present.

4. They replied that their <u>wife</u> *wives* were not invited to join them, even if the women were smart and had <u>Ph.D.</u> *Ph.D.'s*

5. The men assumed the women socialized while shopping at the fruit, vegetable, and meat <u>market</u> *markets*.

6. <u>Eyebrow</u> *Eyebrows* went up when I asked them to teach me the <u>rule</u> *rules* for the game of *nardo,* but they graciously showed me how to play.

7. I saw that the games were played on oval-shaped <u>board</u> *boards* that were held together with <u>hinge</u> *hinges*.

8. Like the American game of backgammon, *nardo* uses two <u>die</u> *dice (or) dies*.

9. Whenever fives and <u>six</u> *sixes* were rolled, the *nardo* players yelled, *"Shesh-besh!"*

10. Meanwhile, on another set of <u>bench</u> *benches*, four men were hunched over a game of <u>domino</u> *dominoes (or) dominos*.

11. All around us, <u>handful</u> *handfuls* of vendors sold <u>sausage</u> *sausages* and hot tea.

12. A musician played soft mandolin <u>solo</u> *solos* elsewhere in the park.

13. I have many wonderful <u>memory</u> *memories* of my visit to Russia.

Extend: Write a short paragraph about a visit you made to a different place—near or far. Include plural words whenever possible, checking to make sure you've spelled them correctly.

Writers INC 510.1–511.5

Spelling 1

Spelling can be tricky. You must learn the rules as well as the exceptions to the rules. Turn to pages 664–671 in *Write Source*.

> **Underline** the words that are misspelled and write the correct words above.

1. I desparately want to make the basketball team.
   desperately

2. I think I have enough heigth and weigth.
   height   weight

3. My strenth and stamina are as good as any of the other kids' in my school.
   strength

4. I'm a good ahtlete.
   athlete

5. Dribbling is more easly done than shooting free throws—at least for me.
   easily

6. If I don't make the team, the coach will ask me to be the "apprentise" again.
   apprentice

7. I'll run errands, get water, distribut towels, congratalate the team members, and
   distribute   congratulate
   hide my misary.
   misery

8. My parents try to sheild me from possible disapointment.
   shield   disappointment

9. Mom says, "It's possibel you won't make the team, but you can always try again."
   possible

10. Dad says, "Prehaps you'll make it this time."
   Perhaps

11. My impatiense grows daily.
   impatience

12. I think I'll join the drum and bugle core if I don't make the basketball team.
   corps

13. I'll have a briused ego, that's for sure—especially if my cousen makes the team and
   bruised   cousin
   I don't.

14. I think I'd like steping out onto the floor following my interduction.
   stepping   introduction

15. Some of the teams we play in our division are feircely competetive.
   fiercely competitive

16. It's finaly Wendesday, and guess what? I made the team!
   finally Wednesday

Extend: Study the rules for spelling on page 664 in *Write Source*. List three to five words that follow each rule.

Spelling 2

To become a better speller, study pages 660–664 and pages 666–667 in *Write Source.*

> **Underline** the incorrectly spelled words in the following sentences. Write the corrections above.

1. Hot dogs are an American ~~fenomenom~~. *phenomenon*

2. In 1996, the National Hot Dog and Sausage ~~Counsel~~ sent more than 37,000 *Council*

   wieners to U.S. troops in Bosnia.

3. ~~Busness~~ people know that hot dogs are ~~asocciated~~ with America and good times, *Business* *associated*

   which is why you see them in so many advertisements.

4. Even British royalty is aware of the "dog's" ~~extrordinary~~ popularity. *extraordinary*

5. President Franklin Roosevelt served Queen Elizabeth II of England hot dogs

   with ~~potatoe~~ salad at a ~~lunchen~~. *potato* *luncheon*

6. ~~Celebritys~~ like Jerry Seinfeld and Demi Moore promote hot dogs. *Celebrities*

7. Hot dogs are the ~~prefered~~ meal when you're in a hurry, since you can hold them *preferred*

   in one hand.

8. Hot dogs, on average, ~~wiegh~~ about two ounces. *weigh*

9. Chili dogs are ~~espesially~~ popular in the Southwest, while southerners favor *especially*

   corn dogs.

10. New Englanders have an ~~appitite~~ for franks and beans, while people from *appetite*

    Kansas City find cheese dogs ~~iresistable~~. *irresistible*

11. Chicagoans load hot dogs with onions, tomatos, pickles, peppers, and a ~~peculier~~ *peculiar*

    bright-green relish.

12. They call this "~~draging~~ the dog ~~thorough~~ the garden." *dragging* *through*

13. What is your ~~favourite~~ way to eat a hot dog? *favorite*

Extend: Write a mouth-watering description of your favorite hot or cold sandwich. Use words you have trouble spelling. Check your spelling.

Writers INC pp. 513–516 and 517–522

Review: Plurals & Spelling

> **Underline** the incorrectly used or misspelled word(s) in each sentence and write the correction above.

1. During the *reign* ~~rein~~ of the *pharaohs* ~~pharoahs~~, Egyptians did not consider death the end, but rather the *beginning* ~~begining~~ of their eternal *lives* ~~lifes~~.

2. They believed that their souls (*bas*) *continued* ~~continnued~~ to live on earth, but their spirits (*kas*) *traveled (or) travelled* ~~traveld~~ back and forth from their *bodies* ~~bodys~~ to the other world.

3. For this reason, the *mummies* ~~mummys~~ and the coffins in which they lay were *extremely* ~~extreemly~~ *important* ~~importent~~.

4. Canopic jars were placed around the dead *pharaohs* ~~pharoahs~~ to hold the brains, *teeth* ~~tooths~~, and all internal *organs* ~~organes~~ except the *heart* ~~haert~~.

5. A pyramid offered protection *against* ~~aganst~~ weather, decay, and *thieves* ~~thiefes~~ who might try to steal the objects buried with the body. (Egyptians *believed* ~~beleived~~ the *kas* and *bas* used the objects in the afterlife.)

6. Before actual construction could begin on a *pyramid* ~~pyromid~~, two weeks of prayers and *sacrifices* ~~sacrificees~~ were made to the gods.

7. Skilled workers and *architects* ~~architectes~~ created the complicated design criteria. They were paid well in food and *clothing* ~~clotheing~~.

8. Unskilled workers were used to move millions of stones, some *weighing* ~~wieghing~~ more than a ton, without horses or *donkeys* ~~donkeyes~~.

9. Most of the pyramids were constructed of limestone found nearby, but some of the granite had to be *shipped* ~~shiped~~ from *quarries* ~~quarrys~~ across the Nile River.

10. Many laborers died from the backbreaking work and unsafe working *conditions* ~~conditiones~~.

Pretest: Using the Right Word

> **Select** the right word from the choices given in parentheses to complete each sentence.

1. Will you __*accept*__ this challenge? *(accept, except)*

2. The __*capitol*__ building is located in our nation's __*capital*__ . *(capital, capitol)*

3. Would you __*lend*__ me sixty-five cents for bus fare? *(borrow, lend)*

4. Ms. Crawford will __*teach*__ us origami in art class. *(learn, teach)*

5. I am __*dying*__ to try that spray-on hair color. *(dyeing, dying)*

6. The __*whole*__ band attended a picnic following their successful road tour.

   (hole, whole)

7. Dominic asked the teacher, "__*May*__ I please go to the cafeteria?" *(can, may)*

8. The teacher answered, "__*All right*__ ." *(all right, alright)*

9. Stay __*here*__ while I make sure this bridge is safe. *(hear, here)*

10. The __*board*__ members soon became __*bored*__ by the long report. *(board, bored)*

11. There was __*altogether*__ too much rain. *(all together, altogether)*

12. The student __*council*__ voted 15–0 in favor of homework limits. *(council, counsel)*

13. After raking a giant pile of leaves, __*it's*__ always fun to jump in them. *(it's, its)*

14. Today the wind and the cold kept us from going __*farther*__ than two miles.

    (farther, further)

15. Liter bottles are larger __*than*__ quart bottles. *(than, then)*

16. The Chihuahuas continued __*their*__ barking for an hour. *(their, they're)*

17. Are you and __*your*__ cousin camping by Devil's Tower tonight? *(you're, your)*

Using the Right Word 1

Turn to pages 678 and 680 in *Write Source* for help.

> **Write** the correct word above each underlined word that is wrong. If an underlined word is correct, write a *C* above it.

          annual

1. This <u>biannual</u> parade is always held on the third Saturday in September.

          between

2. The clowns, who are the crowd favorites, walk <u>among</u> the mayor's car and the

high school marching band.

       C effect

3. The hot sun had a <u>bad</u> <u>affect</u> on one float's fresh flowers.

          isle

4. The Jaycees had an amazing float that looked like a desert <u>aisle</u>.

    C

5. The <u>number</u> of parade entries easily exceeded last year's total of 35.

        adapt

6. One parade watcher said she will gladly <u>adopt</u> to hot weather as long as there is

shade along the parade route.

       C

7. All the antique cars <u>except</u> one jalopy were perfectly restored and polished for

the car show.

    ascent

8. The steep <u>assent</u> to the city park marked the end of the parade route.

9. A huge display wall on the back of the final float fell to the pavement and was

      badly

bent <u>bad</u>.

  A lot

10. <u>Alot</u> of help was needed to clear the street.

        all right

11. Volunteers made sure the float was <u>alright</u> before continuing to the big rally in

the park.

        altogether

12. In spite of the accident, the parade was <u>all together</u> a grand success.

Using the Right Word 2

Turn to pages 682 and 684 in *Write Source* for help.

> **Circle** the correct word from the pair in parentheses to complete each sentence.

1. In ancient Rome, purple *(die, (dye))* for clothing was reserved for emperors.

2. On the other hand, many ordinary Roman citizens often wore *((coarse,) course)*, plain cloth.

3. *((Can,) May)* you imagine wearing only one kind of clothing?

4. Rome, one of the largest cities of its day, was the *((capital,) capitol)* city of the Roman Empire.

5. Roman emperors often sought *(council, (counsel))* from their favorite generals.

6. Julius Caesar fought the Gauls when they tried to *((break,) brake)* away from Roman rule.

7. During the reign of Trajan, the Roman Empire expanded *((farther,) further)* than ever before.

8. Roman generals had their soldiers build numerous roads, walls, and forts to keep them from getting *(board, (bored))*.

9. Roman emperors *(cent, (sent,) scent)* trusted military officers to rule their conquered provinces.

10. The Romans built beautiful structures, but they never built a *(capital, (capitol))* building.

Using the Right Word 3

Turn to pages 686 and 688 in *Write Source* for help.

> **Choose** the correct words from the choices given to fill in the blanks in the following story.

1   Allan wanted to help reforest a hillside. He took a special introductory

2   class to ___learn___ how to plant small trees. Allan already knew Mr. Lawson
          (learn, teach)

3   from the high school would ___teach___ the course. Because Allan wanted to
                           (learn, teach)

4   do a ___good___ job, he listened carefully and took notes. When the instructor
        (good, well)

5   took the class outdoors, Allan practiced using a special tool to make a small

6   ___hole___ in the ground for tree seedlings. To his surprise, Allan found he
    (hole, whole)

7   would be planting trees that were only five inches tall.

8   The next day, Allan was ready to start planting trees. A local tree nursery

9   decided to ___loan___ the class the necessary tools. Allan made a hole and
          (borrow, loan)

10   picked up a ___healthy___ tree. Using his ___heel___ , he pushed the
          (healthful, healthy)   *(heal, heel)*

11   soil around the little tree. He smiled because he could ___hear___ people
                               (hear, here)

12   humming to themselves. A little bit ___later___ , Allan started humming, too.
                    (later, latter)

13   When the planting was finished, Allan looked at the small ___medal___
                                        (medal, meddle)

14   he was given for all of his work. ___Its___ border was gold and ___its___
                         (it's, its)   *(it's, its)*

15   center showed a tall pine tree. The ___whole___ day he had worked hard, but
                           (hole, whole)

16   he felt good. Before he left the planting site, Allan promised to return ___here___
                                          (hear, here)

17   once every year to see how ___well___ the tiny trees were growing.
          (good, well)

Extend: Write a sentence for each of the following words: *latter, it's, healthful,* and *borrow.*

Using the Right Word 4

Turn to pages 690 and 692 in *Write Source* for help.

Choose the correct word from column A to fill in the blank in column B.

Column A   **Column B**

miner   **1.** Jill plans to ___quit___ working on this project tonight.

seem   **2.** I have a walk-on role in the third ___scene___ in Act II of the class play.

quiet   **3.** The Fox River runs ___past___ the county park on the south side of the city.

pour   **4.** Jan ___passed___ the lead runner and surged to victory in the tri-city marathon.

personnel **5.** The last ___petal___ left on that daisy was "he loves me."

past   **6.** Jane carefully sewed the ripped ___seam___ on Jim's letter jacket.

pore   **7.** A coal ___miner___ works at a dangerous job.

piece   **8.** After midnight, even Main Street becomes very ___quiet___.

pedal   **9.** The two old rowboats that those kids are using out on the lake ___seem___ to be sinking!

quit   **10.** The Acre Company expects its ___personnel___ to work overtime.

passed   **11.** Every ___pore___ on his forehead bubbled with perspiration as he did pull-ups.

petal   **12.** Compared to the broken water main, this leak was a ___minor___ problem.

seam   **13.** Janae found the missing ___piece___ of the puzzle under the table.

minor   **14.** Jake said the bike's ___pedal___ wouldn't move.

scene   **15.** Please ___pour___ this bucket of water in the birdbath.

Extend: Write a sentence for each of the following words: *peace, peddle, personal,* and *quite.*

Using the Right Word 5

Turn to pages 694 and 696 in *Write Source* for help.

> **Choose the correct word(s) from the choices given to complete each sentence.**

1. At one time, car manufacturers in the United States used ___*steel*___ beams to make a car's frame. *(steal, steel)*

2. "Remember ___*you're*___ going to need ___*your*___ sleeping bag and ___*your*___ backpack for this weekend's campout," Mr. Graham said. *(your, you're)*

3. After studying the cave's small tunnel, Sherman knew he could squeeze ___*through*___ the opening. *(threw, through)*

4. I think the arrows fell over ___*there*___, next to that big gray boulder, because ___*they're*___ not here. *(their, there, they're)*

5. When Sophie heard I was going hiking, she said, "I want to go, ___*too*___." *(to, too, two)*

6. People never thought much about garbage, but now ___*waste*___ management has become big business. *(waist, waste)*

7. The people on Franklin Street know they will have to ___*wait*___ a few more years for their street to be paved. *(wait, weight)*

8. When the bus was ready to leave for the field trip, Mrs. Lane asked, " ___*Who's*___ missing?" *(who's, whose)*

9. Jack thought he could move the log, but he found out it was heavier ___*than*___ he expected. *(than, then)*

10. Mr. Lee, our science teacher, smiled and asked, " Which will ___*weigh*___ more: a ton of feathers or a ton of bricks?" *(way, weigh)*

Review: Using the Right Word

> **Circle** each word that is used incorrectly in the following sentences and write the correct word above it.

1 I went ~~too~~ *to* an air show last week. The ~~sent~~ *scent* of jet fuel hung in the air, but

2 I loved it because I want to be a pilot someday. I watched the jets zoom by in

3 formation with the capitol building off in the distance. I could ~~here~~ *hear* the engines

4 screaming as the pilots pushed their planes into a steep climb. I wondered how

5 much training the pilots needed to fly those planes.

6 Suddenly, it seemed that the ~~hole~~ *whole* sky was full of planes as jets zoomed

7 left and right, while some dove and others climbed. Then, just as suddenly,

8 they were gone. There was a brief moment of ~~piece~~ *peace*. The pilots didn't make us

9 ~~weight~~ *wait* long; they didn't want us to get ~~board~~ *bored*. Quickly, the planes banked and

10 came back. They ~~seamed~~ *seemed* to be heading right for us. As they zipped ~~passed~~ *past* us,

11 we ducked. Of ~~coarse~~ *course*, we didn't need to do that because the planes weren't that

12 close to us.

13 After the performance was over, I got autographs from some of the

14 pilots. Someone asked me, "Will you ~~borrow~~ *lend* me ~~you're~~ *your* pen so I can get some

15 autographs, ~~two~~ *too*?" ~~Latter~~ *Later*, one of the pilots talked to me about his plane. "Can I

16 look in the cockpit?" I asked. Wow, some of the gauges were ~~quiet~~ *quite* small. There

17 were many switches as well. The pilot told us that his group had to practice ~~alot~~ *a lot*

18 in order to perform ~~good~~ *well*.

19 When the pilots fly in formation, they must follow the leader. They ~~except~~ *accept*

20 his direction as they perform dangerous stunts. The pilots must react quickly.

21 This life-and-death flying leaves no room for performing badly.

22   The pilot I talked to flies an F-16. He said in combat situations the jet can

farther   than

23   fly ~~further~~ ~~then~~ most fighters. At 32 feet, the wingspan seems ~~to~~ short, but it

too

It's

24   helps a pilot outmaneuver almost all challengers. ~~Its~~ hard to believe that the

25   F-16 travels at 1,500 miles an hour and reaches an altitude of 50,000 feet. I

medal

26   bought a ~~meddle~~ with the image of the plane on one side and facts about the

27   plane on the other. I learned that the F-16 is about 50 feet long and 16 feet

28   high.

among

29   I took time to walk ~~between~~ all the jets. I thought about the terrific

dye

30   amount of noise these planes can generate all together. I noticed that red ~~die~~

31   marked a spot for each nosewheel, and I saw how close they stood to each other.

whose

32   I saw that each jet had the pilot's name on the side to identify ~~who's~~ plane it

their

33   was. Pilots are pretty particular about ~~there~~ planes because every aircraft

passed

34   handles a bit differently. As I ~~past~~ each plane, I touched a wing or the fuselage.

steel

35   The metal skin felt like ~~steal~~, but I knew parts of the plane are made of carbon

weight   *weigh*

36   fibers because of their strength and light ~~wait~~. Still, an F-16 can ~~way~~ as much

37   as 37,500 pounds (which includes the pilot and a full fuel tank) at takeoff.

38   I stepped back and took a picture of the five F-16s along the runway. It

quite scene   *way*

39   was ~~quit~~ a ~~seen~~. I'll look at it as I study my math and science on my ~~weigh~~ to

40   becoming a pilot.

Review: Proofreading Activities

Correct errors in numbers and abbreviations in the following paragraphs. Write the corrections above the errors.

1   The Apollo 13 mission to the moon in 1970 began as planned. Until the

                        13

2   movie Apollo ~~Thirteen~~ came out in 1995, many people did not realize what

                                                Jr.

3   a near tragedy it had been. American astronauts James Lovell, ~~Junior~~; Fred

           Jr.   *Florida*

4   Haise, ~~JR~~; and John Swigert, Jr., were launched from Cape Canaveral, ~~Fla.~~, on

              11

5   April ~~eleventh~~, 1970, for a 10-day mission to land on the moon.

6   One part of their mission was to start an experiment called Apollo

                                  ALSEP   *56*

7   Lunar Surface Experiment Package (~~Alsep~~). However, ~~fifty-six~~ hours into the

                              200,000   *miles*

8   flight—about ~~2 hundred thousand mi.~~ from Earth—an oxygen tank exploded,

9   cutting off all the power in the service module. Unless something could be done

10   quickly, the astronauts would not have enough oxygen to return to Earth. Gene

                                    Texas

11   Kranz, the lead flight director in Houston, ~~TX~~, began working on solutions

12   immediately.

Correct errors in punctuation and capitalization in the following paragraphs. Add any missing punctuation.

1   After the crew shut down a lot of the electrical power, they moved from the

                        O   *A*

2   command module, named ó̸dyssey, to the lunar module—called ȧquarius. They

3   were allowed to drink only one glass of water per day. The temperature was

4   near 32 degrees Fahrenheit.

5   Lack of oxygen was the deadliest, most immediate threat. The Aquarius

          '

6   didn't have enough canisters to remove deadly carbon dioxide from the air.

7   The Odyssey did have enough canisters~~,~~ but they were incompatible with the
     V (or) 's   H ,

8   Aquarius system. The engineers in Houston, came up with an ingenious

9   solution,.they taught the astronauts to create a homemade adapter so the

10   Odyssey canisters could be used on the Aquarius. That solved the oxygen

11   problem.

Correct errors in punctuation and usage in the following paragraphs.

1   The next challenge was to get back home. The astronauts had to use
           weighed

2   power from the Aquarius to propel their spacecraft, which ~~wayed~~ almost

3   100,000 pounds, around the moon and back to Earth. Despite the complexity of

4   this maneuver, it was a complete success. The dangerous reentry into Earths
         too

5   atmosphere succeeded, ~~to~~. On Friday, April 17, the crew landed in the Pacific

6   Ocean and were picked up by the navy ship Iwo Jima.
        (or) —   *(or) —*   *their*

7   The astronauts: Lovell, Haise, and Swigert, were heroes. For ~~there~~ bravery,
           Medal

8   President Richard Nixon awarded them the ~~Metal~~ of Freedom. The men were

9   honored with a parade in Chicago. It would be almost a year before the next

10   lunar mission, Apollo 14, would successfully return from the moon on Tuesday,

11   February 9, 1971.

Parts of Speech

The activities in this section provide practice and review of the different parts of speech. Most of the activities also include helpful textbook references. In addition, the **Extend** activities encourage follow-up practice of certain skills.

Pretest: Nouns

Underline the words used as nouns in the following sentences. Label each noun. Use *P* for proper nouns, *C* for common nouns, and *COL* for collective nouns. Next, circle the abstract nouns and draw a second line under the concrete nouns.

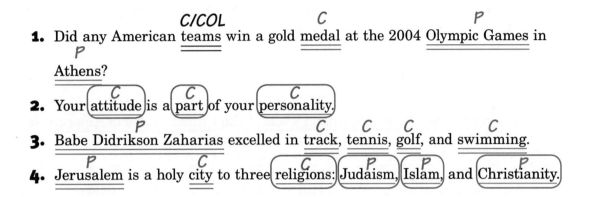

                                          C/COL   C   P

1. Did any American teams win a gold medal at the 2004 Olympic Games in Athens?

2. Your attitude is a part of your personality.

3. Babe Didrikson Zaharias excelled in track, tennis, golf, and swimming.

4. Jerusalem is a holy city to three religions: Judaism, Islam, and Christianity.

Indicate the functions of each of the underlined nouns in the following sentences. Use these symbols: *S* for subject, *PN* for predicate noun, *IO* for indirect object, *DO* for direct object, and *OP* for object of a preposition. Use *POS* for nouns showing ownership.

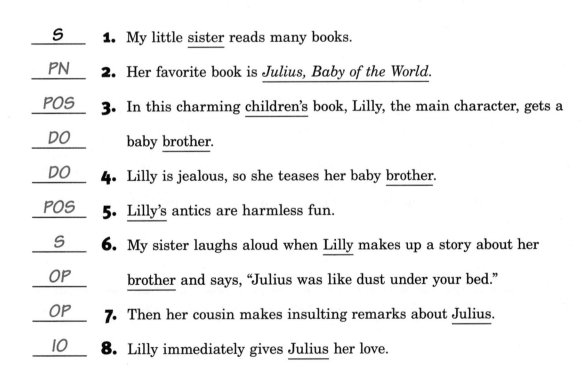

S	**1.** My little <u>sister</u> reads many books.
PN	**2.** Her favorite book is <u>Julius, Baby of the World</u>.
POS	**3.** In this charming <u>children's</u> book, Lilly, the main character, gets a
DO	baby <u>brother</u>.
DO	**4.** Lilly is jealous, so she teases her baby <u>brother</u>.
POS	**5.** <u>Lilly's</u> antics are harmless fun.
S	**6.** My sister laughs aloud when <u>Lilly</u> makes up a story about her
OP	<u>brother</u> and says, "Julius was like dust under your bed."
OP	**7.** Then her cousin makes insulting remarks about <u>Julius</u>.
IO	**8.** Lilly immediately gives <u>Julius</u> her love.

Classes of Nouns 1

A noun is a word that names something: a person, a place, a thing, or an idea. There are five classes of nouns: *proper, common, concrete, abstract,* and *collective.* Turn to 701.1–701.5 in *Write Source.*

> **Underline** the words used as nouns in the following summary. Identify the nouns using *P* for a proper noun, *C* for a common noun, and *COL* for a collective noun. (Collective nouns will have a double classification: *P/COL* or *C/COL.*)

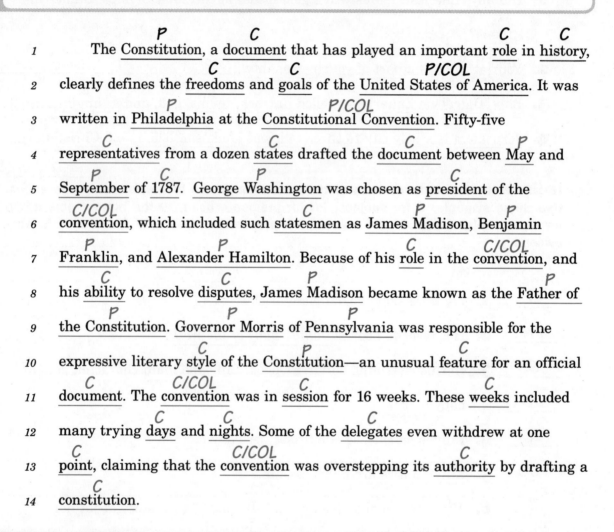

> **List** the nouns from the first sentence in the paragraph above on the correct lines below. (There should be three concrete nouns and four abstract nouns.)

concrete: *Constitution, document, United States of America*

abstract: *role, history, freedoms, goals*

Extend: Study a paragraph from your writing. Underline the nouns. Read "Specific Nouns" on page 534 in *Write Source.* Could you have used more vivid nouns?

Classes of Nouns 2

Proper nouns are always capitalized. Common nouns are not capitalized. Abstract nouns name ideas or feelings, while concrete nouns name tangible things. Learn more about the classes of nouns to improve your writing. Turn to page 701 in *Write Source*.

Complete each pair below with either a proper or a common noun. Use capitalization as needed. Remember to underline the titles of movies and books.

Answers will vary.

	PROPER	COMMON
1.	Tom Hanks	actor
2.	Central Park	park
3.	George W. Bush	president
4.	Gone with the Wind	movie
5.	Oklahoma	state
6.	Jane Eyre	book
7.	Christianity	religion
8.	Spain	country

Make a list of abstract nouns and concrete nouns.

	ABSTRACT		CONCRETE
1.	freedom	1.	apple
2.		2.	
3.		3.	
4.		4.	
5.		5.	
6.		6.	
7.		7.	
8.		8.	

Functions of Nouns

Nouns can be used six different ways. Study the chart below and turn to 702.3 in *Write Source* for more information.

Writers INC	Write Source	Function	Symbol	Example
550.1	738.1	subject	S	*Pilots* fly.
534.3, 539.1	702.3, 714.1	predicate	PN	Pilots are *captains*.
540.1	716.2	direct object	DO	Pilots fly *planes*.
540.1	716.2	indirect object	IO	The pilot gave *passengers* a message.
547	732	object of preposition	OP	The pilot spoke to the *people*.
534.3	702.3	possessive noun	POS	The pilot got the *passengers'* attention.

Identify how the underlined nouns function in the following statements, using the symbols from the chart above.

1. Birds have eyes on the sides of their heads. *(S, DO, OP)*
2. A group of lions is a pride. *(S, PN)*
3. A lion's pride is often his mane. *(POS, PN)*
4. The name for a group of monkeys is a band. *(S, OP, PN)*
5. Only female mosquitoes bite. *(S)*
6. The ostrich is the largest bird; it is also the fastest runner. *(PN, PN)*
7. The smallest bird is the bee hummingbird; it weighs less than a penny. *(S)*
8. Loons, the fastest swimmers, can also dive 160 feet below the surface. *(OP)*
9. A loon can outswim fish and catch them underwater. *(DO)*
10. Loons are shy birds; and their haunting calls give some people goose bumps. *(IO, DO)*
11. Geese, the highest flyers, have been known to fly at 29,000 feet. *(OP)*
12. A peregrine falcon can dive at a speed of 200 miles per hour. *(OP)*
13. The curlew, a long-legged bird related to the sandpiper, can fly 2,000 miles nonstop over water. *(OP, OP)*

Extend: Write four to six sentences about your favorite animals. Include nouns in each sentence; try to use at least three of the six functions listed in the chart above.

Nominative, Possessive, & Objective Cases of Nouns

To determine the case of a noun, look at the way it is used in the sentence. Study the chart below before turning to 702.3 in *Write Source*.

Writers INC	Write Source	Case	Function	Symbol	Example
550.1	738.1	Nominative	subject	S	The *car* wouldn't start.
534.3	702.3		predicate noun	PN	The car is a *lemon*.
540.1	716.2	Objective	direct object	DO	Jake's driving gives me the *creeps*.
540.1	716.2		indirect object	IO	Jake's driving gives *Hannah* the creeps.
547	732		object of preposition	OP	He drives with one *hand*.
534.3	702.3	Possessive	possessive noun	POS	*Hannah's* driving skills are much better.

Label the function of the underlined nouns in the following statements using the symbols from the chart above. Indicate the case of each underlined noun (*N* for nominative, *O* for objective, and *POS* for possessive) on the blanks.

N **1.** *(S)* Dolphins are aquatic mammals related to both whales and porpoises.

O **2.** These amazing creatures live in *(OP)* seas and rivers all over the world.

N **3.** Measuring less than four feet, the *buffeo* is the smallest *(PN)* dolphin known.

N **4.** Most *(S)* dolphins eat nearly one-third of their weight in food every day.

O **5.** For years, humans hunted *(DO)* dolphins for their valuable oil.

POS **6.** Considering their fragile history, the *(POS)* dolphins' survival is remarkable.

O **7.** Between 1959 and 1972, an estimated 4.8 million dolphins were killed when they became entangled in tuna fishing *(OP)* nets.

O **8.** Then, the United States threw *(IO)* dolphins a lifeline and helped stop the tragedy.

O **9.** It pressured both domestic and international tuna *(DO)* canneries to refuse shipments from fleets that did not protect dolphins.

O **10.** The United States passed the *(DO)* Marine Mammal Protection Act of 1972.

O **11.** It prevents the exploitation of aquatic *(OP)* animals, including dolphins.

Review: Nouns

Make lists by filling in the following blanks with the types of nouns called for in the headings. For ideas, think about something that interests you, such as camping, sports, or a subject you're studying.

Answers will vary.

Proper Nouns

1. Structure of Coral Reefs
2. Great Barrier Reef
3. Australia

Common Nouns

1. reefs
2. coral
3. atolls

Collective Nouns

1. group
2. crew
3. species

Abstract Nouns

1. research
2. study
3. goals

Concrete Nouns

1. jellyfish
2. water

Write two sentences using some of the nouns you've listed. (Try to use at least one noun from each of your lists.) Underline and label the nouns in your sentences; use *NOM* for nominative case, *OBJ* for objective case, and *POS* for possessive case.

1. _____

_____

2. _____

_____

Pretest: Pronouns

> **Underline** all of the pronouns in the following sentences. Then label each pronoun **S** for singular or **P** for plural.

             P
1. <u>We</u> talked all night about videos and music.
     S
2. <u>She</u> studied John Steinbeck's *Of Mice and Men*.
                       P
3. Walking along the beach, <u>they</u> saw starfish washed up on the shore.
      S   *S*
4. If <u>he</u> eats burritos or other spicy foods before bedtime, <u>his</u> nightmares return.
      S   *S*   *S*
5. If <u>you</u> don't watch what <u>you</u> are doing, <u>you</u> will hurt <u>yourself</u>.
    S   *S*   *S*   *S*
6. <u>I</u> like <u>my</u> peas on one side of <u>my</u> plate and <u>my</u> carrots on the other side of
   S
   <u>my</u> plate.
    P   *P*
7. <u>Many</u> of the football players wanted <u>their</u> coach to go for a first down.
                     S
8. The car had a hole in <u>its</u> radiator.
                                       S
9. Mardi Gras is also called "Fat Tuesday" because for some people <u>it</u> is the last
                              P
   day to eat certain foods before <u>their</u> Lenten fasting begins.

> **Underline** all of the pronouns in the following sentences. Then label each pronoun with its case (**N** for nominative, **POS** for possessive, or **O** for objective).

     N   *POS*   *O*
1. <u>She</u> took all <u>our</u> towels with <u>her</u> to the beach.
  POS   *POS*
2. <u>Our</u> neighbors' dog is constantly digging up <u>their</u> lawn.
    N   *N*   *O*
3. <u>We</u> wish <u>they</u> would keep <u>it</u> on a leash.
  POS   *POS*
4. <u>Their</u> motorcycle wouldn't fit onto <u>its</u> trailer.
       N *N*
5. Either <u>you</u> or <u>I</u> can get the catcher's mitt later.
      N   *POS*
6. Did <u>anybody</u> see what happened to <u>his</u> car?
  N   *O*   *N*
7. <u>I</u> told <u>them</u> that <u>they</u> were too late.

Types of Pronouns

There are three different types of pronouns: simple, compound, and phrasal. Turn to page 704 in *Write Source*.

> **When Martin Luther King, Jr., was born, *he* was destined to be a great man.**
> (The pronoun *he* is simple.)

> **King knew that people had to believe in *themselves*.**
> (The pronoun *themselves* is compound)

> **King also wanted people to love *one another*.**
> (The pronoun *one another* is phrasal.)

Underline the pronouns in the sentences below. Study the first pronoun in each sentence. In the blank write an *S* if the pronoun is simple, a *C* if it is compound, and a *P* if it is phrasal.

___P___ **1.** Martin Luther King's dream was to have a world where people lived with each other in peace.

___C___ **2.** Everybody who has heard King's brilliant "I Have a Dream" speech is inspired.

___S___ **3.** Long before honor and fame found him, King worked as well as dreamed.

___S___ **4.** After successfully organizing a bus boycott in 1956, he became a leader in the civil rights movement.

___C___ **5.** Martin Luther King studied the practices of Mahatma Gandhi, and King himself followed nonviolent civil disobedience.

___S___ **6.** In 1960 King accepted a co-pastorship with his father at Ebenezer Baptist Church in Atlanta.

___S___ **7.** In 1964 *Time* magazine chose King as Man of the Year, the first black American it had thus honored.

Extend: Write four or five sentences about a famous (or not-so-famous) person. Use at least one pronoun per sentence. Exchange papers with a classmate. Underline and identify the types of pronouns.

Personal Pronouns

A pronoun takes the place of a noun or nouns. By correctly using pronouns, you can avoid repetition and write smoother, more readable sentences. Turn to 704.1 in *Write Source* for the chart "Classes of Pronouns."

 Cleopatra believed laughter reduced fear; Cleopatra had four court jesters to entertain Cleopatra's armies. (This sentence is written without pronouns.)

 Cleopatra believed laughter reduced fear; *she* had four court jesters to entertain *her* armies. (Here is the same sentence written with pronouns.)

> **Replace** the underlined nouns in the following narrative with the appropriate pronouns.

1   Cleopatra, who ruled Egypt from 47 B.C.E. to 30 B.C.E., enjoyed luxury.
                            she   *her*
2   For example, Cleopatra had four court jesters to make Cleopatra laugh and to
                      her   *She*
3   entertain Cleopatra's armies. Cleopatra was rich, extravagant, and demanding.
                                  her   *they*
4   Slaves quickly obeyed Cleopatra's every order. Cleopatra demanded that slaves
              her
5   fill Cleopatra's bathtub with milk every day. Cleopatra believed the milk kept
            her   *She*   *her*
6   Cleopatra's skin soft. Cleopatra also worried about Cleopatra's complexion.
                                                        her
7   One of the legends about Cleopatra demonstrates Cleopatra's concern. The
                            she
8   legend says that Cleopatra once dissolved a large, lustrous pearl in a glass
                        She
9   of vinegar. Cleopatra did this in front of many guests at a banquet.
          They   *they*
10   Cleopatra's guests were astonished! And Cleopatra's guests were even more
                                                        It
11   surprised when Cleopatra drank the mixture. The mixture was supposed
12   to ensure a lustrous complexion. The legends about Cleopatra's riches and
                                              them
13   extravagance are endless. Some of the legends are true; others are mere myth.

Extend: Select a passage from a book or magazine. Exchange passages with a classmate and take turns reading them aloud. Whenever a pronoun is used, don't read it aloud; pause so the listener can supply it. If your classmate has trouble naming the pronoun, tell him or her the antecedent. This exercise requires careful listening.

Writers INC 535.3

Number & Person of Personal Pronouns

The *number* of a pronoun can be either singular or plural. The *person* of a pronoun shows who is speaking (first person), who is spoken to (second person), or who is spoken about (third person). Turn to 708.1–708.2 in *Write Source* for more information.

> **Underline** all of the personal pronouns in the following sentences. Then label each pronoun. Use *S* for singular and *P* for plural. Use *1, 2,* and *3* for first, second, and third person. Label "you" *S-P* when it can be either singular or plural.

1. What makes <u>us</u> laugh? How would <u>you</u> define laughter?
   P/1   *S-P/2*

2. A comedian once said, "<u>I</u> can't define laughter, but <u>I</u> know <u>it</u> when <u>I</u> feel <u>it</u>."
   S/1   *S/1*   *S/3*   *S/1*   *S/3*

3. "<u>It</u> is like a 'happy spasm,'" <u>he</u> added.
   S/3   *S/3*

4. Doctors and psychiatrists say laughter is good for <u>us</u>.
   P/1

5. <u>It</u> stimulates <u>our</u> hearts, increases <u>our</u> circulation, and exercises <u>our</u> stomach
   S/3   *P/1*   *P/1*   *P/1*

   and chest muscles.

6. Research has proven <u>it</u> helps <u>our</u> immune system by increasing the number of
   S/3   *P/1*

   cells that <u>we</u> need for healing and fighting disease.
   P/1

7. <u>I</u> did some research of <u>my</u> own.
   S/1   *S/1*

8. <u>I</u> asked each of <u>my</u> classmates, "How many times do <u>you</u> laugh each day?"
   S/1   *S/1*   *S/2*

9. When <u>you</u> were in kindergarten, <u>you</u> probably laughed as many as 300 times
   S-P/2   *S-P/2*

   a day.

10. By the time <u>we</u> become adults, <u>we</u> laugh only about 15 times daily.
    P/1   *P/1*

11. Laughter is one of the things that makes <u>your</u> life, and <u>mine</u>, worth living.
    S-P/2   *S/1*

12. Another writer took this view: "<u>We</u> laugh in order not to cry."
    P/1

Extend: Write a joke or an anecdote that makes you laugh. Share your writing with a classmate. When you're done laughing, locate the personal pronouns in each piece. Tell each other the number and person for each.

Functions of Pronouns

Pronouns function in the same way that nouns do. Study the chart below and turn to 710.1 in *Write Source*.

Writers INC	Write Source	Function	Symbol	Example
550.1	738.1	*subject*	**S**	*You* need to change your clothes.
538.1	710.1	*predicate nominative*	**PN**	"That is *you*," she remarked about my shirt.
540.1	716.2	*direct object*	**DO**	The river's current pulled *him* under.
540.1	716.2	*indirect object*	**IO**	Frank gave *me* some paperback books.
547	732	*object of preposition*	**OP**	This isn't about *me*.
538.1	710.1	*possessive noun*	**POS**	*His* shoes were ruined by the rain.

Identify how the underlined pronouns function in the following statements, using the symbols from the chart above.

1. Some of the little children lost their coats while on the field trip. — S ... POS

2. They were engrossed with the exhibit and forgot about them. — S ... OP

3. Their teachers helped look for the lost coats. — POS

4. "I know where my coat is," said Sam. — S ... POS

5. "I left it on the bus," he said. — S DO ... S

6. "My lunch is lost," cried a little girl. — POS

7. "She lost her lunch," a little boy said. — S POS

8. "Will you do me a favor?" the bus driver asked. — S IO

9. He asked her to sit quietly while he went to the bus and got her lunch. — DO ... POS

10. "They are so cute," their teacher said. — S ... POS

11. The bus driver nodded his head. — POS

12. "They love field trips," another teacher added. — S

13. "Did you find it," the little girl asked the bus driver. — S DO

14. "Yes, I did," he said. — S ... S

15. "I am one of the children who likes you," the little girl said. — S PN ... DO

Nominative, Possessive, & Objective Cases of Pronouns 1

The case of a personal pronoun is determined by how that pronoun is used within a sentence. Is the pronoun being used as a subject, an object, or a possessive? Turn to 710.1 in *Write Source* for more information and a chart that identifies the case for each pronoun.

Write the case for each pronoun listed below. Use *N* for nominative, *POS* for possessive, and *O* for objective. Watch for pronouns that have more than one case.

N	1. I	**POS**	6. theirs	**POS**	11. its	**O**	16. them
N	2. we	**POS**	7. mine	**N/O**	12. you	**O**	17. me
N	3. she	**N**	8. they	**POS**	13. their	**N/O**	18. it
POS	4. our	**N**	9. he	**POS**	14. his	**POS**	19. my
POS/O	5. her	**O**	10. him	**POS**	15. hers	**O**	20. us

Add the missing pronoun to each of the sentences below as called for in parentheses.

1. ___We___ are going. *(1st person plural, nominative)*

2. ___I___ am going. *(1st person singular, nominative)*

3. She and ___he___ are going, too. *(3rd person singular, nominative)*

4. I asked Ed and Juan, "Are ___you___ joining us?" *(2nd person plural, nominative)*

5. ___They___ said no. *(3rd person plural, nominative)*

6. ___Our___ decision is final. *(1st person plural, possessive)*

7. ___My___ heart is sad. *(1st person singular, possessive)*

8. ___Her/His/Its___ heart rate has slowed. *(3rd person singular, possessive)*

9. We must leave without ___them___. *(3rd person plural, objective)*

10. Do you think ___your___ car is big enough? *(2nd person plural, possessive)*

Extend: Write eight to ten sentences using pronouns from the exercises above. Exchange papers with a classmate. Read each other's sentences to see if the pronouns are used correctly.

Nominative, Possessive, & Objective Cases of Pronouns 2

A pronoun can show ownership (possessive case). A pronoun can also can act as a subject (nominative case) or as an object of a verb or preposition (objective case). For more information on pronouns, turn to 710.1 in *Write Source*.

> **Underline** the pronouns in the sentences below. Label the case for each pronoun. Use *N* for nominative, *POS* for possessive, and *O* for objective.

     N   *O*
1. Most of us know something about tropical rain forests.

   N   *POS*
2. We know their plant and animal life is being destroyed.

        N
3. But did you know there are other kinds of tropical forests?

     N   *POS*
4. Have you and your classmates heard about cloud forests?

   N
5. They are also called tropical montane forests. ("Montane" means mountain.)

   N   *POS*
6. Each of the forests survives under its own special weather conditions.

              N   *O*   *O*
7. Even though I have never seen one, a cloud forest seems as fascinating to me as

    a rain forest.

  POS
8. My biology teacher, Ms. Green, has studied plant life at Costa Rica's

    Monteverde Cloud Forest.

9. The forest is located on top of a mountain range known as the Cordillera de

                   N
    Tilaran; Ms. Green says it is bathed in clouds almost every day.

         N
10. A botanist, who has been studying the Monteverde Cloud Forest for 20 years,

   POS
    was her supervisor and mentor.

                                       POS   *POS*
11. Ms. Green learned a great deal there, and our class will benefit from her

    experience.

Line–Pronoun–Case

8–we–N	12–she–N	13–our–POS	16–I–N
8–our–POS	12–our–POS	14–we–N	17–me–O
11–Our–POS	12–we–N	14–our–POS	
12–We–N	13–we–N	15–I–N	

Extend: Read the second paragraph of the essay on page 87 in this *SkillsBook*. Make a list of the personal pronouns you find. Identify the case for each pronoun.

　　　　　　　　　Writers INC 538.1 and p.193

Pronoun Cases: *I* and *Me*

When do you use "I" and when do you use "me"? Do you get confused when it comes to using *I* and *me*? Turn to 710.1 in *Write Source*.

Pronouns make my eyeballs blur–
He and *she*, *him* and *her*,
She and *I*, *me* and *him*–
My poor noggin starts to swim.

Subject, object what to do?
Here's a rhyme to help you through,
He can go with *her* and *me*
If *she* and *I* go to the sea.

Pronouns change case depending on how they are used in a sentence. There are three cases: nominative (used as subjects), objective (used as indirect and direct objects, or objects of prepositions) and possessive (used to indicate ownership).
Two pronouns that can cause trouble are *I* and *me*.

Choose the correct pronouns in the sentences below.

1. Both he and (*I*, *me*) are determined to learn to speak and write well.

2. Our teachers offered him and (*I*, *me*) recommendations.

3. Both my mother and (*I*, *me*) wanted to dance with Dad.

4. My cat plays more than (*I*, *me*).

5. Ceci and (*I*, *me*) ate all the dill pickles.

6. Thank you for giving Philip and (*I*, *me*) a ride to work.

7. Just between you and (*I*, *me*), I think he's a good friend.

8. Mother wanted to dance more than (*I*, *me*).

9. Niles found out that Julio and (*I*, *me*) are twins.

10. Do you want to go with (*I*, *me*)?

Extend: Using your knowledge about nominative and objective cases (in other words, about using subjects and objects), explain to a classmate why you chose each pronoun. When you disagree, use your handbooks to find information that will help you reach agreement about which pronoun is correct.

Review: Pronouns 1

> **Label** the underlined pronouns either *N* for nominative case, *O* for objective case, or *POS* for possessive case. On the first blank at the left, indicate the number of each pronoun. Use *S* for singular and *P* for plural. On the second blank, indicate the person of each pronoun. Use *1*, *2*, and *3* to indicate first, second, and third person.

P 3   **1.** Chen and Sarah are not sure <u>they</u> *(N)* should see the new movie.

P 1   **2.** Why do you want to go with <u>us</u> *(O)*?

P 3   **3.** The teacher said that <u>they</u> *(N)* should read 25 pages a day.

S 3   **4.** When will <u>she</u> *(N)* come to the house to fix the pipe leak downstairs?

P 2   **5.** Megan and Kevin, <u>you</u> *(N)* need to find another member for the group.

S 2   **6.** Shannon thinks that the ring she found on the floor is <u>yours</u> *(POS)*.

S 3   **7.** Frank thinks that <u>he</u> *(N)* would like to go to the mall instead of the coffeehouse.

S 2   **8.** Jake, what do <u>you</u> *(N)* think the class should do to help the environment?

S 3   **9.** The cat wanted <u>his</u> *(POS)* food immediately.

S 3   **10.** I feel as bad as <u>she</u> *(N)* does.

S 1   **11.** That's what she and <u>I</u> *(N)* would like to know.

P 3   **12.** Margaret and <u>they</u> *(N)* are going on a field trip.

S 1   **13.** Mr. Hatcher gave Mishka and <u>me</u> *(O)* permission.

S 1   **14.** Let's keep it between you and <u>me</u> *(O)*.

P 3   **15.** Reba reminded <u>them</u> *(O)* about the cost of concert tickets.

S 3   **16.** Do you want to come along with <u>him</u> *(O)*?

S 3   **17.** The car wouldn't start because <u>its</u> *(POS)* battery was dead.

S 1   **18.** They knew it was <u>my</u> *(POS)* dog.

S 1   **19.** Nobody hits the bull's-eye more than <u>I</u> *(N)*.

Relative Pronouns

A relative pronoun (*that, who, whom, whose, which*) relates an adjective clause to the noun or pronoun it modifies ("He *who* hesitates misses opportunities."). Turn to 704.1 and 706.2 in *Write Source*.

> **Underline** the relative pronoun in each of the sentences below. Circle the noun or pronoun that it modifies.

1. Carnivorous (plants,) which eat insects and other animals, live mainly in marshy areas.

2. Venus flytrap, a bog (plant) that grows in the Southeast, is the most famous carnivore.

3. (Botanists) who study carnivorous species have found that the plants need minerals from their prey to survive.

4. Most carnivorous plants eat insects and anthropods, but some have also been known to eat (slugs) and (frogs,) which are also nutritious.

5. Carnivorous plants have three different (methods) of trapping, which determine their appearance.

6. The so-called (*pitfalls*,) which have tubular leaves, use a water-filled pit to catch insects.

7. Some carnivorous plants use a sticky substance to trap their dinner—(insects) that are unfortunate enough to get too close.

8. Finally, the third (group) of plants, which includes Venus flytraps, actually move their leaves to enclose their prey and then slowly digest it.

9. Usually the (Venus flytrap,) whose leaves are like jaws, will close a trap after it has caught three insects in it.

Extend: Write the beginning of a desriptive essay. Use relative pronouns correctly.

Indefinite, Interrogative, & Demonstrative Pronouns

Indefinite pronouns represent someone (or something) not specifically named or known (*many, anyone, nobody*). Demonstrative pronouns point out a specific person or a specific thing (for example, *This* is my brother, John). Interrogative pronouns are used in questions (*who? which? what?*). Turn to 704.1 and 706.3–706.5 in *Write Source*.

> **Identify** the pronouns underlined in the sentences below. Use *IND* for indefinite, *DEM* for demonstrative, and *INT* for interrogative.

1   Many historians think the people who invented numbers lived in the Arab
      IND
2   world about 5,000 years ago. Yet <u>nobody</u> knows for certain who used numbers
      INT
3   first. <u>Which</u> of the ancient cultures had the greatest need for numbers? Our

4   answers may indicate who "invented" them.
                    INT   *INT*
5   For instance, <u>who</u> built the pyramids? <u>Who</u> built the Great Wall of China?
      IND
6   <u>Somebody</u> probably needed numbers to build these projects. And what about
                           IND
7   taxes? Even long ago, almost <u>everyone</u> had to pay them. How did the tax
                                 INT   *DEM*
8   collectors keep track of who had paid and <u>who</u> had not? Is <u>that</u> why people

9   invented a numeral system?
                          INT
10   In the current century, <u>who</u> could go through a day without numbers?
      IND   *IND*
11   Almost <u>everyone</u> learns about numbers at an early age. <u>Most</u> of us can hold up
                                                          DEM
12   two fingers to show our age when we are two years old. <u>That</u> may be the first
                                       IND
13   way we learn to use numbers today. <u>Everybody</u> uses numbers in some way;
      DEM
14   <u>these</u> are technological times.
            INT
15   <u>Who</u> invented numbers? Though we don't really know for sure, we know
            IND
16   that <u>whoever</u> it was changed the course of history.

Extend: Choose several indefinite, interrogative, and demonstrative pronouns from the chart on page 704 in *Write Source*. Write a sentence for each pronoun you select. Then read your sentences and have a classmate identify the pronouns.

   Writers INC 536.3–536.5 and p. 535

Review: Pronouns 2

> **Underline** and label the pronouns in the sentences below. Use *P* for personal, *R* for relative, *I* for indefinite, *INT* for interrogative, *DEM* for demonstrative, and *RX* for reflexive.

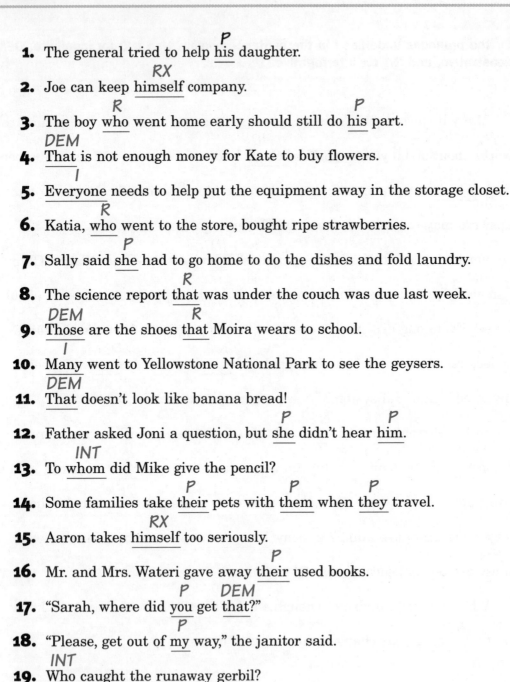

1. The general tried to help <u>his</u> daughter. *(P)*
2. Joe can keep <u>himself</u> company. *(RX)*
3. The boy <u>who</u> went home early should still do <u>his</u> part. *(R) (P)*
4. <u>That</u> is not enough money for Kate to buy flowers. *(DEM)*
5. <u>Everyone</u> needs to help put the equipment away in the storage closet. *(I)*
6. Katia, <u>who</u> went to the store, bought ripe strawberries. *(R)*
7. Sally said <u>she</u> had to go home to do the dishes and fold laundry. *(P)*
8. The science report <u>that</u> was under the couch was due last week. *(R)*
9. <u>Those</u> are the shoes <u>that</u> Moira wears to school. *(DEM) (R)*
10. <u>Many</u> went to Yellowstone National Park to see the geysers. *(I)*
11. <u>That</u> doesn't look like banana bread! *(DEM)*
12. Father asked Joni a question, but <u>she</u> didn't hear <u>him</u>. *(P) (P)*
13. To <u>whom</u> did Mike give the pencil? *(INT)*
14. Some families take <u>their</u> pets with <u>them</u> when <u>they</u> travel. *(P) (P) (P)*
15. Aaron takes <u>himself</u> too seriously. *(RX)*
16. Mr. and Mrs. Wateri gave away <u>their</u> used books. *(P)*
17. "Sarah, where did <u>you</u> get <u>that</u>?" *(P) (DEM)*
18. "Please, get out of <u>my</u> way," the janitor said. *(P)*
19. <u>Who</u> caught the runaway gerbil? *(INT)*
20. Give <u>yourself</u> credit for doing well on this review! *(RX)*

86

Pretest: Verbs

Circle all of the verbs in the following paragraphs. (Be sure not to circle any verbals.)

1   Creative writing (is) the best class! We (try) to activate all of our senses.
2   One day our teacher (gave) us gelatin cubes. We (looked) at them, (felt) them,
3   (smelled) them, (bounced) them, (tasted) them. Perry Thompson (pretended) to have
4   a conversation with his cube after he (named) it Ebenezer. Some days we (go)
5   for a walk around the school or through the halls in order to use all our senses.
6   Mrs. Zechel's home economics class (invited) us to tea. That (required) all our
7   senses and our best manners.
8   Each week we (get) an anthology of our writings: the best satire, the best
9   poem, the best sentence, a list of the best strong nouns and verbs, the piece
10 with the best sentence variety, a list of the most common errors, and so forth.
11 Our teacher (writes) comments on all these pieces; these comments (are) useful.
12 We (can) all (discover) what she (sees) in our writing. Some days we (write) to music.
13 We (read) some of our best writings at the local coffee shop several evenings
14 throughout the semester. Once a week we (measure) our fluency by printing on
15 a banner and then measuring the length of the banner. Last week I (wrote)
16 seven feet! I (am learning) a lot in creative writing. The writing practice (is) good
17 for me.

Provide the following information from the paragraph above.

Answers will vary.

1. List two linking verbs. _is, are_

2. List two auxiliary (helping) verbs. _can, am_

3. List five past tense verbs. _gave, looked, felt, smelled, bounced_

4. List six present tense verbs. _is, try, go, writes, sees, read_

5. In your opinion, what is the strongest verb in the paragraph? _Answers will vary._

6. List an irregular verb. _wrote_

Types of Verbs

A verb is a word that expresses action (*started, declare, ran*) or state of being (*is, are, am*). In this exercise, you will identify action verbs. You probably remember that some action verbs have helping verbs. They have already been underlined in the following narrative. Turn to page 714 and index number 716.1 in *Write Source*.

> **Underline** the action verbs in the following narrative. (Do not underline verbals.)

1   The era of the steam railroad in America <u>started</u> on a Saturday morning in

2   August, 1829, in the forest of eastern Pennsylvania. There Horatio Allen, a

3   bright, twenty-seven-year-old civil engineer and recent graduate of Columbia

4   College, introduced the country to the "Stourbridge Lion," a seven-ton

5   locomotive. Using the "Lion" as his test vehicle, Allen <u>hoped</u> to prove the

6   potential of steam-driven engines as an efficient means of mass transportation.

7   For the test, the locomotive <u>was</u> <u>driven</u> across nearby Lackawaxen Creek on a

8   makeshift wooden trestle that <u>formed</u> a curve nearly a quarter of a mile long.

9   The many eager onlookers <u>believed</u> that the locomotive known as the "iron

10 monster" <u>would</u> either <u>collapse</u> the trestle or <u>jump</u> the track at the curve, <u>go</u>

11 over the edge, and <u>plunge</u> into the creek thirty feet below. Risking no life but

12 his own, Allen, the future president of the Erie Railroad, <u>climbed</u> aboard the

13 "Lion," <u>took</u> the throttle, <u>started</u> down the track, and <u>made</u> the six-mile run

14 without mishap. Despite the success, the "Stourbridge Lion" <u>was</u> <u>declared</u> too

15 heavy for its tracks. It <u>was</u> <u>put</u> into storage and later <u>used</u> for parts. But this

16 one short run <u>opened</u> the way for future railroads to play a vital role in the

17 settlement and development of America.

(Did you find 17 verbs?)

Extend: Study a piece of your own writing. Underline the verbs. After reading about specific verbs on page 538 in *Write Source*, replace any weak verbs in your writing. Do you find any verbs in the above narrative that could be more vivid? If so, write your choice above the verb you would replace.

Auxiliary (Helping) & Linking Verbs

Linking verbs describe a "state of being." They simply tell us how someone or something is (or tastes, feels, looks, and so forth). Turn to 714.1 in *Write Source* for a list of linking verbs. Auxiliary verbs are "helpers." They are added to main verbs to form the perfect tenses and the passive voice. Turn to 714.2 in *Write Source*.

> **Underline** each linking verb or auxiliary verb in the sentences below. On the blanks provided, write *A* for the auxiliary verbs and *L* for the linking verbs.

___A___   **1.** Julius Caesar <u>was</u> born on July 12th or 13th in approximately 100 B.C.E.

___A___   **2.** Never before <u>had</u> Rome experienced an emperor of Caesar's military and political ability.

___L___   **3.** In his early life, Caesar <u>was</u> a military commander for part of the Roman empire.

___A___   **4.** Caesar <u>was</u> gaining political strength and popularity during this time.

___L___   **5.** He <u>looked</u> like a strong leader.

___A___   **6.** After Caesar <u>had</u> turned against Pompey—once his ally—he gained significant power.

___A___   **7.** He <u>may have</u> turned against Pompey for the good of Rome or for personal gain.

___A___   **8.** In 44 B.C.E., Caesar <u>was</u> crowned dictator for life.

___A___   **9.** But a number of prominent Romans <u>were</u> plotting against Caesar.

___A___   **10.** Brutus and other conspirators <u>had</u> plotted to kill Caesar on March 15, 44 B.C.E.

___L___   **11.** Brutus, once Caesar's friend, eventually <u>became</u> his worst enemy.

Extend: Write four or five sentences about a historical figure, using both linking and auxiliary verbs. Underline and label the linking and auxiliary verbs in the sentences you write.

Present, Past, & Future Tense Verbs

Writers use verb tenses to indicate time. The present tense of a verb states an action that is happening now or regularly. The past tense of a verb states an action that happened at a specific time in the past. The future tense of a verb states an action that will take place in the future. Turn to 718.3–718.4 in *Write Source*.

Rewrite the sentence in each group below using the tenses indicated. Keep the meaning of the sentences as close as possible to that of the original.

1. *Present:* Making a movie involves many people.

   Past: Making a movie involved many people.

   Future: Making a movie will involve many people.

2. *Present:* First, a screenwriter writes a script.

   Past: First, a screenwriter wrote a script.

   Future: First, a screenwriter will write a script.

3. *Present:* Next, the casting director picks the actors.

   Past: Next, the casting director picked the actors.

   Future: Next, the casting director will pick the actors.

4. *Present:* Then the crew builds the sets.

   Past: Then the crew built the sets.

   Future: Then the crew will build the sets.

5. *Present:* The director and editors assemble the final film.

   Past: The director and editors assembled the final film.

   Future: The director and editors will assemble the final film.

6. *Present:* Finally, you watch the movie while you eat your popcorn.

   Past: Finally, you watched the movie while you ate your popcorn.

   Future: Finally, you will watch the movie while you eat your popcorn.

Extend: Choose a short passage from a history book and rewrite it in the future tense.

Perfect Tense Verbs

It may take some practice, but you can understand verb tenses perfectly. Like simple tenses, perfect tenses deal with time. To learn about perfect tenses, turn to 720.1 in *Write Source*. Also refer to the past participles for irregular verbs on that page.

> **Write** the past participle for each of the present tense verbs listed below. Then, write the verb in the perfect tense indicated in the parentheses.

Present Tense	Past Participle	Perfect Tense of the Verb
1. be	been	(present perfect): has been (or) have been
2. fly	flown	(future perfect): will have flown
3. show	shown	(present perfect): has shown (or) have shown
4. take	taken	(past perfect): had taken
5. ride	ridden	(future perfect): will have ridden
6. run	run	(past perfect): had run
7. drag	dragged	(present perfect): has dragged (or) have dragged
8. lay	laid	(future perfect): will have laid
9. swim	swum	(past perfect): had swum
10. choose	chosen	(future perfect): will have chosen
11. go	gone	(past perfect): had gone
12. see	seen	(present perfect): has seen (or) have seen
13. shine	shone	(present perfect): has shone (or) have shone
14. freeze	frozen	(past perfect): had frozen
15. give	given	(future perfect): will have given

Extend: Write about yourself in each of the perfect tenses. Past perfect: What did you do last summer? Present perfect: What are you learning in your classes? Future perfect: What would you like to do next summer? (These are only examples—feel free to choose your own subjects.)

Review: Verbs 1

> **Underline** the verbs in the following sentences. Then identify auxiliary verbs with an *A* and linking verbs with an *L*.

1. My favorite meal <u>is</u> *L* meatloaf and sweet potatoes.

2. Chris's younger brother and sister <u>are</u> *L* twins.

3. Yolanda and Eric <u>are</u> *A* always <u>reading</u> advice columns.

4. Grandpa <u>has</u> *A* <u>been</u> *A* <u>forgetting</u> where he <u>puts</u> his eyeglasses.

5. We <u>were</u> *A* <u>studying</u> Emily Dickinson's poems last week.

6. My best friend and I <u>attend</u> the meetings for Young Diplomats.

7. <u>Do</u> *A* you <u>intend</u> to run for re-election in the next presidential race?

8. Her motto <u>is</u> *L* "Every day <u>is</u> *L* an adventure."

9. <u>Would</u> *A* you please <u>wipe</u> your shoes on the mat before coming in?

10. The sandwiches and salads <u>were</u> *L* good.

11. Everyone <u>was</u> *L* sorrowful when Mrs. Greene <u>announced</u> her retirement.

12. We <u>used</u> the Internet to find things to do during the summer vacation.

13. The choir <u>gave</u> a concert, and then they <u>began</u> their singing tour.

> **Write** a sentence using a present, past, or future tense verb.

Answers will vary.

My dad watched the launch of a satellite at Cape Canaveral, Florida.

> **Rewrite** your sentence using a perfect tense verb.

Answers will vary.

My dad has watched the launch of a satellite at Cape Canaveral, Florida.

Active & Passive Voice

A verb is said to be in the *active voice* when the subject is doing something. A verb is in the *passive voice* when the subject of the verb is being acted upon. Turn to 722.2 in *Write Source* for examples and more information.

Underline the verbs in the following sentences. On the blank at the left, write whether the voice is active or passive. Some sentences contain more than one verb.

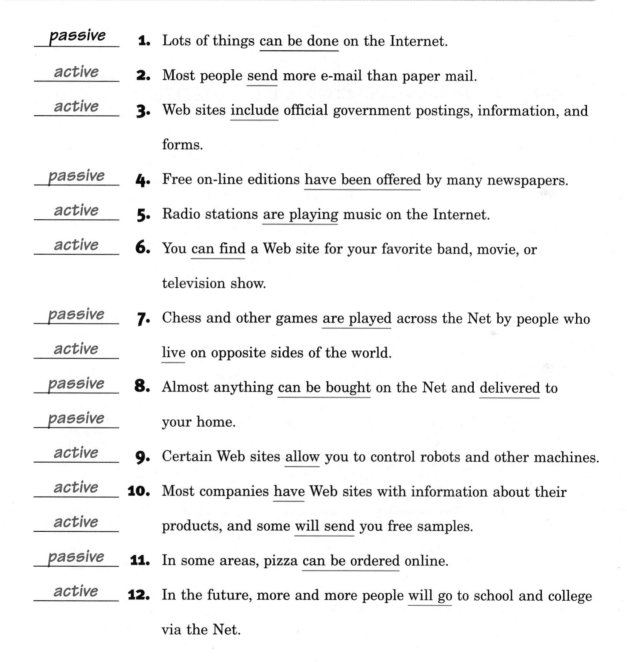

passive **1.** Lots of things <u>can be done</u> on the Internet.

active **2.** Most people <u>send</u> more e-mail than paper mail.

active **3.** Web sites <u>include</u> official government postings, information, and forms.

passive **4.** Free on-line editions <u>have been offered</u> by many newspapers.

active **5.** Radio stations <u>are playing</u> music on the Internet.

active **6.** You <u>can find</u> a Web site for your favorite band, movie, or television show.

passive **7.** Chess and other games <u>are played</u> across the Net by people who
active <u>live</u> on opposite sides of the world.

passive **8.** Almost anything <u>can be bought</u> on the Net and <u>delivered</u> to
passive your home.

active **9.** Certain Web sites <u>allow</u> you to control robots and other machines.

active **10.** Most companies <u>have</u> Web sites with information about their
active products, and some <u>will send</u> you free samples.

passive **11.** In some areas, pizza <u>can be ordered</u> online.

active **12.** In the future, more and more people <u>will go</u> to school and college via the Net.

Extend: Using an active voice, write three sentences about the Internet. Then rewrite them in the passive voice. Mark the sentences that you feel are strong and effective. Did you use active or passive voice in these sentences?

Transitive & Intransitive Verbs

A transitive verb shows action and is always followed by a direct object that receives the action. An intransitive verb refers to an action that is complete in itself. It does not need an object to receive the action. Turn to 716.1–716.2 in *Write Source*.

> **Underline** and label the verbs in the sentences below. Use *T* for transitive, *I* for intransitive. Circle all direct objects.

1. In 1925, Charles Francis Jenkins, an American, envisioned (television.) — *T*

2. Vladimir Kosma Zworykin gave America its first (camera tube,) several years later. — *T*

3. Philo Farnsworth contributed greatly to the invention of television. — *I*

4. Three American scientists invented the (transistor) in 1947. — *T*

5. Inventors worked hard to overcome obstacles. — *I*

6. The first regularly scheduled black-and-white telecasts for the public began in 1939. — *I*

7. In 1941, the Federal Communications Commission (FCC) authorized public (broadcasts) in the United States. — *T*

8. By 1950, six million Americans owned television (sets.) — *T*

9. Color TV became available to most people in the 1960s. — *I*

10. The FCC authorized (companies) to broadcast color images in 1954. — *T*

11. Flat-screen televisions came on the scene in the 1980s. — *I*

12. Now digital signals create cleaner, sharper (images) than previous TV signals. — *T*

Extend: Write five sentences about how your life would be different without television. Use both transitive and intransitive verbs. Exchange papers with a classmate. Underline all the verbs in each other's sentences. Indicate whether the verbs are transitive or intransitive and be prepared to explain why.

Direct & Indirect Objects

Direct objects and indirect objects receive the action of verbs and are usually nouns or pronouns. A sentence must have a direct object before it can have an indirect object. Turn to 716.2 in *Write Source*.

 Patty sang *Mother* a *song*.

Direct Object: song	**Indirect Object:** Mother
Who or *what* receives the action? (Patty sang *what?*)	*To whom* or *to what* was something done? (Patty sang *to whom?*)

> **Underline** and label the objects in the sentences below. Use *DO* for direct objects and *IO* for indirect objects. We've shown you how to use the question method.

1. Ben Franklin witnessed man's first successful <u>flight</u>, *[DO]* which occurred in 1783 in a lighter-than-air balloon invented by the Montgolfier brothers.

   (Ask yourself, "Ben Franklin witnessed **what?**")

2. The lighter-than-air balloon prompted further <u>experimentation</u> *[DO]* with heavier-than-air gliders.

   (Ask yourself, "Balloon prompted **what?**")

3. Soon inventors were testing heavier-than-air flying <u>machines</u>. *[DO]*

4. The wings on these heavier-than-air gliders needed a special <u>shape</u>, *[DO]* one that would force <u>air</u> *[DO]* to flow much faster over the top than across the bottom.

5. Air pressure gives the <u>wings</u> *[IO]* the <u>lift</u> *[DO]* they need to carry heavy objects aloft.

   (Ask yourself, "Air pressure gives **what?**"
   (Ask yourself, "**To what** was something given?")

6. The physical property of lift gave <u>Orville and Wilbur Wright</u> *[IO]* the <u>opportunity</u> *[DO]* to develop the first airplane.

   (Ask yourself, "The physical property of lift gave **what?**")
   (Ask yourself, "**To whom** was something given?")

7. Past glider designs gave the Wright <u>brothers</u> *[IO]* a <u>model</u> *[DO]* for their self-propelled aircraft.

8. An evolution of imaginative experiments formed the modern <u>airplane</u>. *[DO]*

Extend: Write three to five sentences about your favorite activity. Use direct objects and indirect objects and label them *DO* or *IO* (as above).

Verbals: Gerunds, Infinitives, & Participles

Verbals (gerunds, infinitives, and participles) can strengthen your writing. Use them to clarify and describe your ideas. Turn to page 726 in *Write Source* for examples.

Types of Verbals	Noun	Adjective	Adverb
Gerund	X		
Infinitive	X	X	X
Participle		X	

Underline and label the verbals in the sentences below. Use *G* for gerunds, *I* for infinitives, and *P* for participles.

1. *G*
Riding the roller coaster is the biggest thrill at the amusement park.

2. The first roller coaster to *I* thrill Americans was built in 1884.

3. *P*
Built by popular demand, the roller coaster has become a familiar attraction; today you'll find about 2,000 of them in the United States alone.

4. *G*
Standing in line is part of the roller coaster experience.

5. All that *G* waiting can be difficult!

6. Once *P* secured safely in their cars, the riders have no escape.

7. *I*
To be hurtled straight into the air at more than 70 mph challenges the bravest passengers.

8. The clang of wheels on the rail builds tension in passengers *P* anticipating the first *P* dizzying drop.

9. Some people raise their hands to *I* enhance the *P* thrusting force of the ride.

10. Stay away from too much cotton candy to *I* avoid roller-coaster sickness.

11. After the *P* thrilling ride is over, why not get back in line?

12. *G*
Riding the roller coaster ends a perfect day at the amusement park.

Extend: Imagine riding a roller coaster or another amusement-park ride. In a paragraph, describe the sensations, using verbals to enhance your description. You might want to make a list of possible verbals. You could then create sentences using the verbals in your list.

Irregular Verbs 1

It's easy to form the past tense and past participle of regular verbs. You simply add *d* or *ed* to the present tense: *walk, walked,* (have) *walked.* Irregular verbs don't follow these simple rules: *begin, began,* (have) *begun.* You need to memorize the forms of irregular verbs. See the chart "Common Irregular Verbs and Their Principal Parts" at 720.2 in *Write Source.*

> **Write** the correct forms of the irregular verbs below. (The verbs appear in parentheses.)

1. Ernest Hemingway, one of the most influential writers of the early twentieth century, ___*is*___ admired by many writers today. *(am)*

2. In 1917 Hemingway ___*chose*___ a career in journalism instead of attending college. *(choose)*

3. Hemingway's poor eyesight ___*kept*___ him from joining the armed forces. *(keep)*

4. However, Hemingway ___*was*___ a volunteer ambulance driver in World War I. *(am)*

5. He ___*wrote*___ his famous novel The Sun Also Rises in 1926. *(write)*

6. This book ___*brought*___ him fame. *(bring)*

7. Hemingway ___*went*___ to Europe and Africa, where he gathered material for his novels. *(go)*

8. After the United States entered World War II, Hemingway ___*fought*___ German submarines in the Caribbean with an armed cabin cruiser. *(fight)*

9. In 1944, when the Germans ___*fled*___, Hemingway followed as a war correspondent. *(flee)*

10. Hemingway was ___*given*___ the Pulitzer Prize for fiction in 1953, and he received the Nobel Prize for literature in 1954. *(give)*

Extend: Write sentences using the past tense and past participle of the following irregular verbs: *wear, know, do.*

Irregular Verbs 2

Regular verbs form their past and past participle by adding a *d* or an *ed* to the present tense: *talk, talked,* (have) *talked.* Irregular verbs form their past and past participle in some way other than the regular way: *sing, sang,* (have) *sung.* It is necessary to memorize the forms of irregular verbs. Turn to the list on page 720 in *Write Source.*

> **Circle** the correct verb forms in the sentences below.

1. Have you (**seen**, see, saw) the sunrise?

2. We often (seen, **see**, saw) the sunrise and hear the rooster crow.

3. I (seen, see, **saw**) the sunrise yesterday.

4. I have (saw, **seen**) the sunrise many times.

5. Mother asked me to (sit, **set**) the table.

6. I (sit, **sat**) and rested.

7. He (throwed, **threw**, thrown) the letter in the garbage.

8. Brighton will (**shake**, shook, shaken, shakes) with fear during storms.

9. Our dog (shaked, **shook**, shaken, shakes) with fear during the storm last night.

10. Bridget and Cleo have (weave, wove, **woven**) rugs for the craft fair next Friday.

11. The kindergarten class (draw, **drew**, drawn) pictures yesterday.

12. All the fruit salad has been (eat, ate, **eaten**).

13. The full moon (shine, **shone**, shined) on the lake as Margaret (**shined**, shone) her new shoes.

14. Have you (drunken, drank, **drunk**) the lake water?

15. We (fleed, **fled**) before the water rose.

16. Both of them (**come**, came) whenever I call.

17. Both of them (come, **came**) whenever I called.

Extend: Correct all your errors in the sentences above. Read the corrected sentences aloud several times. In this way, you train your ear to hear the correct usage.

Irregular Verbs 3

The principal parts of irregular verbs don't fit a simple pattern, so you need to memorize them. See 720.2 in *Write Source* for a list of some irregular verbs and their parts.

> **Correct** the mistakes below by writing the proper verb above the underlined words.

1. Tornadoes, also known as twisters or cyclones, have took [*taken*] many lives.

2. Tornadoes have tore [*torn*] towns apart and left paths of destruction 50 miles wide.

3. A tornado creates extreme low pressure that can cause buildings to explode as the tornado's effect is feel [*felt*].

4. Tornadoes can dragged [*drag*] objects for miles.

5. When a tornado warning is issued, people went [*go*] to basements for safety.

6. A tornado hanged [*hung*] in the air.

7. Later the huge funnel sinked [*sank*] to the ground, and we run [*ran*] to the basement.

8. One shocked man just sitted [*sat*] and watched the funnel cloud approach.

9. Another man lied [*lay*] in a ditch, covering his head.

10. Dad watched as the tornado dived [*dove*] toward the ground.

11. After the tornado, it was clear that many trees had fell [*fallen*].

12. The neighbor's fence had been threw [*thrown*] down the street.

13. The tornado had blew [*blown*] away one building, while leaving another building a few feet away untouched.

14. People come [*came*] from far away to help the victims of the tornado.

15. A tornado's tremendous destruction has often gave [*given*] many people a feeling of despair.

Extend: Write three sentences for each verb you used incorrectly in the above sentences.

Irregular Verbs: *Lie* and *Lay*

Here are the principal parts of *lie* and *lay*.

	Present	Present Participle	Past	Past Participle
>	**Lie** *(to recline)*	**(am) lying**	**lay**	**(have) lain**
	I want to *lie* down.			
>	**Lay** *(to put down)*	**(am) laying**	**laid**	**(have) laid**
	I *lay* my books on the table.			

> **Circle** the correct word in the parentheses in each of the sentences below.

1. The little baby *(lay, lie)* quietly in the corner of his crib.

2. After their 50-mile march, the soldiers *(lay, laid)* in their tents.

3. Where is my pen? I know I *(laid, lay)* it down here yesterday.

4. They have *(laid, lain)* the blankets on the ground in preparation for the concert.

5. She was *(laying, lying)* clothes out on the bed.

6. Last night I *(laid, lay)* awake in bed, listening to the storm.

7. I *(laid, lay)* my head upon the pillow.

8. If you are tired, *(lay, lie)* down on the sofa.

9. I was so exhausted that I could have *(lain, laid)* in bed all day.

10. Our hens are *(laying, lying)* eggs.

11. Please, *(lie, lay)* the newspaper down and talk to me.

12. Have you *(lain, laid)* the tile in the bath?

13. I'm going home and *(lay, lie)* in the sun.

14. That tree has been *(laying, lying)* in the lake since the storm.

15. Grandma has been *(laying, lying)* on the couch.

16. Does that rug *(lie, lay)* smoothly?

Extend: If you have trouble using *lie* and *lay,* read the sentences above aloud (after you are certain you have chosen the correct form). Read them several times. Hearing the correct form of *lie* and *lay* helps you learn them.

Review: Verbs 2

Underline and label the verbs in the sentences below. (In sentences with more than a one-word verb, be sure to underline the whole verb phrase.) Write *A* above a phrase containing an auxiliary verb and *L* above a linking verb.

1. Francine <u>was helping</u> [*A*] her grandma.

2. The American eagle <u>appears</u> [*L*] on the endangered-species list.

3. Oksana <u>will reach</u> [*A*] the top of the mountain in less than a week.

4. The bear <u>is</u> [*L*] badly injured.

5. At breakfast, the milk <u>smelled</u> [*L*] spoiled.

6. I <u>am telling</u> [*A*] you for the last time.

Underline the verbs below. Write *T* above a transitive verb and *I* above an intransitive verb. If the verb is transitive, write *DO* above the direct object and *IO* above any indirect object.

1. Justin <u>covered</u> [*T*] his book [*DO*] with aluminum foil.

2. The eagle <u>flew</u> [*I*] across the river.

3. Why don't you <u>give</u> [*T*] Peter [*IO*] the assignment [*DO*] at the end of class?

4. Peter <u>strutted</u> [*I*] down the street.

5. Chia <u>baked</u> [*T*] me [*IO*] a loaf [*DO*] of banana nut bread.

6. I <u>threw</u> [*T*] my dog [*IO*] the ball [*DO*].

Underline and label the verbals in the following sentences. Use *G* for gerund, *I* for infinitive, or *P* for participle.

1. <u>Running</u> [*G*] is good exercise.

2. I really like to <u>run</u> [*I*] on a treadmill.

3. The quarterback, <u>faking</u> [*P*] a pass, ran in for the touchdown.

4. I know you are going to track mud all over the house if I let you in.
   (I above track)

5. I enjoy tracking.
   (G above tracking)

6. The hunter tracking the deer stopped to catch his breath.
   (P above tracking)

Write the correct forms of the verbs (in parentheses) in the blanks in the sentences below.

1. He shouldn't have ___lain___ down there. *(lie)*

2. I ___ate___ the turkey sandwich yesterday. *(eat)*

3. The company had ___written___ him a letter. *(write)*

4. Last week the athlete ___swam___ the channel in about an hour. *(swim)*

5. Pat had ___torn___ his shirt while working on the car. *(tear)*

6. The magician ___showed___ me her sleeve before she performed the trick. *(show)*

7. The game was canceled because it had ___begun___ to rain. *(begin)*

8. The man ___took___ the stray dog to the animal shelter. *(take)*

Fill in the missing principal parts for the following irregular verbs.

	Present Tense	Past Tense	Past Participle
1.	go	went	gone
2.	wear	wore	worn
3.	keep	kept	kept
4.	sing	sang	sung
5.	speak	spoke	spoken
6.	take	took	taken
7.	show	showed	shown
8.	swing	swung	swung
9.	do	did	done

Pretest: Adjectives & Adverbs

> **Underline** the adjectives (except for any articles: *a*, *an*, or *the*) and draw arrows to the nouns they modify. **Circle** each adverb and draw an arrow to the verb, adjective, or adverb that it modifies.

1. Theodore Roosevelt advised, "Walk softly, but carry a big stick."

2. The singer filled the immense hall with a magnificent voice.

3. Pumpkins and corn grow well in the Midwest.

4. Harsh winters in the Alaskan wilderness claimed many lives during the Gold Rush.

5. It certainly appears that the tournament is running smoothly.

6. Obi-Wan Kenobi said quietly, "May the Force be with you."

7. The Italian restaurant sold more deep-dish pizzas this year than last year.

8. The turbo-charged car swerved dangerously around the corner.

> **Write** out the positive, the comparative, and/or the superlative forms of the following adjectives and adverbs.

	Positive	Comparative	Superlative
1.	fantastic	more fantastic	most fantastic
2.	tall	taller	tallest
3.	closely	more closely	most closely
4.	hungry	hungrier	hungriest
5.	badly	worse	worst
6.	pretty	prettier	prettiest
7.	likely	more likely	most likely
8.	soon	sooner	soonest

Adjectives

An adjective describes or in some way modifies a noun or pronoun. The articles—*a, an, the*—are always considered adjectives. Turn to page 728 in *Write Source*.

> **Insert** an appropriate adjective on each blank below. Use interesting and powerful adjectives to make the information come alive. Try not to repeat adjectives.

Answers will vary.

1   A couple of years ago, I started working at the high school radio station.

2   It's a ___wonderful___ experience. I help out by teaching ___interested___ students

3   and disc jockeys how to be ___excellent___ speakers. On the radio, it isn't

4   ___effective___ to talk in a ___monotone___ voice. A DJ has to be ___alert___

5   and ___energetic___. Only by having a ___lively___ voice does the DJ keep

6   ___some___ listeners from tuning out between ___the___ ___latest___ hits.

7   Many people scoff at the idea that the DJ matters, but don't you have _a_

8   ___favorite___ DJ on the station you listen to? The question is, "What makes him

9   or her so ___popular___?" Is she very ___upbeat___? Is he unusually ___funny___?

10   I give examples of ___good___ speaking voices. I know that each person will

11   have his or her own ___personal___ style, but my ___professional___ pointers help

12   the student DJ's see the effect of their styles. I would much rather listen to a

13   DJ who is ___talkative___ than one who seems ___sleepy___ or ___bored___.

14   The next time you listen to your radio, see if you can pick out the

15   ___professional___ DJ's from ___the___ ___amateur___ ones.

Extend: Choose an author you enjoy and select a passage from one of her or his books. Make a list of the adjectives you find there. Share your list with a classmate. Ask questions such as "How often does this author use adjectives?"; "Which adjectives are the most powerful?"; or "How do the adjectives add to the passage?" To help answer these questions, read each sentence aloud, leaving out all the adjectives.

Predicate Adjectives

Any adjective that follows a form of the verb "be" (or other linking verb) and describes the subject is a predicate adjective. Turn to 728.1 in *Write Source*.

> **Put** parentheses around the sentence in each pair that does not contain a predicate adjective. In the other sentence, underline the simple subject once and underline a predicate adjective twice.

1. a. (Ever since the fifth grade, I have played the saxophone in the school band.)

   b. Band <u>class</u> seemed <u>challenging</u> then, but I met a real challenge in high school.

2. a. (Marching band replaced band class as the hardest thing I'd ever done.)

   b. It may look <u>easy</u>, but <u>marching</u> while playing an instrument is very <u>difficult</u>.

3. a. (Not only did I (and everyone else in the band) have to memorize the music, but we also had to remember how we had to move on the field.)

   b. <u>That</u> was <u>hard</u> to do, especially when we practiced the music only a few times in the band room before starting to learn the marching maneuvers.

4. a. I know some people think marching <u>bands</u> are <u>silly</u>.

   b. (I travel with a great group of friends, visiting places I wouldn't see on my own.)

5. a. (Last year we traveled to Boston for a parade that honored war veterans.)

   b. Our <u>band</u> felt <u>honored</u> when the Rolling Along Veteran Band, all in wheelchairs, asked <u>us to play</u> a concert with them.

6. a. <u>We</u> sound <u>great</u> at sporting events, and <u>we</u> look <u>good</u> in our uniforms.

   b. (Everyone's friends and family come to watch us and cheer us on.)

Extend: Write three to five sentences about playing in a band (based on your experience or your imagination). Use linking verbs with predicate adjectives in your sentences. Then try to think of some action verbs to use in place of the linking verb + predicate adjective combination. Which version do you prefer?

Forms of Adjectives

Adjectives take three forms: *positive* (describing a noun or pronoun without comparing it to anything), *comparative* (comparing two nouns), and *superlative* (comparing three or more persons, places, things, or ideas). Turn to 728.2 in *Write Source*.

> **Read** each sentence below. Then rewrite it using the positive, comparative, and/or superlative form of the underlined adjective.

Answers will vary.

1. *Positive:* Michael Jordan was a <u>good</u> basketball player.

2. *Comparative:* Michael Jordan was a better basketball player than Larry Bird.

3. *Superlative:* Michael Jordan was the best basketball player ever.

4. *Positive:* Dracula is a scary creature.

5. *Comparative:* Dracula is a <u>scarier</u> creature than Godzilla.

6. *Superlative:* Dracula is the scariest creature of all.

7. *Positive:* That was a good meal.

8. *Comparative:* That was a better meal than I had yesterday.

9. *Superlative:* That was the <u>best</u> meal I've ever eaten.

10. *Positive:* I feel <u>silly</u> today.

11. *Comparative:* I feel sillier than I did yesterday.

12. *Superlative:* I feel the silliest I've ever felt.

13. *Positive:* This is a remarkable painting.

14. *Comparative:* This is a more remarkable painting than that one.

15. *Superlative:* This is the <u>most remarkable</u> painting I've seen all day.

Extend: Compose three to five sentences containing positive adjectives. Next rewrite each sentence using the comparative and superlative forms. Would one of your sentences be an excellent beginning statement for a piece of writing?

Review: Adjectives

> **Underline** all the adjectives in the sentences below. Write *C* above a comparative adjective, *S* above a superlative adjective, and *P* above all predicate adjectives.

1. That dog is exceptionally <u>friendly</u>. ^P

2. A <u>family</u> dog should be both <u>well-trained</u> and <u>cooperative</u>. ^{P   P}

3. I think <u>golden</u> retrievers are <u>better</u> than greyhounds as <u>family</u> dogs. ^{C/P}

4. <u>Labrador</u> retrievers are also <u>good</u> pets, especially for children.

5. If you like <u>gentle</u>, <u>intelligent</u> dogs, then nothing can compare to <u>the</u> collie.

6. Poodles can be <u>large</u> or <u>small</u> and are frequently crossbred with <u>other</u> dogs. ^{P   P}

7. A <u>graceful</u>, <u>quick</u> dog, the Siberian husky is also <u>alert</u> and <u>strong</u>. ^{P   P}

8. <u>Loyal</u>, <u>gentle</u>, and <u>intelligent</u> sheepdogs herd and guard sheep.

9. The <u>Chinese</u> shar-pei has <u>loose</u> skin, <u>many</u> wrinkles, and <u>a</u> <u>blue-black</u> tongue.

10. <u>Every</u> dog needs <u>nutritious</u> food and <u>fresh</u> water <u>every</u> day.

11. Most dogs are <u>energetic</u> and enjoy walking, running, and playing. ^P

12. Dogs require <u>more</u> care than cats. ^C

13. Some dogs are <u>intelligent</u>; others are <u>strong</u>. ^{P   P}

14. <u>Many</u> people think <u>the</u> <u>smallest</u> dog is <u>the</u> Chihuahua. ^S

15. <u>Most</u> dogs are <u>loyal</u> companions, and they need owners who are equally <u>faithful</u>. ^P

16. Perhaps <u>the</u> <u>biggest</u> challenge for <u>busy</u> owners is spending time with their dog. ^S

17. You can often find <u>a</u> <u>suitable</u> dog at <u>an</u> <u>animal</u> shelter.

18. Having <u>a</u> dog is <u>hard</u> work, but it can be very <u>enjoyable</u>. ^P

Adverbs

Adverbs modify a verb, an adjective, or another adverb. They tell the reader *how, when, where, why, how often,* or *how much* something happens. This exercise will help you identify adverbs. Turn to page 730 in *Write Source*.

> **Underline** the adverbs in the following sentences. The correct number of adverbs in each sentence is given in parentheses.

1. My parents <u>regularly</u> invite friends over for dinner. (*1*)

2. I <u>rarely</u> help prepare for the dinners, but I <u>badly</u> needed to make some money and I knew my parents would <u>really</u> appreciate the help. (*3*)

3. My mother left me a list of "things to do," and I <u>very</u> <u>diligently</u> worked my way through it. (*2*)

4. I <u>precisely</u> measured and <u>carefully</u> chopped the ingredients for the meal. (*2*)

5. I had almost everything ready when the phone <u>suddenly</u> rang. (*1*)

6. I <u>quickly</u> jumped <u>up</u> to answer it and <u>accidentally</u> knocked the cutting board and three full bowls of ingredients to the floor. (*3*)

7. I stood <u>completely</u> stunned for a moment and <u>then</u> answered the phone. (*2*)

8. My mother <u>cheerily</u> said she'd called to see how I was doing and that she'd return <u>shortly</u>. (*2*)

9. I <u>reluctantly</u> said okay, <u>slowly</u> hung up the phone, and <u>dejectedly</u> looked at the mess covering the floor. (*3*)

10. I sulked for a moment, <u>then</u> <u>busily</u> cleaned up the mass of ingredients that covered the floor. (*2*)

11. We had enough extra ingredients in the house for me to <u>hurriedly</u> duplicate all my work . . . without my mother <u>ever</u> knowing what had happened. (*2*)

Extend: List the adverbs in the above exercise on a piece of your own paper. Catalog each adverb by time, place, manner, or degree. See 730.

Types of Adverbs

An adverb modifies a verb, an adjective, or another adverb. Adverbs can be cataloged in four basic ways: time, place, manner, and degree. Turn to 730.1 in *Write Source*.

> **Rewrite** the sentences below following the instructions in parentheses. In the blank at the left, tell whether the italicized adverb shows time, place, manner, or degree.

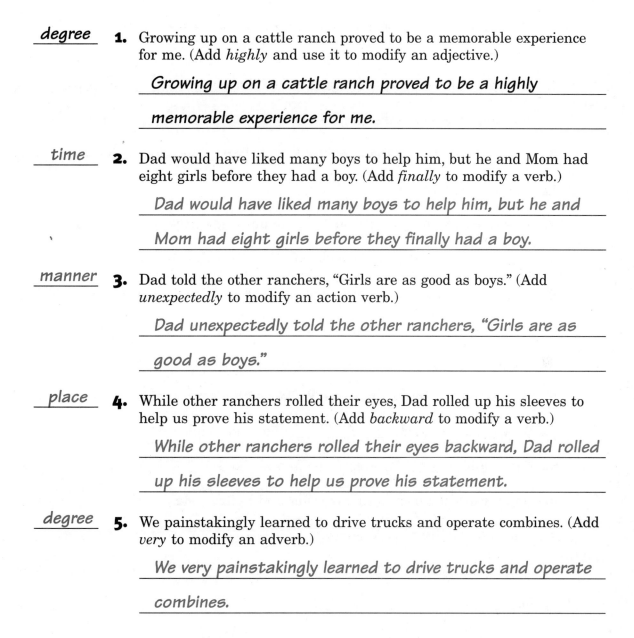

degree   **1.** Growing up on a cattle ranch proved to be a memorable experience for me. (Add *highly* and use it to modify an adjective.)

Growing up on a cattle ranch proved to be a highly

memorable experience for me.

time   **2.** Dad would have liked many boys to help him, but he and Mom had eight girls before they had a boy. (Add *finally* to modify a verb.)

Dad would have liked many boys to help him, but he and

Mom had eight girls before they finally had a boy.

manner   **3.** Dad told the other ranchers, "Girls are as good as boys." (Add *unexpectedly* to modify an action verb.)

Dad unexpectedly told the other ranchers, "Girls are as

good as boys."

place   **4.** While other ranchers rolled their eyes, Dad rolled up his sleeves to help us prove his statement. (Add *backward* to modify a verb.)

While other ranchers rolled their eyes backward, Dad rolled

up his sleeves to help us prove his statement.

degree   **5.** We painstakingly learned to drive trucks and operate combines. (Add *very* to modify an adverb.)

We very painstakingly learned to drive trucks and operate

combines.

Extend: Use the five italicized adverbs in parentheses above in sentences of your own. Circle each adverb and draw an arrow to the verb, adjective, or adverb it modifies.

Forms of Adverbs

Adverbs, like adjectives, have three forms: *positive*, *comparative*, and *superlative*. (Turn to 730.2 in *Write Source*.) Use the comparative form to compare two things, the superlative to compare three or more. Most one-syllable adverbs take the endings -er or -est (soon, sooner, soonest) to create the comparative and superlative forms; but longer adverbs and almost all those ending in -ly use *more* and *most* or *less* and *least* (more ambitiously, most ambitiously; less ambitiously, least ambitiously).

Add an adverb to each sentence below. Be sure to use the correct form.

Answers will vary.

1. The part of growing up on a ranch that I liked ____*best*____ of all was having acres and acres of native prairie to roam.

2. One part of ranching that I did very ____*well*____ was riding horses.

3. The horses moved quite ____*swiftly*____.

4. Whenever my horse veered suddenly to put a cow back in the herd, I had to try ____*hard*____ to stay in the saddle.

5. Susan, my sister, was a great rider, and she could control horses ____*better*____ than I could.

6. For pleasure riding, we used several horses, and I liked Goldie ____*best*____ of all because she was a Tennessee Walker with a smooth gait.

7. We went on trail rides ____*sooner*____ than most children.

8. Dad would ____*carefully*____ carry us in a blanket.

9. On an early summer morn, my sister and I often rode ____*slowly*____ to the top of Juneberry Hill to pick berries.

10. Mom, compared to all the rest of us, was the ____*most*____ likely to drive our pickup.

11. She packed picnic breakfasts ____*better*____ than I did.

12. After eating, we would ____*quickly*____ fill our buckets with berries and head for home.

Using *Good* and *Well*

Good is always used as an adjective. *Well* can be used as either an adjective or an adverb. Turn to page 686 in *Write Source*.

> **I get *good* grades.** (*Good* is an adjective; it modifies the noun *grades*.)

> **I am *good*.** (*Good* is a predicate adjective that describes *I*. *Good* is used as an adjective to mean "able" or "not bad.")

> **I am *well*.** (*Well* is a predicate adjective that describes *I*. *Well* is used as an adjective to mean "healthy.")

> **He sang *well*.** (*Well* is an adverb; it modifies *sang*.)

Circle the correct word (*good* or *well*) in the following sentences. Draw an arrow to the word that *good* or *well* modifies.

1. The circus had a number of very (*good*, *well*) acts.
2. The trained seals performed exceptionally (*good*, *well*)!
3. It must take a long time to train seals that (*good*, *well*).
4. The ringmaster introduced the acts (*good*, *well*).
5. It is (*good*, *well*) that the lions are well-trained.
6. The lion tamer seems to know each lion (*good*, *well*).
7. The flying trapeze acts went (*good*, *well*).
8. Every band member plays several instruments (*good*, *well*).
9. Laughing at the clowns felt (*good*, *well*).
10. The hot dogs always taste so (*good*, *well*) at a circus.
11. It was (*good*, *well*) that we took our little sisters and brothers with us.
12. They behaved surprisingly (*good*, *well*).
13. It must take a lot of practice to be a (*good*, *well*) clown.
14. Roasted peanuts smell (*good*, *well*).
15. Going to the circus makes everyone feel (*good*, *well*).

Extend: Write three to five sentences using *good* and *well*. Exchange papers with a classmate and discuss whether you have used these words correctly.

Review: Adverbs

Circle all the adverbs in the following narrative. There are 40 adverbs.

1   It was (so) hot! We sweated as we marched (slowly) under the scorching sun.

2   Our wool band uniforms grew heavier and heavier, clinging (more) and (more)

3   (tightly) to our bodies. (Suddenly,) the tuba player fell (backward.) Several

4   paramedics rushed to him and (quickly) moved him to the sideline. (Still) we

5   marched (on,) (regally) and (precisely.)

6   (Then,) a flute player fell (down.) The front three rows marched (away)

7   because they had (not) seen the girl faint. The rest of the band stopped,

8   however. Watching the chaos, the band director blew his whistle (sharply.) (Now)

9   the front rows stopped (abruptly)—a half-dozen paces (away.) Several parents

10 began (vigorously) fanning the flute player. The band director told us to take (off)

11 our jackets and hats. (We laid them (neatly) on the curb.) Firefighters and

12 paramedics began passing cups of water (around.) (Finally,) the flute player

13 revived, and someone (carefully) helped her to the curb.

14   When the mayhem was over, the band director blew his whistle (twice,) and

15 we (quickly) re-formed. We had (just) marched past the reviewing stand when

16 (suddenly) water was swirling (everywhere!) The firefighters had opened a

17 hydrant. Spectators, both young and old, began to splash one another with

18 water. Some people sat (down) in the cool spray. We stood frozen in our rows,

19 waiting for a whistle blast that would tell us what to do (next.) The band

20 director (just) stood (silently,) staring (blankly.) (Apparently) he had (never)

21 encountered anything like this. "Go (back) to the gym," he said. "(Quickly) get

22 into your street clothes, and let's get cool."

Pretest: Prepositions, Conjunctions, & Interjections

> **Underline** the prepositional phrases in the following sentences. Then circle each preposition and write *O* above each object of the preposition.

1. Step behind the line so that you can shoot the free throw.

2. Yikes! What is in the attic?

3. Since you seem to have so many of the answers, you do it.

4. Though she had polio as a child, Wilma Rudolph won gold medals during the 1960 Olympic Games in Rome.

5. Organ donors give the gift of life, yet many people do not have the donor sticker placed on their drivers' licenses.

6. Good grief! Both the emu and the ostrich are born with weird legs.

7. Throughout history, people have studied the stars and the planets.

8. Either pull the weeds out of the flower bed or shovel the grain into the grainery.

9. If you look out the bus window and peer down the street, you can see the tower on top of the John Hancock Building.

> **List** the interjections and conjunctions from the sentences above, placing each in the appropriate column below.

Interjections	Coordinating Conjunctions	Subordinating Conjunctions	Correlative Conjunctions
Yikes	and	so that	Both, and
Good grief	yet	Since	Either, or
	and	Though	
		If	

Prepositions & Interjections

A preposition is a word (or group of words) that shows the relationship between its object (a noun or a pronoun that follows the preposition) and another word in the sentence. Turn to page 732 in *Write Source*.

An interjection is included in a sentence in order to communicate emotion or surprise. Interjections are set off from the rest of the sentence with either a comma or an exclamation point. Turn to page 734 in *Write Source*.

> **Underline** the prepositional phrases in the following narrative and then circle the prepositions. Write *INT* above any interjections.

1   *INT*
     "Hey, Rita!" Bill called as he saw Rita limping toward him on crutches.

2   "Why are you wearing a cast? What happened to you?"

3   "Hi, Bill," Rita said as she looked up at him. "I guess you didn't hear that I

4   was in a car accident last week."

5   *INT*
     "Wow! No, I didn't hear. I'm sorry. Was anyone else in the car with you?"

6   *INT*
     "Yeah, my little brother," she said.

7   "I hope he wasn't hurt! I can't imagine the amount of trouble I'd get in if

8   my little brother got hurt while I was driving," Bill said.

9   *INT*
     "No kidding! My brother was actually thrown out of the car when the

10   passenger door popped open. He landed about 15 feet from the car in an

11   overgrown ditch. But he wasn't hurt, except for a few scrapes."

12   *INT*
     "Whew! Thank goodness for that," said Bill.

13   "I'd just gotten done telling him to wear his seat belt," Rita said. "Mom

14   really yelled at him when she found out he hadn't been wearing it." Rita

15   leaned back against the wall and moved her crutches so she could lean on

16   them.

Extend I: Copy a passage from a book or write down lyrics to a song and then underline all the prepositional phrases. In a small group, compare your work. Were prepositional phrases used a lot?

Extend II: Try to go an entire day without using any interjections. Or, write down every interjection you use in a day.

Coordinating Conjunctions

Words, phrases, and clauses are often connected to one another by coordinating conjunctions such as *and, but, or, for, nor, so,* and *yet.* Coordinating conjunctions link words, phrases, or clauses that are equal or of the same type. Turn to page 734. Study the chart "Kinds of Conjunctions."

Underline all of the coordinating conjunctions in the following passage.

1 I've been playing soccer a long time, <u>so</u> it seems like second nature to me.

2 I started when I was only eight <u>and</u> have played every year since then. At first

3 my parents were worried that I might get hurt, <u>but</u> when they saw me play,

4 they were impressed <u>and</u> encouraged me to continue. I have never been injured

5 while playing, <u>nor</u> have I ever missed a game. (Actually, I did miss one game

6 for a family vacation, <u>but</u> I told my coaches ahead of time.)

7 I think it's odd that soccer is so popular in other countries, <u>yet</u> in the

8 United States it's one of the least popular team sports. I realize that it has

9 become more popular over the past few years, <u>but</u> I think soccer is much more

10 fun <u>and</u> interesting than baseball, football, <u>or</u> hockey. Some people say it's a

11 boring sport <u>and</u> has no strategy to it, <u>but</u> I think those people aren't truly

12 familiar with the game.

13 Soccer is all about strategy, <u>but</u> it's not the slow, plodding strategy of

14 football. Soccer demands a fast-paced, think-on-your-feet strategy: *Where's the*

15 *ball? Who's most likely to get the next pass? Can I intercept <u>or</u> should I pull*

16 *back <u>and</u> defend? What is the main weakness <u>or</u> bad habit of the opposing*

17 *goalie?* All of these questions race through my mind as I'm playing, <u>and</u> I have

18 to decide what's best for the team <u>and</u> which options will ultimately pay off in

19 the form of a goal.

Extend: Write a paragraph about how you can use coordinating conjunctions in sentences to improve your writing. Include examples to illustrate your point. You might begin, "I often use coordinating conjunctions to join two sentences."

Writers INC 548.1

Correlative Conjunctions

Correlative conjunctions are conjunctions used in pairs. Turn to 734.2 in *Write Source* for examples and more information. Also use the chart "Kinds of Conjunctions" on page 734.

> **Write** sentences using the correlative conjunctions that are listed in the parentheses.

Answers will vary.

1. *(not only, but also)*

I not only like oatmeal for breakfast, but I also like it for lunch.

2. *(both, and)*

Both my brother and my sister are graduating today.

3. *(either, or)*

Either we celebrate your birthday today, or we celebrate it on the weekend.

4. *(neither, nor)*

This table is neither stable nor level.

5. *(whether, or)*

He decided he would enjoy the vacation whether he took it in the summer or he took it in the fall.

6. *(both, and)*

When the tornado siren began, both my mom and I headed to the basement.

7. *(not only, but also)*

Not only was Jenny the captain of the varsity soccer team, but she was also the president of the student council.

Extend: Edit a piece of your writing. Try to join short sentences with correlative conjunctions to make longer, stronger statements.

Subordinating Conjunctions

A subordinating conjunction connects a dependent clause to an independent clause. Turn to 734.3 in *Write Source*. Also use the chart "Kinds of Conjunctions."

> **Join** the following sentence pairs using a subordinating conjunction. **Consider which sentence should become the subordinate clause, and whether it should begin or end the sentence.**

Answers may vary.

1. My mother gave me guitar lessons for a gift. It was my birthday.

Since it was my birthday, my mother gave me guitar lessons for a gift.

2. I could take them any time I wanted. I began my first lesson in the summer.

Although I could take them any time I wanted, I began my first lesson in the summer.

3. I went to the music store. My teacher showed me different kinds of guitars.

I went to the music store where my teacher showed me different kinds of guitars.

4. He showed me the six different strings on the guitar. He explained the guitar's other parts.

After he showed me the six different strings on the guitar, he explained the guitar's other parts.

5. My first lesson went well. My mother took me to get some frozen yogurt.

Since my first lesson went well, my mother took me to get some frozen yogurt.

6. I practice an hour every day. I want to join a band.

Because I want to join a band, I practice an hour every day.

Extend: Write five to eight sentences, each containing a different subordinating conjunction. Read your sentences to a classmate and ask him or her to identify each subordinating conjunction.

Review: Prepositions, Conjunctions, & Interjections

Underline each interjection once and each preposition twice in the sentences below. Then circle each conjunction and identify it by writing coordinating, correlative, or subordinating on the blank at the left.

coordinating   **1.** Yeah, I have the ball (and) the bat in my basement.

coordinating   **2.** Hey! Where do you think you're going with my bat (and) ball?

correlative   **3.** In spite of all the time I've spent on the shores of Lake Michigan, I have learned (neither) how to swim (nor) how to sail.

subordinating   **4.** (After) we went to the basketball game, I wanted a basketball hoop in my backyard.

subordinating   **5.** Yipes, that bee nearly stung you (while) you weren't looking.

correlative   **6.** I think we can see (both) the Badlands (and) Yellowstone National Park during our two-week vacation.

subordinating   **7.** No! I will not eat mashed potatoes with gravy (after) the gravy gets cold.

subordinating   **8.** I'll go to the store (while) you're gone.

subordinating   **9.** Oh, well! Jevon will have to go home (before) the game is over (if) he doesn't want to get into trouble.

coordinating   **10.** I went down the hole, through the tunnel, (and) into the water to finally retrieve my hat.

subordinating   **11.** My gosh, you have grown (since) I last saw you.

coordinating   **12.** Yes, my brother threw three touchdown passes, (but) we still lost the game.

subordinating   **13.** I don't want to hear about any problems the babysitter had with you (while) I was gone.

subordinating   **14.** Ouch! I burnt my tongue (when) I tasted the pizza..

correlative   **15.** The Pony Express riders made their deliveries (whether) it snowed (or) not.

Review: Parts of Speech Activities

> **Identify** the part of speech that each underlined word represents. Use the following labels: *N* for noun, *V* for verb, *PRO* for pronoun, *ADJ* for adjective, *ADV* for adverb, *PREP* for preposition, *C* for conjunction, and *I* for interjection.

1   This summer I'm going on a *backpacking* [ADJ] trip with my friend Aaron

2   *and* [C] his *dad* [N]. We're going to hike *through* [PREP] Yellowstone National Park for

3   five days. Backpacking is a lot *like* [PREP] camping, *but* [C] you have to carry

4   everything *you* [PRO] need while you hike.

5   Aaron has been *backpacking* [V] *before* [ADV], *so* [C] last weekend he *helped* [V] me load my

6   new backpack so I could practice using it. The first thing *we* [PRO] packed was

7   clothing, including a *warm* [ADJ] sweater and jeans for when we go up into the

8   *mountains* [N]—it gets cold *there* [ADV]! Next I added a *small* [ADJ] bag *with* [PREP] my flashlight,

9   my toothbrush, and some sunscreen. Then I *attached* [V] my sleeping bag to the

10   bottom *of* [PREP] the pack.

11   I will *have* [V] to carry more than just my personal *gear* [N], though. *Our* [PRO] camp

12   stove *and* [C] a big cooking pot went *into* [PREP] my pack next. They're *really* [ADV] heavy, *but* [C]

13   *Aaron* [N] has to carry something even heavier: our tent.

14   *Though* [C] I don't think I'll be able to make it for long, Aaron *says* [V] that I'll be

15   walking around *easily* [ADV] once I get used to the pack on my shoulders. He says

16   the trails are *not* [ADV] exactly like sidewalks in our neighborhood. In fact, *some* [PRO]

17   may be *snow-covered* [ADJ], rocky, and steep. *When* [C] we go up into the mountains,

18   we will have to adjust to the *higher* [ADJ] elevations. *Wow* [I], I can't wait.

Complete the following statements.

1. A _____noun_____ is a word that names a person, a place, a thing, or an idea.

2. When a noun or a pronoun is used as a direct object, an _____indirect object_____, or an _____object of the preposition_____, it is in the objective case.

3. When a noun or a pronoun shows ownership, it is in the _____possessive_____ case.

4. A _____pronoun_____ can be used in place of a noun.

5. A _____noun_____ or a _____pronoun_____ is used as the subject of a sentence or a clause.

6. *Who, whose, whom, which,* and *that* are _____relative pronouns_____ .

7. A _____verb_____ expresses action or a state of being.

8. *I see* is an example of the _____present_____ tense; *I saw* is an example of the _____past_____ tense; *I will see* is an example of the _____future_____ tense.

9. In the following sentence, the word _____skateboard_____ is the direct object: *The boy proudly showed me his skateboard.*

10. In the following sentence, the word _____me_____ is an indirect object: *Ruth-Anne gave me an extravagant birthday present.*

11. Adjectives describe or modify _____nouns_____ or _____pronouns_____ .

12. Adverbs modify _____verbs_____ , _____adjectives_____ , or _____other adverbs_____ .

13. The word *smart* is a predicate _____adjective_____ in the following sentence: *Tarzan is smart.*

14. In the phrase *behind the door,* the word *behind* is a _____preposition_____ .

15. The words *and, but, or, nor, for, yet,* and *so* are coordinating _____conjunctions_____ .

16. A _____conjunction_____ connects individual words or groups of words.

17. An _____interjection_____ shows strong emotion or surprise.

Sentence Activities

The activities in this section cover three important areas: (1) the basic parts, types, and kinds of sentences as well as agreement issues; (2) methods for writing smooth-reading sentences; and (3) common sentence errors. Most activities include practice in which you review, combine, or analyze different sentences. In addition, the **Extend** activities will give follow-up practice with certain skills.

Pretest: Subjects & Predicates

Underline the simple subject once and the simple predicate twice in the following sentences. If the subject is understood, as in the first statement, insert the understood subject within parentheses.

1. *(You)* <u>Bring</u> the chair over here, please.

2. The <u>cat</u> <u>ate</u> the tuna-fish sandwich.

3. <u>What</u> <u>is keeping</u> them?

4. <u>They</u> <u>are playing</u> soccer on field number four.

5. <u>You</u> <u>can help</u> your dad with the laundry.

6. Where <u>is</u> Jacqui's blue-sequined <u>dress</u>?

7. <u>Thomas Alva Edison</u> <u>invented</u> the phonograph and the electric lightbulb.

8. *(You)* <u>Put</u> more slack on the sail!

Underline the complete subject once and the complete predicate twice in the following sentences. If either the subject or the predicate is compound, write **C** above it.

1. <u>Red, yellow, and orange tulips</u> <u>grow and flourish in Holland.</u> *C*

2. <u>From small, plain caterpillars come</u> <u>bright and beautiful butterflies.</u>

3. <u>Hamburgers, hot dogs, and tacos</u> *C* <u>are my favorite foods.</u>

4. <u>Fly-fishing and canoeing</u> *C* <u>are popular activities in Wisconsin and Minnesota.</u>

5. <u>Students</u> <u>should walk quickly to the exits if the alarm sounds.</u>

6. <u>Are</u> <u>you and Rosa</u> *C* <u>walking or riding your bikes to the park?</u> *C*

7. <u>Evel Knievel</u> <u>jumped motorcycles over cars, buses, walls, and even buildings.</u>

8. <u>Elk, moose, and other large mammals</u> *C* <u>inhabit Yellowstone National Park.</u>

9. <u>Ginger Rogers and Fred Astaire</u> *C* <u>tap-danced and tangoed their way through</u> *C* <u>many old films during the '30s and '40s.</u>

Simple Subjects & Predicates

All sentences must have a subject (noun or pronoun) and a predicate (verb) and express a complete thought. A simple subject is the subject without the words that modify it. A simple predicate is the verb without the words that modify it. Turn to 738.1 and 740.1 in *Write Source* for examples.

> **Underline** the simple subjects once and the simple predicates twice in the following sentences.

1. Many aspects of daily life depend upon electricity.

2. Electricity is a basic part of the matter in the universe.

3. In the human body, electrical signals carry information to and from the brain.

4. Electrical signals tell the brain what the eyes see, what the ears hear, and what the fingers feel.

5. The brain, using electrical signals, tells muscles to move.

6. During the 1800s, people learned to use electricity to do work.

7. Soon inventors learned to generate electrical energy in large quantities.

8. Electricity has many practical applications.

9. Lighting, one practical application, has changed the way people live.

10. Could you imagine life without electricity?

11. Computers use electricity to process information.

12. Without electricity, modern manufacturing would be impossible.

13. Satellites use electrical energy to send information around the world.

14. Most cars depend on an electric spark to start the engine.

15. Yes, electricity makes our lives more productive.

Extend: Write a paragraph about what your life would be like without electricity. Underline each simple subject once and each simple predicate twice. Look carefully at your subjects and predicates. Could you use a more specific noun for some subjects or a stronger verb for some predicates?

Simple, Complete, & Compound Subjects and Predicates

A simple subject or predicate is the subject or predicate without the words that describe or modify it. The complete subject or predicate includes the simple subject or predicate and all the words that modify or explain it. Compound subjects or predicates are composed of two or more simple subjects or predicates. Turn to 738.1 and 740.1 in *Write Source* for examples.

> **Circle** the simple subjects and underline the simple predicates in the following sentences. Draw a line between the complete subject and the complete predicate. Write *CS* above compound subjects and *CP* above compound predicates.

1. (Scientists) | conduct research in Antarctica.

2. (Antarctica)—the world's coldest, windiest, highest continent—is not an easy place to work.

3. Harsh (conditions) | face the men and women who go there.

4. The world's biggest laboratory, (Antarctica) | is reserved for science by international agreement.

5. (Scientists) | recorded the world's lowest temperature there: –89.2° C (–128.6° F).

6. Antarctic (winds) | average 44 miles per hour, but (they) | can gust to 120 miles per hour.

7. Most (scientists) and support (staff) | conduct research from spring through fall *CS* *CP* and head home for the winter (which is actually summer in the Northern Hemisphere).

8. Complete (darkness) and extreme (cold) | isolate Antarctica and discourage *CS* *CP* research during the six-month-long winter.

9. Antarctica's dry, cold (climate) and unusually clear summer (skies) | create *CS* excellent conditions for astrophysicists and other scientists.

Extend: Select a passage from your own writing. Identify both the simple and complete subjects and predicates. If you frequently write fragments or run-on sentences, this practice (finding the subjects and predicates) can help you identify and correct such errors.

    Writers INC 550.1 and 551.2

Review: Subjects & Predicates

Expand the simple subjects and predicates in the following sentences.

Answers will vary.

1. Parents hesitate.

   My parents hesitate to give me advice about how to succeed in life.

2. Advice can be rejected.

   Advice and good counsel can be accepted or rejected by anyone.

3. She will vote in the next election.

   Because of all the debates on television, she will vote in the next election.

4. Dogs bark.

   Our neighbors' dogs bark in the middle of the night.

5. Fireworks explode.

   On New Year's Eve, fireworks explode from the top of Granddad's Bluff overlooking La Crosse, Wisconsin.

Write three sentences using complete subjects and predicates. Circle the simple subjects and underline the simple predicates in the sentences you wrote. Draw a line between the complete subject and the complete predicate in each sentence.

Answers will vary.

1. The lost (backpacker) wondered when she would find her way to safety.

2. Tired and sore from the long hike, (he) crawled into his sleeping bag without eating supper.

3. The (janitors) opened the gym door for the dance.

Pretest: Phrases

> **Identify** the underlined phrases using *G* for gerund, *I* for infinitive, *P* for participial, and *A* for appositive. Circle all the prepositional phrases. A prepositional phrase is often part of another kind of phrase. Study the first sentence to learn how to mark such constructions.

1. Shaking violently (from the cold,) Janis couldn't wait outside any longer.   [*P*]

2. To earn a grade based (on effort) seemed fair (to the students.)   [*I*]

3. Leonardo da Vinci's famous painting, *the Mona Lisa*, portrays an unknown woman.   [*A*]

4. Walking alone (at night) is not safe.   [*G*]

5. The entire building, the two shops and the bank, was being renovated.   [*A*]

6. The town's safety codes (about renovating old structures) are outdated.   [*G*]

7. His empty stomach, rumbling (like an avalanche,) needed food.   [*P*]

8. The alarm clock told him it was time to get up and work (in the shop.)   [*I*]

> **Underline** and identify the phrases in the following sentences. Use the same symbols as above and circle the prepositional phrases.

1. (In the game) of baseball,) stealing first base is impossible.   [*G*]

2. Why is it so hard to steal first base?   [*I*]

3. Raising the coffin's lid, Dracula, that scary monster, peered (into the darkness) (at the other cloaked figures.)   [*P*] [*A*]

4. Weaving her way (around the floating buoys,) she swam (to the boat.)   [*P*]

5. Her face, puckered (from age and countless worries,) broke (into a wide grin) (at the sight) (of her granddaughter.)   [*P*]

6. To save the child, the paramedic performed CPR (inside the wrecked automobile)   [*I*]

7. Feeding the birds is becoming a year-round activity.   [*G*]

8. Do you like to feed the birds?   [*I*]

Verbal Phrases

A verbal phrase is a phrase based on one of the three types of verbals: gerund, infinitive, or participle. Turn to 742.1 in *Write Source* for explanations and examples.

Answers will vary.

1. <u>Having caught the ball</u>, he took off for the end zone.

  Participial phrase used as an adjective.

  Watching the horizon, I spotted the funnel cloud.

2. <u>To cry</u> at the movies is human.

  Infinitive phrase used as a subject.

  To live happily is my goal.

3. I grew tired of his <u>stomping around</u>.

  Gerund phrase used as an object of a preposition.

  You can get to the treehouse only by walking through the woods.

4. <u>Smiling at everyone</u> is one of her habits.

  Gerund phrase used as a subject.

  Going to the movies is my hobby.

5. <u>Ranting and raving about the poor rehearsal</u>, the director stomped offstage.

  Participial phrase used as an adjective.

  Raising her voice, Mother again said, "No!"

6. Grandma baked raisin pie <u>to please Grandpa</u>.

  Infinitive phrase used as an adverb.

  He wore boots to satisfy his father.

Extend: Write three to five sentences about playing a game. Include at least one of the three types of verbal phrases in each sentence, and identify what kind it is.

Prepositional Phrases

A prepositional phrase consists of a preposition, its object, and any modifiers. Turn to pages 732 and 744 in *Write Source* for examples and more information.

> **Underline** the prepositional phrases below. Then circle each preposition and connect it to its object with an arrow. (Note: Sometimes "to" is part of an infinitive.)

1. Members (of) professional or recreational groups—(from) pilots (to) bowlers—often use special slang or technical words called *jargon.*

2. (In) the jargon (of) airline pilots, passengers may be called "geese."

3. (To) truckers—who have invented a lot (of) colorful slang (through) the years—an accelerator is a "hammer," and a state trooper is a "smokey."

4. Some slang comes (from) those who live (in) the shadowy underworld.

5. This special slang, known (as) *argot* or *cant,* is designed to protect criminals who might be overheard talking (about) their crimes.

6. The words "joint" (a cheap bar or restaurant) and "scram" (to get away quickly) came (into) our vocabulary (from) criminal jargon.

7. *Idioms* are special phrases whose meanings cannot be determined simply (through) the definitions (of) their individual words.

8. (For) example, consider the following idioms: "kick the bucket" (to die) and "(up) the creek" (in) trouble).

9. (Over) the years, many slang words have become part (of) our standard language.

10. "Hairdo" was invented (in) the 1920s (as) a slang term (for) *coiffure,* but it became a standard word (within) 20 years.

11. Some slang terms are very old—"grub" (food) dates back (to) the 1600s and "lousy" (bad) dates (from) the 1700s.

Extend: Write three to five sentences about slang words or phrases that are popular at your school (no vulgarity allowed). Include at least one prepositional phrase in each sentence, and identify them with underlining.

Writers INC 547.1 and 552.1

Appositive Phrases

An appositive phrase, consisting of a noun and its modifiers, immediately follows another noun and renames it. Although the phrase adds new information, it functions as a noun and does not modify any word as an adjective would. Turn to 742.1 in *Write Source*.

Underline the appositive phrases in the following sentences.

1. The Internet, the world's largest computer network, became possible with the evolution of personal computers.

2. On the Net, information resources—national news services, stock reports, and libraries—can place a wealth of facts and details at your fingertips.

3. Newsgroups, a popular Internet destination, enable you to share ideas with people who are interested in a particular subject.

4. Abbe Don, "the electronic-storyteller-lady," conducts two digital storytelling projects on the Internet.

5. Digital storytelling, a rapidly growing phenomenon on the Internet, connects authors with their readers, who actually help develop the stories.

Practice writing appositive phrases. Add more information about each noun.

Answers will vary.

1. My mother, _a true horse lover_, rode a horse in the parade.

2. My father, _a rancher_, stood on the sidewalk and waved to her.

3. My little sister, _the girl in the red dress_, told everyone, "That's my mother."

4. The mayor, _Mrs. Jean Hefty_, rode a camel in the parade.

5. The parade, _an amazing display of bands and floats_, went down Main Street.

Extend: Read a page in one of your textbooks and count the number of appositive phrases you find. Are they used frequently? Do you use them in your writing?

Review: Phrases

> **Identify** each phrase. Write sentences using the following phrases: prepositional, appositive, infinitive, participial, and gerund.

Answers will vary.

1. in the hall _prepositional phrase_

We passed in the hall between classes.

2. my favorite sport _appositive phrase_

Volleyball, my favorite sport, attracts big crowds at my school.

3. driving the truck _gerund phrase_

Driving the truck through traffic made me nervous.

4. to find the address _infinitive phrase_

We tried and tried to find the address.

5. beyond the city limits _prepositional phrase_

We drove beyond the city limits to see the stars.

6. shattered into a thousand pieces _participial phrase_

Shattered into a thousand pieces, the antique vase was

worthless.

7. to keep trying _infinitive phrase_

To keep trying was her only option.

Pretest: Clauses

> **Underline** the independent clause once and the dependent clause twice in the following sentences.

1. She bicycled around the lake <u>while the race was in progress</u>.

2. <u>After the cast took their bows</u>, the curtain descended.

3. The pessimist sees a half-empty glass <u>while the optimist notices it is half-full</u>.

4. The ballpark's maintenance crew covered the diamond with a plastic tarp <u>as soon as the umpire called the rain delay</u>.

5. <u>Though Morgan had been down the street many times before</u>, he was not sure which house was Delphine's.

> **Circle** the noun clauses, underline the adverb clauses once, and underline the adjective clauses twice in the following sentences.

1. <u>Although it wasn't a long speech</u>, the coach's pep talk sparked her team to victory.

2. Nate skied down the mountain <u>as if he were being chased</u>.

3. The working time <u>that falls between midnight and dawn</u> is sometimes called the "graveyard shift."

4. (What the father said) <u>as he walked her down the aisle</u> made his daughter smile.

5. <u>As long as you stay on Main Street</u>, you can't miss it.

6. The quarterback, <u>whose shoulder pads were twisted out of his jersey</u>, blindly heaved the football toward the end zone.

7. Take out the garbage <u>after you scrape all the plates</u>.

8. You will never believe (what Carolina did next.)

Independent & Dependent Clauses

A clause is a group of words that includes both a subject and a predicate. An independent clause presents a complete thought and can stand alone as a sentence. A dependent clause does not present a complete thought and cannot stand alone. Dependent clauses often begin with a subordinating conjunction or relative pronoun. Turn to 744.1–744.2 in *Write Source*.

> **Draw** one line under the independent clauses and two lines under the dependent clauses in the following sentences. Write *S* above each simple subject and *P* above each simple predicate.

1. Sleep is a time of rest (when) the sleeper loses awareness of his or her surroundings.

2. All human beings need sleep; only those (who) get enough high-quality sleep can perform at their best.

3. To study sleep, scientists use a machine called an electroencephalograph, (which) measures the electrical activity of the brain.

4. (While) people are relaxed and awake, their brains emit about 10 small electrical waves per second.

5. (As) they fall into a deep sleep, their brains emit slower and larger waves.

6. The slowest, largest waves occur during the first two or three hours of sleep, (which) is the phase known as "slow-wave sleep."

7. (When) they are dreaming, people's eyes move rapidly, and their brains emit small, fast waves.

8. Scientists call this dreaming phase "REM," (which) stands for "rapid eye movement."

9. During an eight-hour sleep, most people experience three to five periods of dreaming.

Extend: Circle the subordinating conjunctions and relative pronouns in the sentences above. Use these words in three to five sentences of your own. Each should contain both an independent and a dependent clause.

Adverb, Adjective, & Noun Clauses

An adverb clause is used like an adverb, an adjective clause is used like an adjective, and a noun clause is used in place of a noun. Turn to 744.2 in *Write Source* for examples and more information.

> **Find** the dependent clauses in the following sentences, and underline and identify them. Use *ADV* for adverb clauses, *ADJ* for adjective clauses, and *N* for noun clauses.

1. What happens to a person <u>while he or she sleeps</u>? *ADV*

2. <u>When a person falls asleep</u>, all activity decreases and the muscles relax. *ADV*

3. A sleeping person, <u>who becomes less and less aware of what is happening around her or him</u>, changes positions at least a dozen times. *ADJ*

4. <u>Although some may shift their entire bodies</u>, most sleepers move just their heads, arms, or legs. *ADJ*

5. <u>While one experiences REM (rapid eye movement) sleep</u>, the body cannot move. *ADV*

6. This means <u>that your body does not move during your dreams</u>. *N*

7. The pathways <u>that carry nerve impulses from the brain to the muscles</u> are blocked during REM sleep <u>so that no movement can occur</u>. *ADJ* *ADV*

8. The cerebral cortex, <u>which is the part of the brain involved in higher mental functions</u>, is much more active during the dreaming state. *ADJ*

9. Dreams include places, situations, and feelings <u>that the dreamer may have experienced</u>. *ADJ*

10. Incidents <u>that happen in the hours before sleep</u> may appear in dreams. *ADJ*

11. In other words, what you dream is probably related to things <u>that happen throughout the day prior to the dream</u>. *ADJ*

12. Many experts <u>who study dreams</u> also believe <u>that dreams are related to the deep wishes and fears of the dreamer</u>. *ADJ* *N*

Extend: Compose three sentences—one for each of the three types of clauses reviewed above. Exchange papers with a classmate and identify the clauses in each other's sentences.

Review: Clauses

> **Write** sentences following the directions below.

Answers will vary.

1. Write a sentence containing a dependent clause used as a noun.

The researchers discovered <u>that young adults use seat belts more often than their parents</u>.

2. Write a sentence containing a dependent clause used as an adjective.

My report, <u>which is based on my best friend's experiences</u>, is about living with asthma.

3. Write a sentence containing a dependent clause used as an adverb.

<u>Unless I get better grades</u>, I won't be able to play on the tennis team.

4. Adjective clauses are introduced by <u>relative pronouns</u> .

5. Adverb clauses are introduced by <u>subordinating conjunctions</u> .

> **Underline** the adjective and adverb clauses in the following sentences. Write *ADJ* above each adjective clause and *ADV* above each adverb clause.

1. <u>Although most of Antarctica lies beneath snow and ice</u>, [ADV] sand dunes exist in the dry valleys of the Transantarctic Mountains.

2. Strong winds <u>that blow the snow away</u> [ADJ] <u>before it can accumulate</u> [ADV] ripple the sand in Victoria Valley, one of the dry valleys.

3. Volcanoes <u>that are found in West Antarctica</u> [ADJ] are a part of a string of volcanoes in the Pacific Ocean known as the Ring of Fire.

4. Smoke drifts up from Mount Erebus <u>because it is an active volcano</u>. [ADV]

Review: Phrase or Clause?

Describe on the lines below the difference between a phrase and a clause.

Both phrases and clauses are groups of related words, but a clause has both a subject and a predicate, while a phrase lacks either a subject or a predicate.

Identify each group of words below. Use *P* for phrase and *C* for clause.

P **1.** into the darkness   *P* **6.** at noon

P **2.** of Antarctica   *P* **7.** to hunt seals and whales

C **3.** winds blow the sand   *C* **8.** researchers collect fossils

C **4.** volcanoes exist   *P* **9.** above sea level

P **5.** of the brave scientists   *C* **10.** temperatures plunge

Indicate whether the underlined portions of each of the sentences below are clauses or phrases. Use *C* for clause and *P* for phrase.

1. Antarctica has not always been buried *P* in ice.

2. *P* Millions of years ago, Antarctica *C* was a much warmer place.

3. Gondwanaland, a land mass *C* that included Antarctica, Africa, Australia, India, and South America, began to break apart *P* about 140 million years ago.

4. Antarctica *C* began drifting south, and ice *C* began building up.

5. This *C* happened approximately *P* 30 million years ago.

6. Evidence *C* that supports this finding comes *P* from fossil studies.

7. Antarctica *C* is inhabited today *P* by a number of scientists.

8. The scientists come from *P* many different nations, yet *C* they all work together.

Pretest: Sentences

> **Label** the following sentences: write *D* for declarative, *I* for interrogative, *IP* for imperative, *E* for exclamatory, or *C* for conditional. Add end punctuation.

E (or) D   **1.** You can't be serious! (or) .

IP   **2.** Please pass the salt.

D   **3.** The senior prom queen was also the school's valedictorian.

I   **4.** Have you ever fished before?

C   **5.** If the squirrel didn't work so hard in the fall, it wouldn't eat so well in the winter.

E (or) D   **6.** She just broke the world record! (or) .

I   **7.** Is there enough flour to make two loaves of bread?

> **Write** *S* for simple, *CD* for compound, *CX* for complex, or *CD-CX* for compound-complex for each of the following sentences.

CD-CX   **1.** Charity begins at home, but it would be nice if you did some community volunteer work, too.

CX   **2.** After I read the whole book, I finally understood its title.

CD-CX   **3.** Although she worked hard for the promotion, she got it because of her strong people skills; however, she was disappointed when she found out she had to relocate.

S   **4.** Hillary and Anya jogged around the track for 10 laps.

CD   **5.** Scottish terriers are solid black, and West Highland terriers are solid white.

CX   **6.** Wishful thinking won't get you any closer to your goals unless you also make a plan and follow it.

CD   **7.** The producer liked the recording; it reminded him of a cross between Will Smith and Garth Brooks.

S   **8.** Now I understand the four kinds of sentences.

Basic Sentence Patterns

A sentence consists of a subject and a predicate and expresses a complete thought. Basic sentences follow certain patterns. If you use these patterns, your sentences will almost always be clear and correct. Study the examples below, and turn to page 760 in *Write Source*.

> **Judy ran.**
> (Subject + Action Verb [Predicate])

> **Josh ate carrots sticks.**
> (Subject + Action Verb + Direct Object)

> **Clowns give audiences enjoyment.**
> (Subject + Action Verb + Indirect Object + Direct Object)

> **The clown looks funny.**
> (Subject + Linking Verb + Predicate Adjective)

> **Ms. Maggie-Moo is a clown.**
> (Subject + Linking Verb + Predicate Noun)

Write a sentence for each pattern. Use the above examples for models.

Answers will vary.

1. Subject + Action Verb

   Marion laughed.

2. Subject + Action Verb + Direct Object

   Terry played tennis.

3. Subject + Action Verb + Indirect Object + Direct Object

   Mary Anne gave Jeremy advice.

4. Subject + Linking Verb + Predicate Adjective

   The bread tastes stale.

5. Subject + Linking Verb + Predicate Noun

   My basketball coach is a triathlete.

Extend: Now experiment with expanding the basic sentences you wrote above. Use the suggestions on page 554 in *Write Source*. When you can write a basic sentence, you are a writer. When you can expand a basic sentence, you are a better writer.

Kinds of Sentences

The four most common kinds of sentences are declarative, interrogative, imperative, and exclamatory. A fifth kind of sentence, conditional, expresses wishes ("if . . . then" statements). Turn to 746.1 in *Write Source*.

> **The history of golf still remains a mystery.** *(declarative)*

> **In what country did golf originate?** *(interrogative)*

> **Go to Scotland and find out.** *(imperative)*

> **Arnold Palmer did not invent golf!** *(exclamatory)*

> **If I ever get a hole in one, I'll dance on the green.** *(conditional)*

> **Identify** the kind of sentence below by writing declarative, interrogative, imperative, exclamatory, or conditional in the blank. Add the appropriate end punctuation.

interrogative **1.** What changes have golf balls gone through?

exclamatory **2.** I can hardly believe the changes!

declarative **3.** Golf balls have been made of wood, leather, and rubber.

interrogative **4.** Did you know that some balls have titanium cores?

declarative **5.** Research continues in the hope that an improved design will enable golfers to hit golf balls farther.

conditional **6.** If golf-ball design continues to improve, people will improve their scores.

declarative **7.** Golf clubs have evolved, too.

imperative **8.** Look at old clubs to see the differences.

declarative **9.** Originally, golf clubs were made of wood.

declarative **10.** In the 1920s, steel replaced wood.

interrogative **11.** What are they using today to make golf clubs?

declarative **12.** Golf clubs are made out of graphite, titanium, and other metals.

Extend: Write five sentences about a sport or hobby you're interested in. Each sentence should be a different kind.

Types of Sentences

A sentence may be *simple, compound, complex,* or *compound-complex* depending on the relationship between independent and dependent clauses. Turn to 748.1 in *Write Source* for more information and examples.

> **Label** each sentence below. Use *S* for simple, *CD* for compound, *CX* for complex, and *CD-CX* for compound-complex.

1   Do you know the theory of black holes? __*S*__ Objects in space have

2   gravitational pull, so smaller objects are attracted to larger objects. *CD*

3   Throw a rock into the air, and it falls to earth when gravity pulls the rock

4   down. *CD-CX* Imagine throwing a rock so far and fast that it escapes the

5   earth's gravitational pull. __*CX*__ The exact speed necessary to escape

6   gravitational pull is called *escape velocity.* __*S*__

7   Escape velocity and age contribute to the creation of black holes. __*S*__

8   A large star grows old and can't withstand the force of its own gravity, so it

9   collapses. __*CD*__ The star collapses to a fraction of its former size, but its mass

10 and gravity remain the same. __*CD*__ A concentrated field of gravity is created

11 because the forces of mass and gravity stay strong despite the collapse, and a

12 black hole is formed. *CD-CX*

13   With an escape velocity beyond light speed, a black hole prevents light from

14 escaping and this gives the black hole its name. __*CD*__ Replacing the name

15 "frozen star," John Archibald Wheeler coined the term "black hole." __*S*__ You

16 can't escape a black hole unless you can travel faster than light, and man

17 cannot travel at such speeds. *CD-CX* The existence of black holes is difficult to

18 prove, but scientists continue trying. __*CD*__

Extend: Compose one of each of the four types of sentences. To double-check your work, label all the dependent and independent clauses in each sentence. For help, turn to 744.1 in *Write Source.*

Writers INC 554.2 and 553.1

Modeling a Sentence 1

Writing your own version of a sentence by a famous author, imitating it part by part, teaches you ways to put personality, rhythm, balance, and variety into your sentences. Turn to page 560 and 750.1 in *Write Source*.

> **Read** each sentence below and follow the directions to learn procedures for modeling sentences.

1. "Soon a glow began in the dark, a tiny circle barely red."
   —Joseph Krumgold, *Onion John*

   a. Underline the main clause in the sentence above.

   b. Copy the prepositional phrase: _____.

   c. What word in the first part does the last part describe? _____

   d. Model the sentence above. Write a main clause, add a prepositional phrase, then add a detail that describes something in the main clause:

   _____

   _____

2. "Then, stomach down on the bed, he began to draw."
   —Katherine Patterson, *Bridge to Terabithia*

   a. Underline the main clause in the sentence above.

   b. What part of speech introduces this sentence? _____

   c. Copy the prepositional phrase used in this sentence. _____

   _____

   d. What word in the main clause does the second part ("stomach down on the bed") describe? _____

   e. Model the sentence above: _____

   _____.

Extend: Find a sentence in a book or magazine that you think sounds especially good. Give it to a classmate to model.

Modeling a Sentence 2

Writers often use specially designed sentences to emphasize a detail, to expand a thought, or to begin or end a piece of writing. They add various kinds of phrases and clauses to the main thought to create stylistic sentences. If you want to know the names for different stylistic sentences, turn to 750.1 in *Write Source*. This exercise will help you create stylistic sentences.

> **Model** the sentences below. If you have not modeled sentences before, use the suggestions on page 560 in *Write Source*. The main clause in each sentence is in italics.

Answers will vary.

1. On his stomach, an inch at a time, *he came to me and laid his head in my hand.*　　　　　　　—Wilson Rawls, *Where the Red Fern Grows*

On two wobbly legs, a step at a time, she came toward me and

placed the bouquet of dandelions in my hand.

2. *There's still snow on the ground,* a dirty filigree, though the winter is losing its hardness and glitter.　　　　　—Margaret Atwood, *Cat's Eye*

There's now white foam on the sand, a bubbly lace, as though the

sea is unraveling its crocheting and knitting.

3. *Charles sat there on the floor of the corridor whimpering,* not a small boy's sound, but a fearful, animal noise.　　　—Madeleine L'Engle, *A Wrinkle in Time*

The hobo stood there in the door of the barn crying, not a grown

man's sobbing, but a sorrowful, little-boy sound.

4. *Then he turned and left,* a tired and bruised old man who somehow represented the pride and dignity of a whole race.　　—Hal Borland, *When the Legends Die*

Then she stood and smiled, a slim and vibrant young winner who

somehow represented the endurance and courage of all the racers.

5. With his face burning and his head bowed, *he walked through court after court,* hearing that voice roaring ahead.　　　—Pearl Buck, *The Good Earth*

With his hands shaking and his shoulders hunched, he walked

down street after street, hearing her voice screaming within.

Review: Sentences

Identify the following sentences as either declarative, interrogative, imperative, exclamatory, or conditional. Add the correct end punctuation.

<u>declarative</u>   **1.** I saw my brother take the remote control to his bedroom.

<u>conditional</u>   **2.** If you picked the color, then I should choose the shape.

<u>interrogative</u>   **3.** What did you do with my new soccer ball?

<u>exclamatory</u>   **4.** That was a terrific shot!

<u>imperative</u>   **5.** Go home and take the roast out of the oven.

Write a stylistic sentence using the sentence below as a model. The main thought is in italics.

Answers will vary.

Or a tornado would twist down and do strange tricks to the things it hit, carrying someone fifty yards and leaving him barely hurt, or driving straws into car tires like needles. . . .   —Willie Morris, *Good Old Boy*

Or a mother could bend over and whisper wonderful words to the

child she loves, building the child's confidence and leaving her boldly

empowered, or fueling sparks of her dreams like fireworks. . . .

Write sentences that demonstrate the following structures.

Answers will vary.

1. (Simple) *My ankles and wrists are sore and swollen.*

2. (Compound) *I tried to get in shape before basketball season, but obviously I hadn't worked out enough.*

3. (Complex) *Even though I biked 10 miles a day for several weeks, my stamina did not last for an entire practice.*

Pretest: Subject-Verb Agreement

Underline the verb that agrees in number with its subject.

1. Neither he nor she *(is, are)* strong enough to lift the barbell.

2. The teacher as well as the students *(is, are)* required to attend the assembly.

3. Mathematics *(has, have)* always been my favorite subject.

4. Most of the picture *(was, were)* covered in blue and red paint.

5. There *(is, are)* disagreements among the committee members.

6. Some of the ice-cream cones in the pack *(was, were)* crushed.

7. Neither one of them *(is, are)* qualified to make that decision.

8. All of the collie's fur *(was, were)* knotted with burdocks.

9. Honesty and integrity *(was, were)* just two of Abraham Lincoln's most famous characteristics.

10. *Jack and the Beanstalk* *(is, are)* the first graders' favorite story.

11. There *(is, are)* more to their stories than either witness *(is, are)* willing to say.

12. The cleaners promised that his trousers *(was, were)* going to be cleaned, pressed, and delivered in time for the award ceremony.

13. The paper plates, napkins, and coleslaw *(was, were)* brought to the picnic by the Sungs.

14. It *(was, were)* the Crain family that *(was, were)* supposed to bring the ice and chicken.

15. None of the 3-D movies *(is, are)* much fun without the special glasses.

Subject-Verb Agreement 1

A verb must agree in number (singular or plural) with its subject. Study the examples below. Turn to pages 752–754 in *Write Source*.

> **A student sings the national anthem.** (*Student* and *sings* are both singular.)

> **Students sing the national anthem.** (*Students* and *sing* are both plural.)

Study the sentences below. Underline the subject and circle the correct verb.

1. <u>Cynthia Moss</u> (study, (studies)) and (protect, (protects)) elephants.

2. Her <u>research</u> (have, (has)) been done in Kenya's Amboseli National Park.

3. <u>Moss</u> ((is,) are) tracking more than 1,000 elephants.

4. Wild African <u>elephants</u> (leads, (lead)) extraordinary social lives.

5. Elephant <u>families</u>, made up of adult females and their young, (is, (are)) led by the oldest female of the group.

6. Each <u>family</u> (rely, (relies)) on this leader and her memory.

7. <u>Life</u> and <u>death</u> ((depend,) depends) on her skills during droughts when both <u>food</u> and <u>water</u> (is, (are)) scarce.

8. <u>Katy Payne</u>, who (record, (records)) songs of humpback whales, ((is,) are) helping Moss record elephant sounds.

9. <u>Payne</u> and <u>Moss</u> (is, (are)) learning what <u>elephants</u> (says, (say)) to each other.

10. <u>Moss</u>, <u>who</u> also (protect, (protects)) the elephants from poachers, (say, (says)) 85 <u>percent</u> of the world's wild elephants (was, (were)) killed between 1979 and 1989.

11. Tribal <u>people</u>, the Masai, (helps, (help)) her protect the elephants.

Extend: Write eight sentences, one for each verb in the following pairs: *is, are; attend, attends; know, knows; was, were*. Make your subjects and verbs agree.

Writers INC 558.1–559.3

Subject-Verb Agreement 2

> **Underline** the subjects and circle the correct verbs in the sentences below. All the subjects will be either plural nouns (turn to 702.1 and 718.1) or collective nouns (754.1).

1. The construction <u>crew</u> *(is,)* *are)* continuing work on the new bridge.

2. The <u>scissors</u> *(is,* *are)* still missing.

3. The counseling <u>committee</u> *(was,)* *were)* providing new services for students.

4. The rescue <u>squad</u> along with several police cars *(was,)* *were)* at the scene of the accident almost immediately.

5. The <u>crowd</u> *(grows,)* *grow)* restless before the musicians appear.

6. <u>Mathematics</u> *(is,)* *are)* my favorite subject.

7. The <u>news</u> always *(is,)* *are)* on at 6:00 p.m.

> **Underline** the subjects and circle the correct verbs in the sentences below. Some of the subjects will be indefinite (turn to 706.3) and relative pronouns (706.2).

1. <u>Many</u> of America's scenic highways *(curves,* *curve))* through mountains.

2. The scenic <u>roads</u>, <u>which</u> *(is,* *are))* found in all parts of America, *(requires,* *require))* alert drivers.

3. <u>One</u>, Highway 12 in Utah, *(makes,)* *make)* you think of another planet.

4. <u>Somebody</u> who drives Highway 12 every day *(says,)* *say)* everyone should drive it by the light of the full moon.

5. <u>Some</u> of Highway 12 *(passes,)* *pass)* through vast open spaces.

6. <u>Groups</u> of visitors <u>who</u> *(travels,* *travel))* America's scenic highways *(thinks,* *think))* these roads are engineering marvels.

Extend: Compose five to eight sentences using plural and collective nouns and indefinite and relative pronouns. Make certain your subjects and verbs agree. Exchange papers with a classmate and check each other's work.

Subject-Verb Agreement 3

> **Underline** the subjects and circle the correct verbs in the sentences below. Some of the subjects will be delayed (turn to 738.2).

1. There *(is, are)* a number of homeless cats at the Humane Society.

2. Whooping cranes *(is, are)* an endangered species.

3. Jackie's study habits *(is, are)* deplorable and distressing!

4. Here *(is, are)* the CD you left at my house yesterday.

5. *(Wasn't, Weren't)* Jen or George supposed to help you clean?

6. *(Has, Have)* the rain stopped yet?

7. There in the distance *(was, were)* the remains of the ghost town.

8. The tortoise *(is, are)* the animal with the longest life span.

> **Underline** the subjects and circle the correct verbs in the sentences below. Most of the subjects will be connected with conjunctions. Turn to 734.1–734.3.

1. Mike and Mary *(spend, spends)* most of their spare time fishing.

2. Both the bonfire and the canoe trip *(was, were)* the campers' favorite activities.

3. The bifocal lens and lightning rods *(was, were)* invented by Ben Franklin.

4. The forked tongue of the lizard and the snake *(is, are)* used to smell.

5. Neither Jim nor Earl *(complains, complain)* about mowing the grass.

6. The floor and the ceiling *(need, needs)* painting.

7. The floor or the ceiling *(needs, need)* painting.

8. Do you or I *(has, have)* the house keys?

Extend: Choose a hobby you enjoy. Write three to five sentences joining subjects with conjunctions. Write several sentences using a linking verb. Also try to write at least one sentence with a delayed subject. Be sure your subjects agree with your verbs.

Review: Subject-Verb Agreement

1. Deep-sea diving <u>equipment</u> (*gives,* give) individuals the ability to explore a vast underwater world.

2. Two main <u>techniques</u> for diving (is, *are*) diving with a JIM suit or diving with a helmet.

3. Marine <u>geologists</u> and <u>biologists</u> (uses, *use*) these two techniques.

4. Around the corner (is, *are*) several fresh <u>footprints</u> in the cement.

5. <u>Cindy</u> or <u>Jose</u> (*was,* were) in charge of the food drive.

6. <u>None</u> of his friends (wants, *want*) to see Javier move away.

7. <u>All</u> of the senators (wants, *want*) the president to call a special session.

8. The clean-up <u>committee</u> (*tries,* try) to keep the sidewalks clean.

9. Here (is, *are*) the <u>books</u> that you ordered from the book club.

10. The <u>dolphins</u> (is, *are*) following our boat.

11. <u>One</u> of the preschoolers (*is,* are) crying.

12. <u>Many</u> of the preschoolers (is, *are*) crying.

13. The neon <u>lights</u> (was, *were*) lighting up the whole street.

14. <u>Two</u> of the couples (was, *were*) waiting for the bus.

15. Often <u>families</u> (is, *are*) separated during a war.

16. Both the <u>toy</u> and the granola <u>bar</u> (is, *are*) for you.

17. <u>Both</u> of the editors (has, *have*) proofread the next chapter.

18. There (*is,* are) in the closet a <u>pair</u> of cross-country skis.

19. <u>Few</u> of the wolves (kills, *kill*) cattle.

20. Not <u>one</u> of the wolves (*kills,* kill) cattle.

Pretest: Pronoun-Antecedent Agreement

Underline the pronouns and draw an arrow to each antecedent. If a pronoun does not agree with its antecedent, cross out the pronoun and write the correct pronoun above.

1. Ella made sure her roller skates fit correctly before taking <del>it</del> *them* to the rink.

2. The politicians had made up <del>his</del> *their* minds long before the bill made its way out of the committee.

3. The stockbrokers on the trading-room floor had their arms up, yelling words that made the traders sound like <del>we</del> *they* were from a foreign country.

4. If Jerrill wants this project done right, he will have to do <del>them</del> *it* himself.

5. Mia and her soccer team won <del>her</del> *their* match with Franklin High to win the city tournament.

6. The baseball was signed by Alez Rodriguez after he clobbered it into the right-field bleachers.

7. Was the accountant driving a company car to her meeting?

8. The president had already served two terms, so he was not eligible to run for the presidency again.

9. The radio station ran <del>their</del> *its* yearly contest to see if listeners could correctly name a few old songs.

10. The king and <del>their</del> *his* court moved from the castle to his stronghold in the East.

11. I, George Washington, cannot tell a lie; I cut down the cherry tree with <del>our</del> *my* little hatchet.

12. No worker is required to pay for <del>their</del> *his or her* own transportation.

Pronoun-Antecedent Agreement 1

Pronouns must agree in number and gender with their antecedents, the words to which the pronouns refer. Turn to page 756 in *Write Source*.

> **Underline** the antecedent for each pair of pronouns below; then choose the pronoun that agrees in number with its antecedent. Write that pronoun on the line provided. For an indefinite pronoun (like "everyone") use the phrase "his or her" or "her or his."

1. <u>Each</u> of the female runners in the race bettered *(her, their)* previous best time. ___her___

2. Not <u>everyone</u> should include a four-year college in *(his or her, their)* future. ___his or her___

3. <u>Both</u> of the girls told *(her, their)* parents about the dance. ___their___

4. The <u>team</u> has chosen Waldo as *(its, their)* mascot. ___its___

5. Many of <u>Jack's</u> errors reveal *(his, their)* lack of practice. ___his___

6. Can <u>anybody</u> do this worksheet correctly without *(his or her, their)* handbook? ___his or her___

7. The <u>assembly</u> voted to raise *(its, their)* salaries by 10 percent. ___their___

8. Has <u>anybody</u> gotten *(her or his, their)* parents to chaperone the dance? ___her or his___

9. Either <u>Ramona</u> or <u>Christine</u> will have to bring *(her, their)* toboggan if we hope to have enough room for everyone. ___her___

10. <u>No one</u> going on the trip needs to bring *(his or her, their)* own lunch. ___his or her___

11. If <u>Carmen</u> budgets time carefully, *(she, they)* will have little trouble finding time for both work and play. ___she___

12. If you find my <u>notes</u> or <u>outline</u>, please bring *(it, them)* to me. ___it___

13. <u>Mario</u> and <u>Paulo</u> showed slides of *(his, their)* home in Brazil. ___their___

14. The <u>players</u> and <u>manager</u> were asked to give *(her or his, their)* predictions about the coming season. ___their___

15. Either <u>the drummer</u> or <u>the tuba player</u> left *(his or her, their)* sheet music in the band room. ___his or her___

Extend: Write a sentence for each of the following words, and make each pronoun agree with its antecedent: *each, any, everybody, none,* and *one.*

Pronoun-Antecedent Agreement 2

> **Circle** the correct pronoun and underline its antecedent.

1. Has either <u>Toya</u> or <u>Heather</u> remembered *(their,* **her** *)* backpack?

2. <u>Everyone</u> on the girls' team discovered *(* **her** *, their)* own special strengths.

3. In all the excitement, <u>one</u> of the first contestants lost *(their,* **his or her** *)* shoes.

4. <u>Somebody</u> must have completely lost *(* **her or his** *, their)* mind!

5. When <u>Amber</u> left the cafeteria, *(they,* **she** *)* must have forgotten her backpack.

6. Neither Jordan nor his <u>parents</u> wanted *(his,* **their** *)* dessert.

7. Every <u>dog</u> has *(* **its** *, their)* day.

8. If <u>Tina</u>, <u>Lena</u>, or <u>Sabrina</u> would visit us, *(they,* **she** *)* would have a big surprise.

9. Because of a soccer <u>player's</u> schedule, *(* **he or she** *, they)* cannot run cross-country.

10. Even after a long debate, the student <u>senate</u> could not make up *(their,* **its** *)* mind.

11. Either <u>Mr. Green</u> or <u>Mr. Slade</u> backed *(their,* **his** *)* car into the sculpture.

12. <u>Max</u> and <u>Ali</u> were very concerned about *(his,* **their** *)* hair loss.

13. Each <u>woman</u> in the room had completed *(their,* **her** *)* questionnaire.

14. Many <u>people</u> cannot express *(* **their** *, his or her)* true feelings.

15. Will <u>anyone</u> come forward and claim *(* **her or his** *, their)* prize?

16. Because of all the uncertainty, <u>nobody</u> dared to offer *(their,* **his or her** *)* opinion.

17. <u>Each</u> of the academic teams had *(* **its** *, their)* own human computer.

18. <u>Someone</u> tell <u>Kent</u> or <u>Chantal</u> to bring *(their,* **his or her** *)* soccer ball tomorrow.

19. <u>Both</u> of the returning travelers are eager to describe *(her,* **their** *)* trip.

20. When I locate your black <u>jacket</u> or your down <u>coat</u>, I will send *(* **it** *, them)* to you.

Extend: Write sentences using each of these pronouns: *his, her, them, theirs, he, she, it, you, they.* Be certain to also include antecedents for the pronouns. Exchange papers with a classmate and check each other's sentences for pronoun-antecedent agreement.

Review: Pronoun-Antecedent Agreement

> **Underline** each pronoun's antecedent in the following paragraphs and circle the correct pronoun.

1   The members of our high school track <u>team</u> have chosen *(its,* (*their*)) mascot

2   for the coming year. Each <u>member</u> was involved in the selection process and

3   was able to voice (*(his or her,)* *their)* opinion. A <u>committee</u> first narrowed

4   (*(its,)* *their)* choices to three animals: a greyhound, a cheetah, and an opossum.

5   The opossum was the first candidate to lose its standing by a majority vote.

6   <u>Each</u> of the other candidates had (*(its,)* *their)* strong points, but in the end, the

7   greyhound won.

8   Next, <u>we</u> had to name (*(our,)* *their)* new mascot. The <u>team</u> voted to name

9   (*its,* (*their*)) mascot Wilbur. Wilbur has already charmed <u>everyone</u> into bringing

10   (*(his or her,)* *their)* leftovers to him. If you should wander into the locker room on

11   the day of a meet, don't be shocked to find Wilbur taking a shower with the

12   rest of the team. As far as <u>Wilbur</u> is concerned, (*it's,* (*he's*)) human.

13   Everyone who knows <u>Wilbur</u> loves (*her,* (*him*)). From (*their,* (*his*)) wet, cold

14   nose to (*(his,)* *their)* furiously wagging tail, <u>Wilbur</u> is a bundle of joy. Even the

15   coach's <u>family</u>, famous for (*(their,)* *its)* cat lovers, have changed (*its,* (*their*)) tune.

16   <u>They</u> have adopted Wilbur and have given him a place to sleep in (*its,* (*their*))

17   kitchen. <u>Wilbur</u>, of course, has other accommodations in mind; he's been seen

18   napping on (*its,* (*his*)) favorite spot—the Perez's sofa.

Pretest: Sentence Combining

Combine the following sentences. You may want to use the method in parentheses.

Answers may vary.

1. The Berlin Wall was built in 1961. It was about 42 kilometers (26 miles) long. *(Use a relative pronoun.)*

   The Berlin Wall, which was built in 1961, was about 42 kilometers

   (26 miles) long.

2. The wall divided a city into two distinctly different communities. The city was Berlin, East Germany. *(Use an appositive.)*

   The wall divided Berlin, a city in East Germany, into two distinctly

   different communities.

3. Communist East Berlin built the wall to prevent its citizens from emigrating to West Berlin. East Berlin was backed by the Soviet Union. *(Use an introductory phrase.)*

   Backed by the Soviet Union, Communist East Berlin built the

   wall to prevent its citizens from emigrating to West Berlin.

4. The wall was constructed of 15-foot-high concrete slabs. It made escape to West Berlin extremely difficult. *(Use a participial phrase.)*

   The wall was constructed of 15-foot-high concrete slabs, making

   escape to West Berlin extremely difficult.

5. Armed guards and guard dogs were used to secure the wall. Barbed wire, trenches, and electric alarms were also used. *(Use a series.)*

   Armed guards, guard dogs, barbed wire, trenches, and electric

   alarms were used to secure the wall.

6. More than 170 people died trying to cross the wall. Most of them were killed by the border guards. *(Use a semicolon.)*

More than 170 people died trying to cross the wall; most of them

were killed by the border guards.

7. In 1989, more freedom was demanded by East Germans. They wanted the freedom to emigrate and the freedom to travel. *(Use a key word.)*

In 1989, more freedom was demanded by East Germans—freedom

to emigrate and freedom to travel.

8. By 1990, demolition of the wall was well under way. The unification of East and West Germany was also taking place. *(Use correlative conjunctions.)*

By 1990, both the demolition of the wall and the unification of

East and West Germany were well under way.

Sentence Combining 1

Combining some of your simple sentences can result in variety, a characteristic of good writing. Here are some ways to combine sentences. Also see pages 555–556 in *Write Source*.

> **Practice** combining the following simple sentences. Try to use as many of these ways to combine sentences as you can. Label each sentence with the combining method you used.

Answers may vary.

1. (1) One of the mountains in the Teton Range is Grand Teton. (2) Another mountain is Mount Owen. (3) A third mountain is Mount Moran.

Mountains in the Teton Range include Grand Teton, Mount Owen,

and Mount Moran. (series)

2. (1) One bird of prey in the Tetons is the osprey. (2) Ospreys have superb fishing skills. (3) Ospreys are dark brown and white.

The dark-brown-and-white osprey is one of the birds of prey in the

Tetons; it has superb fishing skills. (semicolon)

3. (1) Buffalo are the largest land mammals in the United States. (2) Overhunting and mindless slaughter almost wiped out the buffalo.

Overhunting and mindless slaughter almost wiped out the

buffalo, which is the largest land mammal in the United States.

(relative pronoun)

4. (1) Coyotes contribute to the Teton/Yellowstone ecosystem by eating mice, voles, and ground squirrels. (2) This keeps the rodent population under control.

Coyotes contribute to the Teton/Yellowstone ecosystem by eating

mice, voles, and ground squirrels, keeping the rodent population

under control. (participial phrase)

5. (1) River otters live along the streams in Grand Teton National Park. (2) They are weasel-like mammals. (3) They have short legs and webbed feet.

River otters, weasel-like mammals with short legs and webbed

feet, live along the streams in Grand Teton National Park.

(appositive)

6. (1) Trumpeter swans live in Grand Teton National park during the winter. (2) They live throughout Canada during the summer. (3) They hatch their young in Canada during the summer.

Trumpeter swans live in Grand Teton National Park during the

winter, but they live and hatch their young throughout Canada

during the summer. (coordinating conjunction)

7. (1) A number of moose live in Grand Teton National Park. (2) Their long legs and wide hooves make it easy for them to move through swamplands. (3) They also make it easy for them to walk through deep snow.

Because of their long legs and wide hooves, the moose who live in

Grand Teton National Park move easily through the swamplands

and deep snow. (introductory clause)

Extend: Use the sentences you wrote to form a paragraph about the animals and birds that live in Grand Teton National Park. Follow the guidelines on page 555–556 in *Write Source*. You may choose to re-combine some of the sentences in order to create a clear paragraph.

Sentence Combining 2

Writing that contains too many short sentences often seems choppy and immature. To correct this problem, you can combine some of the sentences to create a variety of sentence lengths and types. Turn to pages 555–556 in *Write Source*.

> **Combine** the short sentences in each group below to create a single, more effective sentence. (You may edit the text as long as the basic meaning remains unchanged.)

1. Bees build amazingly strong honeycombs. The walls are only 1/80 inch thick. These walls can support 30 times their own weight.

Bees build amazingly strong honeycombs; although the walls are only 1/80 inch thick, they can support 30 times their own weight.

2. A bee colony contains from 50 to 60,000 bees. They are made up of workers, drones, and one queen bee.

A bee colony, which is made up of workers, drones, and one queen bee, contains from 50 to 60,000 bees.

3. Some bees are just 1/12 inch long. Some grow to be as long as an inch.

While some bees are just 1/12 inch long, others grow to be as long as an inch.

4. It takes a great deal of work for bees to make a pound of honey. They must travel a combined distance of 13,000 miles. This is about four times the distance across the United States.

To make a pound of honey, bees must travel a combined distance of 13,000 miles, which is about four times the distance across the United States.

Extend: Rewrite each of your sentences, combining the parts in another way.

Review: Sentence Combining

Use at least 10 of the facts listed below in five (or fewer) sentences. How you combine ideas is entirely up to you, but try to vary the combining methods you use.

Answers will vary.

Ravens
- appear to be serious birds
- are very playful
- are related to jays and magpies
- have fantastic memories
- have a wingspan of four feet
- mate for life
- live in stable flocks
- are related to crows
- are highly intelligent
- like to do midair acrobatics
- can recognize a gun from a great distance
- can learn to count
- know 60 different birdcalls
- can remember more than 1,000 hiding places for food

1. Ravens are highly intelligent birds with fantastic memories that enable them to remember more than 1,000 hiding places for food.

2. Not only do they know 60 different birdcalls, but they can also learn to count and even recognize a gun from a great distance.

3. Although ravens appear serious, they are very playful and like to do midair acrobatics.

4. Ravens, which are related to crows, jays, and magpies, mate for life and live in stable flocks.

5.

Pretest: Sentence Problems

Correct the comma splices in the following sentences. (One sentence is correct.)

1. The conveyor belt was not working properly, it fed the parts to the assemblers too fast. *(or) ⊙ I* ∧;

2. Casually whistling a tune, the tow-truck driver hooked up the car, it was parked illegally in a handicapped space. *(or) ⊙ I* ∧;

3. Thundering through the narrow canyon, the wild mustangs instinctively knew that wranglers were close behind.

Rewrite the following sentences to correct any dangling modifiers.

1. Wildly flapping its miniature wings, the heavy tomcat stalked the baby robin.

   The heavy tomcat stalked the baby robin, which was wildly flapping

   its miniature wings.

2. Trying to swallow a wad of bubble gum, the teacher peered suspiciously at the student.

   The teacher peered suspiciously at the student trying to swallow

   a wad of bubble gum.

3. Barry picked up the injured bird who had compassion for all living things.

   Barry, who had compassion for all living things, picked up the

   injured bird.

4. Tiptoeing gracefully across the stage, the director enjoyed watching the ballet dancers.

   The director enjoyed watching the ballet dancers tiptoeing

   gracefully across the stage.

Cross out any double negatives or nonstandard language in the following sentences. Write any necessary corrections above.

1. If you will just wait ~~up~~, I will be ready in a moment.

2. She ~~hadn't~~ *had* scarcely made it through the door when the dog jumped into her arms.

3. Mandy and Roberto went ~~off~~ to do research for their social-studies project.

4. Try to save your money so you can go ~~with~~ next time.

5. The teacher should ~~of~~ *have* let us use our notes on the test.

6. Try ~~and~~ *to* get it right the first time, okay?

7. Don't use ~~none~~ *any* of the warped boards.

Correct the fragments and rambling and run-on sentences in the passage below. Besides correcting punctuation, you may add, delete, or rearrange words as necessary.

Answers may vary.

1 Nancy snuggled deeper under the blanket and smiled because of her

2 pleasant dream. ~~and~~ *She* turned over and managed to crack open one eye to

3 peek at the clock. Eight o'clock! Both of Nancy's eyelids snapped open. The

4 chapter 7 trigonometry test *was* This morning!

5 She raced to the bathroom, grabbed her toothbrush and toothpaste,

6 and leaned over to turn on the shower. *P*ressing a glob of paste onto the

7 brush, she tossed the toothpaste tube back toward the sink. ~~and~~ *I*t bounced

8 off and landed on the floor. Nancy stepped on the tube. *T*oothpaste

9 squirting between her toes and onto the bath mat.

10 So far, the morning was a real disaster. *and it* Didn't look like it was going

11 to improve any time soon. A broken hair dryer, a lost shoe, and a missing

12 button. What else could go wrong?

Comma Splices & Run-On Sentences 1

A comma splice is a sentence error that results when two independent clauses are joined together with only a comma. A run-on sentence is a sentence error that results when two independent clauses are joined without any punctuation. Both of these errors can be corrected in one of several ways. Turn to page 557 in *Write Source*.

> **Place** an *RO* in front of each run-on sentence, a *CS* in front of each comma splice, and a *C* in front of each correct sentence. Correct each faulty sentence. Use the proofreading marks inside the back cover of *Write Source*.

Answers may vary.

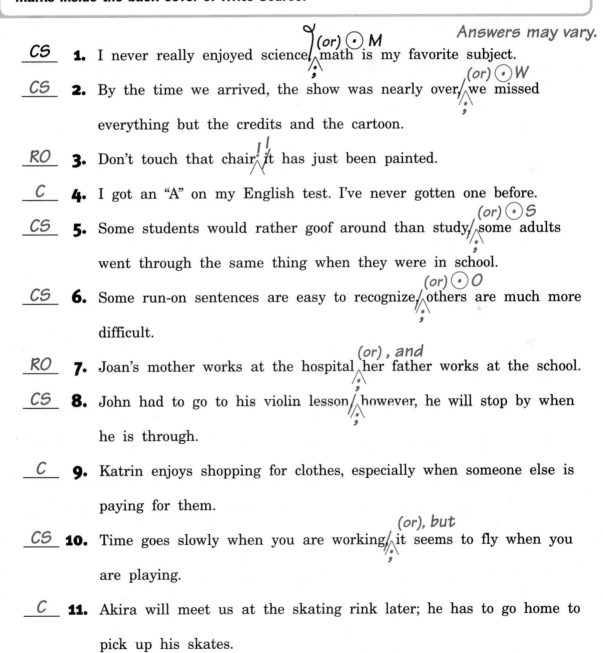

__CS__ **1.** I never really enjoyed science, math is my favorite subject.   *(or) ⊙ M*

__CS__ **2.** By the time we arrived, the show was nearly over, we missed   *(or) ⊙ W*

everything but the credits and the cartoon.

__RO__ **3.** Don't touch that chair, it has just been painted.

__C__ **4.** I got an "A" on my English test. I've never gotten one before.

__CS__ **5.** Some students would rather goof around than study, some adults   *(or) ⊙ S*

went through the same thing when they were in school.

__CS__ **6.** Some run-on sentences are easy to recognize, others are much more   *(or) ⊙ O*

difficult.

__RO__ **7.** Joan's mother works at the hospital, her father works at the school.   *(or) , and*

__CS__ **8.** John had to go to his violin lesson, however, he will stop by when

he is through.

__C__ **9.** Katrin enjoys shopping for clothes, especially when someone else is

paying for them.

__CS__ **10.** Time goes slowly when you are working, it seems to fly when you   *(or) , but*

are playing.

__C__ **11.** Akira will meet us at the skating rink later; he has to go home to

pick up his skates.

Extend: Write two run-on sentences and two sentences with a comma splice. Exchange papers with a classmate and correct each other's sentence errors.

Comma Splices & Run-On Sentences 2

There are three basic ways to correct comma splices and run-ons: (1) use a comma and a coordinating conjunction, (2) use a semicolon, or (3) make the clauses into separate sentences. Turn to page 557 in *Write Source*.

> **Correct** the following sentences by inserting a semicolon, a period and a capital letter, or a comma and a coordinating conjunction. Use each method at least twice.

Answers will vary.

1. Psychology is the science that studies all kinds of behavior. The behavior may be normal, *or* the behavior may be abnormal.

2. Psychologists try to find answers to questions about thoughts, feelings, and actions. *T*heir findings help us understand why people behave as they do.

3. In the late 1800s, psychology developed into a science based on observation and experimentation; prior to that, there were no systematic studies of the mind.

4. Sigmund Freud introduced the theory that behavior is determined by the unconscious mind, *and* he developed techniques to uncover repressed feelings.

5. Many psychologists disagree with some of Freud's ideas, *but* most accept that the unconscious has a major effect on behavior.

6. Cognitive psychologists concentrate on thinking processes and self-awareness. *T*hey believe there's more to human nature than a response to a stimulus.

7. Humanistic psychologists trust that people's values and choices affect their behavior. *T*hey believe the psychologist helps people to realize their unique possibilities.

8. Understanding of individuals and groups has broadened because of these psychological studies; the insights from these studies can benefit people in their everyday lives.

Extend: Write three run-on sentences about whatever you believe influences your behavior. Exchange papers with a classmate and correct each other's work.

Comma Splices & Run-On Sentences 3

Another way to revise a run-on sentence or a comma splice is to restructure the sentence. If one of the independent clauses is less important than the other, change it into a subordinate clause or a phrase. Turn to page 557 and 744.1 and 744.2 in *Write Source*.

> **Correct** the following sentences by using subordinate clauses or phrases.

Answers may vary.

1. An airship is different from a manned balloon it has an engine and steering equipment.

An airship, which is different from a manned balloon, has an

engine and steering equipment.

2. The main body of an airship is a balloon filled with a lighter-than-air gas, the gas raises the airship and keeps it in the air.

The main body of an airship is a balloon filled with lighter-than-air

gas, which raises the airship and keeps it in the air.

3. A series of explosions was caused by the hydrogen gas used in airships, this led to the use of helium gas in United States craft in the 1920s.

A series of explosions, which were caused by the hydrogen gas

used in the airships, led to the use of helium gas in United States

craft in the 1920s.

4. Airships were also called dirigibles, zeppelins, or blimps they were used in World War I as bombers and as cargo and passenger carriers.

Airships, also called dirigibles, zeppelins, or blimps, were used in

World War I as bombers and as cargo and passenger carriers.

5. The *Hindenburg* was one of the largest airships ever built it exploded when its hydrogen gas somehow ignited, killing 36 people.

The Hindenburg, one of the largest airships ever built, exploded

when its hydrogen gas somehow ignited, killing 36 people.

Extend: Write three run-on sentences about airplanes or air travel. Exchange papers with a classmate or work together. Experiment with a variety of ways to correct each sentence.

     Writers INC p. 88, 553.1 and 553.2

Sentence Fragments 1

A fragment is a group of words often mistaken for a sentence. A fragment is either a phrase or a dependent clause that looks or sounds like a sentence. Remember: A sentence contains a subject and a predicate and expresses a complete thought. Turn to page 558 in *Write Source*.

> *Complete Sentence:*
> **The polar bear is a curious animal.**

> *Fragments:*
> **Can be quite a clown** (subject missing)
> **When the bear is safely confined** (dependent clause, not a complete thought)
> **Of captive bears exceeding 1,000 pounds** (both subject and predicate missing)

Identify the following groups of words by writing *S* for sentence or *F* for fragment on the line before each. Put periods at the end of all sentences.

S **1.** The polar bear is a large carnivore that does not fear humans.

F **2.** Deliberately stalks and kills humans for food

F **3.** Has been called the "King of the North"

S **4.** When wounded, the polar bear can be a deadly adversary.

F **5.** Covered 60 yards in a charge after being shot through the heart several times

S **6.** On the other hand, this bear can bring delight to its viewers.

S **7.** Once a coast guard vessel in the Canadian Arctic received a visit from an adult male polar bear.

F **8.** The bear, traveling atop a drifting ice floe

S **9.** The crew, who did not know better, decided to feed the curious critter floating alongside the boat.

F **10.** A case of black molasses from the ship's storeroom

S **11.** Soon the bear and the ice floe were black and sticky with the sweet stuff.

S **12.** After the molasses came the apples.

Extend: Make each of the five sentence fragments into a complete sentence. Always proofread your writing for sentence fragments.

Sentence Fragments 2

Fragments, once found, need to be changed into sentences that contain a subject and a predicate and express a complete thought. Turn to page 558 in *Write Source*.

> **Make** the following fragments into complete sentences. Use the appropriate end punctuation.

Answers will vary.

1. Henry "Hank" Aaron, baseball's all-time home-run champion by hitting a total of 755 homers

Hitting a total of 755 homers, Henry "Hank" Aaron became baseball's all-time home-run champion.

2. broke Babe Ruth's record—714 homers—in 1974

Aaron broke Babe Ruth's record—714 homers—in 1974.

3. playing professionally for all-black teams when drafted by the Milwaukee Braves

Aaron was playing professionally for all-black teams when he was drafted by the Milwaukee Braves.

4. with a lifetime batting average of .305 and 2,297 runs batted in and led the National League four times in runs batted in

With a lifetime batting average of .305 and 2,297 runs batted in, he led the National League four times in runs batted in.

5. the National League's most valuable player in 1957, elected to the Baseball Hall of Fame in 1982

Aaron, the National League's most valuable player in 1957, was elected to the Baseball Hall of Fame in 1982.

6. as a right fielder won three Gold Glove awards for his fielding skills

He won three Gold Glove awards for his fielding skills as a right fielder.

Rambling Sentences

Rambling sentences go on and on, and readers can find them confusing. Overusing the word *and* is one cause. Turn to page 558 in *Write Source*.

> **Rewrite** the following sentences so they are clear. Sometimes you may need to divide a rambling sentence into two sentences, or you may need to reword portions. Experiment with a variety of correction methods.

1. I took a trip to the Apostle Islands and they are in Lake Superior and getting there was both exciting and scary and we crossed some very choppy water.

I took a trip to the Apostle Islands in Lake Superior. Getting there was both exciting and scary because we crossed some very choppy water.

2. I went kayaking with a friend known as Frederick the Great Fisher, so we brought our fishing supplies, our maps and some food and tents and mosquito repellent and camped near Lake Superior.

I went kayaking with a friend known as Frederick the Great Fisher. We brought our own fishing supplies, maps, food, tents, and mosquito repellent and camped near Lake Superior.

3. We paddled to Oak Island and Sand Island and we hiked on the trails and saw three deer and we ate lunch on the beach and went swimming afterward.

We paddled to Oak Island and Sand Island, hiked on the trails, saw three deer, and ate lunch on the beach. Afterward, we went swimming.

4. After swimming we tried fishing but even Frederick the Great Fisher didn't catch anything so we put the kayaks into the water and paddled back to camp and complained about having to eat bologna for supper again.

After swimming we tried fishing, but even Frederick the Great Fisher didn't catch anything. So we put the kayaks into the water, paddled back to camp, and complained about having to eat bologna for supper again.

Extend: Write one long rambling sentence about a fishing or swimming experience. Show two different ways to rewrite the sentence so it is clear.

Review: Sentence Problems 1

> **Identify** the sentence errors below by writing *F* for fragment, *RO* for run-on, *CS* for comma splice, and *R* for rambling. Change the sentences so that they are complete and effective.

Answers may vary.

_RO_ **1.** We are in the midst of the computer revolution even our cars are computerized.

> *We are in the midst of the computer revolution; even our cars*

> *are computerized.*

_R_ **2.** Computers can make life easier by doing our everyday tasks and helping us buy groceries and pump gas and do banking.

> *Computers can make life easier by doing our everyday tasks*

> *like helping us buy groceries, pump gas, and do banking.*

_R_ **3.** Computer technology changes almost daily and thousands of creative minds are at work and new uses for computers are found.

> *Computer technology changes almost daily as thousands of*

> *creative minds work to find new uses for computers.*

_F_ **4.** Overwhelmed by all this new technology.

> *Some people are overwhelmed by all this new technology.*

_F_ **5.** When considering the latest developments in the personal computer.

> *When considering the latest developments in the personal*

> *computer, I wonder what's next.*

_CS_ **6.** The first computers were giant machines housed in special air-conditioned rooms, now they are often tiny machines, we carry them in our pockets.

> *The first computers were giant machines housed in special*

> *air-conditioned rooms, but now they are often tiny machines*

> *we carry in our pockets.*

Misplaced Modifiers

When a modifier is incorrectly placed in a sentence, the meaning of the sentence becomes confusing. This type of writing error is called a misplaced modifier. Generally the way to fix a misplaced modifier is to reorganize the sentence so that the modifier clearly describes or modifies the correct item. Turn to page 559 in *Write Source* for more information.

Rewrite each sentence so that the modifier clearly modifies the correct word.

Answers may vary.

1. Jana bought four tickets for the concert this weekend at the grocery store.

Jana bought four tickets at the grocery store for the concert this weekend.

2. Shavonn walked into a class that was discussing bookkeeping by mistake.

By mistake, Shavonn walked into a class that was discussing bookkeeping.

3. The flight attendants served cookies to the passengers after warming them.

After warming the cookies, the flight attendants served them to the passengers.

4. Maryjean made computer greeting cards using a special software program personalized for her friends.

Using a special software program, Maryjean made computer greeting cards personalized for her friends.

5. The student council has been planning to hold a pizza sale for two months.

The student council has been planning for two months to hold a pizza sale.

6. The school needs someone to clean the cafeteria badly.

The school badly needs someone to clean the cafeteria.

Extend: Write three to five sentences containing misplaced modifiers. Exchange papers with a classmate and correct each other's work.

Dangling Modifiers

When a modifying phrase or clause does not clearly and sensibly modify a word in a sentence, the result is called a dangling modifier. Dangling modifiers are difficult to recognize, especially in your own writing, but they are often easy to fix. Turn to page 559 in *Write Source*.

> **Fix** the dangling modifiers. Follow the suggested method given in parentheses.

Answers may vary.

1. Upon entering the science lab, the dangling skeleton caught my eye.
(Use "I" somewhere in this sentence.)

As I entered the science lab, the dangling skeleton caught my eye.

2. After pouring the coffee, her dog jumped on one of Grandma's guests.
(Name the person doing the acting in the introductory clause.)

After Grandma poured the coffee, her dog jumped on a guest.

3. Having had three teeth knocked out, mother suggested that Josh quit the soccer team. *(Create a relative clause.)*

Mother suggested that Josh, who had three teeth knocked out, quit the soccer team.

4. Using a computer to help diagnose engine problems, our car was repaired by Omar. *(Name a person as the subject.)*

Using a computer to help diagnose engine problems, Omar repaired our car.

5. Just after eating lunch, a strange-looking bird landed on our windowsill.
(Name a person as the subject.)

Just after eating lunch, Maya saw a strange-looking bird land on our windowsill.

Extend: Select two sentences from the exercise above and fix the dangling modifiers using a different method.

Writers INC p. 90

Wordiness & Deadwood

Make your sentences more concise by eliminating unnecessary or redundant words. Also see pages 170 and 224 in *Write Source*.

> **Place** parentheses around the unnecessary words or phrases in the following sentences.

Answers may vary.

1. The former tenant (who had lived in the apartment before we moved in) had painted all the walls (with a coat of) pink (paint).

2. A typical basketball court is (normally) 90 feet long.

3. (The main reason) he didn't pass the test (is) because he didn't study his notes carefully (or look over his notebook).

4. (There are) six students (who) volunteered (on their own) to clean up after the homecoming dance (is over).

5. The injured climber was unable to descend (down) the mountain by himself, so he relied on (the help of) another climber to assist him.

6. The fragile vase (, which would surely break if mishandled,) was shipped "Special Handling" (so that it would be handled with care).

7. The (cancelled) game has been rescheduled for 8:00 p.m. tomorrow (evening).

8. A portable radio (can be carried anywhere and) is (especially) handy (to use) when jogging, biking, or doing other outdoor activities.

9. (As a general rule,) he usually spends about one hour (of his time) reading each day.

10. (Needless to say,) wordiness (is a writing problem that) should be eliminated from all writing, (which goes without saying).

Extend: Carefully read a paper you have written. Put parentheses around unnecessary words and phrases. Read your revised work to a classmate. In your opinion, is your paper better now?

Nonstandard Language

Nonstandard English is not recommended for formal writing. Consider both your subject and your audience before deciding to use formal or informal language. Turn to page 559 in *Write Source*.

> **Cross out** the nonstandard language and double negatives in the sentences below. Write a correction, when needed, above the words. (Two sentences are correct as written.)

1. Not long ago, a team of divers went ~~off~~ to Texas to explore the Gulf of Mexico.

2. They wanted to locate a certain sunken ship.

3. It had settled ~~in~~ at a 12-foot depth and was covered with silt.

4. They didn't ~~barely~~ know where to begin.

5. The public believed the team didn't have *any* ~~no~~ idea where that ship was ~~at~~.

6. They had begun diving when one diver yelled, "Sharks!"

7. They thought they had *done* ~~went and did~~ it this time.

8. You should *have* ~~of~~ seen them try to get back to the boat!

9. The divers had not done *anything* ~~nothing~~ to protect themselves from sharks.

10. ~~Man, oh man,~~ *T,*they should *have* ~~of~~ taken precautions.

11. "I would *have* ~~of~~ enjoyed this expedition except for the sharks," one of the divers said.

12. Another diver said, "We won't ~~never~~ forget this day."

13. "I was so scared I *could* ~~couldn't~~ hardly swim," said the youngest diver.

14. He added, "Don't *ever* ~~never~~ let *anyone* ~~no one~~ convince you that diving has no hazards."

15. Evidently the sharks were not ~~hardly~~ man-eaters, for they swam away.

16. Meanwhile, a storm almost sank the divers' vessel ~~—like freaky, man!~~

17. The divers went home, but next time they go exploring, I plan to go ~~with~~.

Extend: Can you name any fictional characters who use nonstandard language? Select a passage in which a character speaks nonstandard English and rewrite it using formal language. What happens?

Unparallel Construction 1

Parallelism is the repetition of similar patterns or word groups—either words, phrases, or clauses—within a sentence. Turn to pages 550 in *Write Source*.

> **We went *to the park, to the game,* and *to the dance.***
> (The repetition of the prepositional phrases creates parallel structure.)

> **The dog *ran to the fence, jumped in the air,* and *barked at the squirrels.***
> (In this sentence, the repeated pattern is an action verb + a prepositional phrase.)

Underline the parallel parts of the sentences below. Then explain what word groups are repeated in each sentence.

1. I think that I <u>should get some juice</u>, you <u>should make the pizza</u>, and Marie <u>should decorate the house</u>.

The repeated word group is a clause with a subject + an action verb + a direct object. Also, each clause contains the word "should."

2. I met someone who could <u>ride a unicycle</u>, <u>juggle three balls</u>, and <u>whistle "The Star-Spangled Banner"</u> at the same time.

The repeated word group is an action verb + a direct object.

3. At age 12, it seems our dog is either <u>eating</u> or <u>sleeping</u>.

The repeated word group is a verb that ends in "ing."

4. When you <u>turn 16</u>, <u>pass a math class</u>, and <u>stop bugging your little sister</u>, we will talk about getting a car for you.

The repeated word group is an action verb + a direct object.

Extend: Write two sentences that show examples of parallel structure. Have a classmate, identify what types of word groups are repeated in each sentence.

Unparallel Construction 2

Parallel structuring is the repetition of similar words, phrases, or clauses. Inconsistent (unparallel) construction occurs when the kinds of words, phrases, or clauses change in the middle of a sentence. Turn to page 550 in *Write Source*.

Underline the parallel structures in the following sentences. Then write sentences using similar constructions.

Answers will vary.

1. Hamlet wondered whether to live or to die.
   Jeremy wondered whether to play football or to join band.

2. Give me a day with sunshine and a strong wind, with a boat and a mended sail, with a lake and a distant horizon.
   Give me a restaurant with outdoor seating and a lakeside setting, with great pasta and crusty bread, with a dessert bar and live music.

3. This is the dress, the hat, and the mask I will wear to the costume dance.
   This is the card, the gift, and the balloon I will take to the surprise party.

4. In the little town where I grew up, people pass the time chatting in the post office, walking the trails by the river, and counting the deer in the woods.
   On the farm where I grew up, we enjoyed reading in our tree house, camping under the pine trees, and riding our ponies across the fields.

5. Benjamin Franklin was not only an inventor but also a statesman.
   My mother is not only a great cook but also a great singer.

6. Walking strengthens your legs, swimming develops your lungs, and trusting expands your heart.
   Reading expands your vocabulary, thinking stimulates your imagination, and writing captures your story.

Follow the directions below to create sentences with parallel structures.

1. Complete the sentence using a series. Each part of the series should contain a past tense verb followed by a prepositional phrase.

Mr. Ortego was the kind of person who _arose at six, ate at seven, and_ _left at eight._

2. Complete the sentence using a series of phrases.

To be a great point guard you need to be able to _dribble with both hands,_ _pass with great accuracy, and hustle back on defense._

3. Complete the sentence using a series of clauses.

He was worried that _the car would break down, the roads would be_ _under construction, or afternoon traffic would be very heavy._

4. Complete the sentence using a series of prepositional phrases.

Somehow Breanne got paint _under her fingernails, on her jeans, and in_ _her hair._

5. Complete the sentence using three gerunds.

Swimming, canoeing, and biking are my _____ favorite summer pastimes.

6. Complete the sentence using gerund phrases.

Singing in the shower, _playing video games_ , and _jogging five miles at a time_ —that's how my brother relaxes.

7. Complete the sentence using action words with direct objects.

I peeled the potatoes, _diced the tomatoes_ , and _sliced the cheese_ .

Extend: Watch for parallel structure in everything you read. Copy especially fine parallel sentences into a notebook or computer folder. Try writing sentences with similar constructions.

Review: Sentence Problems 2

Rewrite the sentences below to correct the following problems: deadwood and wordiness, dangling or misplaced modifiers, nonstandard language, and unparallel construction.

Answers will vary.

1. Looking more confused than ever, Mr. Brown told Michael to come in during study hall for help.

Because Michael looked more confused than ever, Mr. Brown told

him to come in during study hall for help.

2. Trent tried to sell a set of clubs to beginning golfers with oversized heads.

Trent tried to sell beginning golfers a set of clubs with oversized

heads.

3. I could of made it to the movie on time if my tire hadn't of gone flat.

I could have made it to the movie on time if my tire hadn't gone

flat.

4. The night was filled with the howls of unknown beasts, with moaning winds, and the shadows were dark and menacing.

The night was filled with the howls of unknown beasts, with

moaning winds, and with dark and menacing shadows.

5. While moving the couch, the dog ran out the door and down the street.

While moving the couch, we saw the dog run out the door and

down the street.

6. Chasing the dog with her hair in a ponytail, Marta raced down the street.

With her hair in a ponytail, Marta raced down the street chasing the dog.

7. They should have tried harder to get here on time and left earlier and called us when they realized they were going to be late and had more consideration.

They should have tried harder to get here on time by leaving earlier. They should have shown consideration by calling when they realized they were going to be late.

8. We rode our bikes to the post office and to the store, and then our bikes were ridden off to the park.

We rode our bikes to the post office, the store, and the park.

9. By the time we were through chopping firewood, we had nearly chopped a full cord of wood.

By the time were were through, we had chopped nearly a full cord of firewood.

10. My brother's room is full of half-eaten sandwiches, empty water bottles, and laying all over the place are dirty clothes.

My brother's room is full of half-eaten sandwiches, empty water bottles, and dirty clothes.

Pretest: Shifts in Construction

Shifts in construction may occur in four different ways: number (changing from singular to plural or vice versa), tense (mixing present, past, and future tenses), person (mixing 1st, 2nd, and 3rd persons), or voice (mixing active and passive voice).

Write the correction above the second underlined part in each sentence. The underlined words in the following sentences show incorrect shifts in construction.

1. When you know it wasn't your fault, it is hard for one *you* to apologize.

2. Resisting your classmate's invitation to skip out may be the first step toward improving one's *your* self-image.

3. Momentarily escaping their trainer, the circus elephants headed down the street, single file and trunk to tail, just as they are *were* taught.

4. The oil riggers drilled deep under the ocean floor and were watching *watched* as a column of saltwater and sand sprayed high in the air.

5. Janelle will sculpt the clay carefully so that it had *will have* all the details of the original.

6. The archaeologists are looking for pottery that will give him *them* clues about how the natives prepared food.

7. Swooping from its nest on the cliff, the bald eagle snatched its eaglet in midair, just before it hits *hit* the ground.

8. The weather last week was incredible—major snowstorms hit the Midwest and tornadoes had been hitting *hit* the South.

9. If the skateboard park were built, then the boarders would have a place to practice his or her *their* techniques.

10. When they told you they were going to be here "in a little while," she *they* should have been more specific.

11. The large raccoon poked his masked face into the garbage can while three little "masqueraders" were watching *watched* intently.

Shifts in Construction

A *shift in construction* is a change in the structure or style midway through a sentence. These shifts can occur in number, tense, person, or voice. For more information about agreement see pages 752, 754, and 756 in *Write Source*.

> **Study** the underlined shifts in number, tense, person, or voice in the following sentences. You may cross out words and write in new ones as necessary to correct the shifts. See the first sentence to understand how some of the sentences can be corrected in more than one way.

Answers may vary.

1. Before a <u>driver</u> backs out of a driveway, <u>they</u> should make sure that the road is
   she or he

   clear.

(or) Before a <u>driver backs</u> out of a driveway, <u>they</u> should make sure that the road is
   drivers back

   clear.

2. If you cannot finish painting the house before winter, <u>one</u> should wait until
   you

   spring to start.

3. Because Lauren <u>waited for just the right moment,</u> many opportunities were
   she missed

   ~~missed by her~~.

4. In the story, Zenon <u>stole</u> a load of manure; then he <u>starts</u> feeling guilty—and
   steals

   smelly.

5. The Masked Marvel <u>saved a busload of students</u> in the morning, and a
   he rescued

   planeload of senior citizens ~~were rescued by him~~ in the afternoon.

6. <u>One</u> should refrain from speaking if <u>you</u> cannot control your temper.
   You

7. The next <u>person</u> to walk through the door will become our secretary if <u>they</u> can
   he or she

   write legibly.

8. Renaldo <u>tested</u> over a dozen boom boxes before he <u>will buy</u> just the right one.
   bought

9. Make sure that <u>each of you</u> has a full set of stakes for <u>their</u> tent.
   your

10. Why does <u>everyone</u> think that <u>they are</u> the absolute center of the universe?
    he or she is

Extend: Use the following indefinite pronouns in compound or complex sentences: *someone, everything, neither.* Make sure your sentences do not contain a shift in number.

Shifts in Verb Tense 1

Consistent verb tenses clearly establish time in sentences. When verb tenses change without warning or for no reason, readers become confused. Turn to 718.3–720 in *Write Source* for information about the six different "times" that verb tenses communicate to the reader.

> **Underline** the verb in the first sentence of each pair. Change the verb tense in the second sentence to be consistent with the first. Finally, identify the tense that is used.

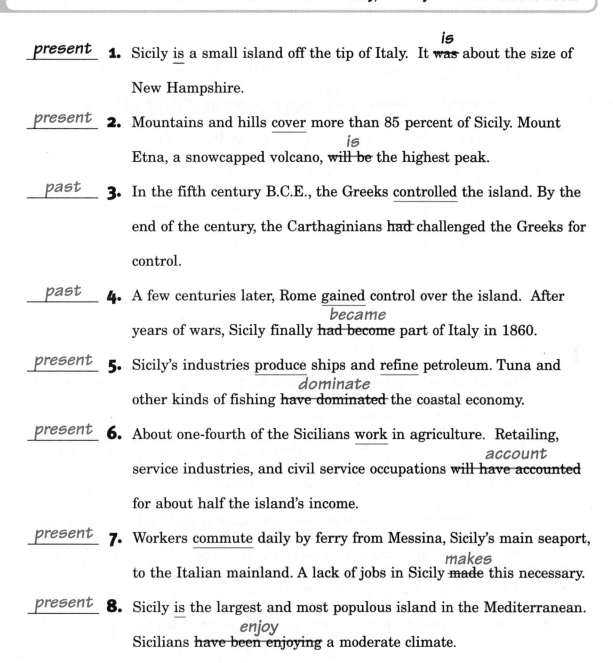

present   **1.** Sicily <u>is</u> a small island off the tip of Italy. It ~~was~~ *is* about the size of New Hampshire.

present   **2.** Mountains and hills <u>cover</u> more than 85 percent of Sicily. Mount Etna, a snowcapped volcano, ~~will be~~ *is* the highest peak.

past   **3.** In the fifth century B.C.E., the Greeks <u>controlled</u> the island. By the end of the century, the Carthaginians ~~had~~ challenged the Greeks for control.

past   **4.** A few centuries later, Rome <u>gained</u> control over the island. After years of wars, Sicily finally ~~had become~~ *became* part of Italy in 1860.

present   **5.** Sicily's industries <u>produce</u> ships and <u>refine</u> petroleum. Tuna and other kinds of fishing ~~have dominated~~ *dominate* the coastal economy.

present   **6.** About one-fourth of the Sicilians <u>work</u> in agriculture. Retailing, service industries, and civil service occupations ~~will have accounted~~ *account* for about half the island's income.

present   **7.** Workers <u>commute</u> daily by ferry from Messina, Sicily's main seaport, to the Italian mainland. A lack of jobs in Sicily ~~made~~ *makes* this necessary.

present   **8.** Sicily <u>is</u> the largest and most populous island in the Mediterranean. Sicilians ~~have been enjoying~~ *enjoy* a moderate climate.

Extend: Tell why the tense used for each pair of sentences is appropriate. For example, the present tense is appropriate in the first sentence because it speaks of a state of being that exists right now. Use the information about verb tenses on 718.3–720 in *Write Source* to help you with this activity.

Shifts in Verb Tense 2

In most cases, writers use the same verb tense throughout a sentence, a paragraph, or an entire piece of writing. Maintaining verb-tense consistency establishes the time of the actions being described. Readers know "what happened when" and are not confused. Turn to 718.3–720 in *Write Source*.

> **Underline** the first verb in the sentences below. Then change the other verbs to match the tense of the first verb.

1. Ultrasonics <u>is</u> the study of sound waves that ~~occurred~~ *occur* above our hearing capacity; today ultrasonics ~~was~~ *is* used in a variety of different ways.

2. In the early 1900s, ultrasound <u>was</u> a novelty, but by 1930, ultrasonics ~~will become~~ *became* an important field of study.

3. Beginning in the 1960s, ultrasonic devices <u>were</u> used to detect flaws in metals, wood, and other materials, and the devices also ~~start~~ *started* to replace the use of X-rays.

4. Ultrasonic waves <u>are</u> able to detect objects that ~~did~~ *do* not transmit light, so they ~~were~~ *are* used to find objects underwater.

5. This process <u>is</u> called *sonar*. Sonar ~~identified~~ *identifies* submarines, has ~~mapped~~ *maps* the ocean bottom, and ~~will measure~~ *measures* the thickness of ice packs.

6. Ultrasonic devices <u>have</u> many medical applications; these ~~included~~ *include* using ultrasound to shatter kidney stones and gallstones.

7. Today, ultrasound's primary medical use <u>is</u> the procedure called *imaging*, in which ultrasonic waves ~~were~~ *are* used to create images of internal body structures or monitor tumors, cysts, and even fetuses.

8. Imaging <u>is</u> a painless process and ~~took~~ *takes* only a few short minutes to complete.

9. Doctors <u>diagnose</u> diseases and ~~will evaluate~~ *evaluate* internal organs using ultrasound.

Extend: Read a section of a history textbook. Identify the tense of the verbs. Does the book's use of tense create a clear picture for you?

Pronoun Shifts

Pronoun shifts occur when a writer "shifts" from using a singular pronoun to a plural pronoun or vice versa, from a masculine pronoun to a feminine pronoun or vice versa, and from a neutral-gender pronoun to a masculine or feminine pronoun or vice versa. Turn to 708.1 and 708.2, 710.2 and 756.2 in *Write Source*.

Circle the correct pronoun in the following sentences.

1. My grandparents seem to like *(his and her,* (their)) new surround-sound system.

2. My grandpa especially likes ((his,) *their)* personal remote headset.

3. Grandpa now thinks that everyone should have ((his or her,) *their)* own headset.

4. My grandma likes to listen to ((her,) *their)* radio program while grandpa watches his game shows.

5. Both can watch or listen to whatever *(he or she,* (they)) want.

Cross out pronoun shifts in the following passage and write the correct pronoun above. Remember to be consistent throughout the passage. You may also need to change the number of some verbs.

Answers may vary.

1   Teenagers everywhere have favorite activities and favorite foods, but in

         they have
2   Hawaii ~~he or she has~~ some that are quite different. In Hawaii teens often learn

3   to use surfboards or body boards. On the surfboard, you stand up; and on the

         you lie
4   body board, ~~one lies~~ down. Some teens learn the hula, an ancient Hawaiian

         their   *their*
5   dance. Hula dancers use ~~her or his~~ hands to tell a story while moving ~~her~~ legs

         they
6   and hips. And Hawaiian teens often learn how to snow ski. Yes, ~~he or she~~ can

7   ski in Hawaii! It snows at the top of Mauna Kea during the winter. All this

         you get
8   activity makes them hungry, and in Hawaii when you order fast food, ~~one gets~~

9   burgers, fries, and shakes as well as Portuguese sausages and Hawaiian noodle

10   soup. Hawaii sounds like a great place to live.

Writers INC 537.1, 537.2, 538.2, and 560.2

Review: Shifts in Construction

Cross out shifts in the following sentences and write the corrections, if necessary, above. Watch for shifts in person, voice, number, and verb tense.

1. Darrick called the grocery store to see if it ~~has~~ *had* closed for the night.

2. The photographers shot several pictures of cheetahs, antelopes, and zebras, but ~~he~~ *they* saw no lions.

3. She walked through the refuge, and ~~they~~ *she* observed the damage caused by the broken dam.

4. Tara is working in Department 307 but ~~hoped~~ *hopes* to be transferred soon.

5. People who look on the bright side in a bad situation are the ~~one~~ *ones* you generally want to be with when things go wrong.

6. I was ready to leave at 9:30, but then I ~~get~~ *got* a phone call.

7. We visited the museum, we saw the dinosaurs, and then ~~souvenirs were bought.~~ *we bought souvenirs.*

8. Each person must sign the application form, or ~~they~~ *he or she* will not be admitted.

9. Nutritious food gives a person energy, and a good night's sleep ~~produced~~ *produces* a positive attitude.

10. The chipmunks raced across the park and ~~will fight~~ *fought* over the spilled bag of popcorn.

11. Howling winds from the north swept over the tiny cabin and ~~swirl~~ *swirled* the snow into giant drifts.

12. Dad bought tickets, so we took the train and ~~the fall scenery was viewed with excitement.~~ *viewed with excitement the fall scenery.*

Review: Sentence Activities

Complete the following statements.

1. A(n) _comma splice_ is the error of connecting two simple sentences with only a comma.

2. A(n) _rambling_ sentence is one that seems to go on and on.

3. A(n) _misplaced_ modifier is one that is placed too far away from the word it modifies in the sentence.

4. A(n) _run-on_ happens when two sentences run together without punctuation or connecting words.

5. _Deadwood/wordiness_ is wording that fills up lots of space but does not add anything important or new to the overall meaning.

6. A sentence _fragment_ is a group of words that is not a complete sentence.

7. In the sentence *There goes a magnificent specimen of humankind,* the simple subject is _specimen_ .

8. _Parallelism_ is the repeating of phrases or sentences that are similar in structure.

9. _Dangling_ modifiers appear to modify the wrong word or a word that isn't in the sentence.

10. A complete sentence must have a(n) _subject_ and a(n) _predicate_ and express a complete thought.

11. A(n) _periodic_ sentence postpones the crucial or most surprising idea until the end.

12. In the sentence *Can you guess my age?,* the simple predicate is _can guess_ .

13. A(n) _____compound_____ sentence contains two simple sentences joined by a semicolon or by a comma with a(n) _____coordinating conjunction_____ .

14. Sentences make five different kinds of statements: declarative, _____interrogative_____ , _____imperative_____ , _____exclamatory_____ , or conditional.

15. In the sentence *Mr. Kotter, my favorite teacher, is back,* the phrase *my favorite teacher* is a(n) _____appositive_____ .

16. *Why do I bother?* is what kind of sentence? _____interrogative_____

17. Sentences have four different basic structures: simple, _____compound_____ , _____complex_____ , and _____compound-complex_____ .

18. A pronoun must agree with its antecedent in _____number_____ , _____person_____ , and _____gender_____ .

19. A(n) _____complex_____ sentence contains one independent clause and one or more dependent clauses.

20. _____Imperative_____ sentences give commands.

21. The three basic types of subordinate clauses are _____noun_____ , _____adverb_____ , and _____adjective_____ .

22. The subject and verb of any clause must agree in both _____number_____ and _____person_____ .

23. *Team, crowd,* and *pair* are _____collective_____ nouns; whether they take a singular or a plural verb depends on how they are used.

24. Sentences can be combined in the following ways: by using _____a key word_____ , _____a participial phrase_____ , _____a semicolon_____ , _____an appositive_____ , _____a relative pronoun_____ , _____correlative conjunctions_____ , _____a series of words or phrases_____ , _____or an introductory phrase or clause_____ .

POSTTEST Activities

The posttests help teachers and students assess what they have learned and what they still need to learn. The final posttest uses the PSAT format, providing learners an opportunity to become familiar with the PSAT format.

Posttest: End Punctuation

> **Place** periods, question marks, and exclamation points where they are needed in the following narrative. Capitalize the first word in a sentence.

1   *H*ave you heard of Alaska's famous dog-sledding race, the Iditarod**?**

2   each sled team includes 7 to 18 dogs usually the dogs line up in pairs,

3   with one dog on each side of the gangline (a gangline—also called a

4   towline—is the tether or rope that links the team to the sled)

5   sledders usually train several dogs to lead that's because each dog

6   may have a different strength or weakness some lead dogs don't like to

7   face the wind, for instance others dislike working their way through the

8   forest some don't accept commands well, but they keep the gangline nice

9   and taut still others maintain a fast pace on straightaways, only to cause

10   tangles when they round a turn an all-around leader—one who does

11   everything well—is a rarity

12   sledders, or mushers, use special terms to describe their lead dogs can

13   you guess what a "pacesetter" does it keeps the team moving fast on

14   straight portions of the trails what do you think a "command leader" does

15   it steers tightly on turns

16   a lead dog becomes both the brain and the "steering wheel" of its

17   team it must listen for the driver's special commands *haw* means "go left"

18   *gee* means "go right" the lead dog must also set a good pace and keep

19   the gangline taut if the leader fails to do this, the other dogs will have

20   trouble running in sync, and utter chaos may result it's easy to see why

21   a good lead dog may be a sledder's most valuable asset

Posttest: Commas

> **Add** commas where they are needed.

1. Black Elk, an Oglala Sioux from South Dakota, became one of the most respected American Indian leaders in the twentieth century.

2. In a vision, Black Elk saw the sky filled with dancing horses a spotted eagle a flowering tree and a tepee with a rainbow door.

3. The symbols in Black Elk's vision—the eagle the flowers and the rainbow—meant humankind would one day live in peace.

4. Black Elk who was nine years old then did not tell anyone about his vision.

5. He was afraid no one would believe him so he kept his vision to himself.

6. When the white men came they said to the Oglala Sioux "You may keep your land as long as grass shall grow and the water flow."

7. A few years later the white men discovered gold in the Black Hills and in their fervor to obtain it they forgot their promise to the Indians.

8. The discovery of gold in the Black Hills of South Dakota a beautiful sacred place to the Indians started a chain of events—events that led to tragedy and hardship events that saddened Black Elk.

9. The Battle of the Little Bighorn which occurred on June 25 1876 was a major turning point.

10. After the Battle of the Little Bighorn the Indians traveled from place to place became desperate for food and gradually succumbed to sickness.

11. In 1931, Black Elk told his life story to John G. Neihardt a writer who published the book *Black Elk Speaks*.

12. Black Elk died in 1950 on Pine Ridge Reservation South Dakota saddened that humankind still was not living in peace.

Posttest: Semicolons & Colons

> **Add** semicolons and colons where they are needed.

1. Pluto, a cold chunk of rock and ice, is a small planet ; it measures about 1,500 miles in diameter.

2. Pluto resembles Earth in two ways it has a moon, and its orbit is tilted.

3. If you lived on Pluto, you would never have a birthday it takes 248 Earth-years for this planet to revolve once around the sun!

4. Some scientists want to classify Pluto as an asteroid they don't feel it is large enough to be a planet.

5. Astronomers have never agreed on a single definition for the word "planet" however, most scientists consider celestial objects to be planets if they are round, if they directly orbit a star, and if they are large enough to shine in the night sky.

6. Pluto might be called an asteroid for three reasons it is smaller than other planets, its gravity is very weak, and its orbit is tilted.

7. Many scientists argue that Pluto should remain a planet they say it has enough gravity to keep its spherical shape.

8. Scientists also point out that Pluto has a solid surface Jupiter, on the other hand, is just a giant ball of gas.

9. On February 3, 1999, the International Astronomical Union ended the debate this way they declared Pluto a planet.

10. Students can still use "My Very Educated Mother Just Served Us Nine Pizzas" to remember the sequence of planets Mercury, Venus, Earth, Mars, Jupiter, Saturn, Uranus, Neptune, and Pluto.

Posttest: Hyphens & Dashes

> **Add** hyphens and dashes where they are needed.

1. We made a U-turn when we realized we had forgotten something—my brother, Zach.

2. The Humphrey-Hawkins bill passed last week.

3. At the age of five—*five,* mind you her daughter speaks three languages.

4. Three-fourths of the student body doesn't know the school song and doesn't care!

5. The Bobcats lost the game 24-18.

6. Was that a B-flat he just played on the violin?

7. The gas tank is three-quarters empty.

8. People are still experiencing the effects of the first H-bomb.

9. My brother-in-law loves to play pool.

10. Neighbors, friends, family—what would a wedding be without them?

11. Many of us enjoy being average, run-of-the-mill people.

12. When a person is shell-shocked, it means he or she is exhausted because of excessive stress.

13. He lived through the crash—just barely—and he'll never be the same.

14. For the rest of his life, someone else will have to fasten the buttons on his shirt sleeves, tie his shoes, and cut his fingernails—all the little things we take for granted.

15. I sometimes wonder why it's so difficult to appreciate—really appreciate—being able to walk and talk and see and hear.

Posttest: Apostrophes

> **Write** the contraction or the possessive form needed to correct the underlined words.
> Write *C* in the blank if the sentence is already correct.

_____*Alice's*_____   **1.** Alice brother did not understand the experiment.

_____   **2.** My brother-in-law mother is a kind lady.

_____   **3.** José garage is filled with spare tires.

_____   **4.** Your prize is a year supply of crunchy dog food!

_____   **5.** It's time for my appointment.

_____   **6.** I dont want to be late.

_____   **7.** Ann and Chris uncle will be here tonight.

_____   **8.** The hat doesn't belong to me; it's somebody else.

_____   **9.** Jerry, Hunter, and Ali car is parked in the driveway.

_____   **10.** Are there three *R* in the word "referred"?

_____   **11.** Couldnt you forget about yesterday?

_____   **12.** Shanika is driving the boss car.

_____   **13.** The three waitresses are late for work.

_____   **14.** The secretary of defense wife hosted the party.

_____   **15.** Ceci and Carol bicycles are here. (Each owns a bike.)

_____   **16.** The professor nose is chubby.

_____   **17.** The Tucson High School Theater Association banquet is tonight.

_____   **18.** My aunt and uncle house was sold last week.

_____   **19.** The king of Siam wife was interviewed on the news.

_____   **20.** We arent finished yet.

Posttest: Quotation Marks & Italics (Underlining)

> **Add** quotation marks where they are needed. Underline words that should be in italics.

1. "I studied for that test and still didn't pass it," complained George.

2. Did she discuss Whittier's poem The Eternal Goodness?

3. Age of Gold is a phrase in Emerson's poem Character.

4. Who's staring at you? he asked.

5. Claire, Mr. Langdon said, please concentrate on one thing at a time.

6. Improvisation for the Theater is a fine book written by Viola Spolin.

7. Are you planning to sail on the Kansas City Clipper?

8. Miss Berg asked, Did you ever read London's short story To Build a Fire?

9. The only narrative poem Jerry read is Old Christmas; now he's reading Sweet and Low, a lyric poem.

10. My mother subscribes to both Time and Newsweek.

11. Mr. Ryken's conversation is always sprinkled with ah's and ahem's.

12. Professor Lenken used the book Zen and the Art of Motorcycle Maintenance in his psychology class.

13. Ms. Jensen asked whether we had studied Rölvaag's book Giants in the Earth.

14. In 1955, four different singers recorded the same song. Amazingly, all four versions of It's Almost Tomorrow made the Top Forty.

15. In the late fifties and early sixties, some of the new and unusual dance fads were named by songs: The Stroll (1957), The Walk (1958), The Bunny Hop (1959), and The Twist (1960).

Posttest: Punctuation

> **Proofread** the paragraphs below. Add punctuation marks where they are needed (and capital letters at the beginnings of sentences).

1   The development of America's railroad as a dependable means of

2   transportation was a long, frustrating process. many people helped make

3   the railroad a reality but one man stood out Horatio Allen

4   As a young college graduate Allen gazed with awe upon the strange

5   steam powered vehicles being tested in Englands coalfields during the

6   1820s he and others like him did their best to introduce the locomotive to

7   America In return they faced the scorn of those who advocated horsepower

8   mule power sail power waterpower and even foot power

9   Allen persevered however it was not until the 1860s and the end of

10   the Civil War that his dream building an American railroad was truly

11   realized Then as the nations attention shifted from the South to the

12   wide open West the railroad suddenly became a vital means of

13   transportation with much enthusiasm railroad companies undertook the

14   task of satisfying the new demand for rail power the invention of steel

15   rails in 1865 made it possible to meet this growing need and four years

16   later the first transcontinental railway was completed.

17   The now famous scene depicting the driving of the golden spike in

18   Promontory Point Utah marked the beginning of a new era in United

19   States history the railroad quickly became the main transportation system

20   of an expanding nation

Posttest: Capitalization

> **Cross** out each lowercase letter that should be capitalized and write your correction above it.

1. *M* *P* *V* *I*
   marco polo was born in venice, italy, in about 1254.

2. his father, nicolò, was a wealthy merchant who purchased goods in the orient and resold them to european markets.

3. when marco was about 17, he traveled with his father and his uncle to the court of the mongol conqueror kublai khan in china.

4. they sailed down the adriatic sea, across the mediterranean sea, to the city of jerusalem.

5. the polos stopped there because the khan (*khan* is a title like *prince*) wanted holy oil from the tomb of jesus christ.

6. even though the khan wasn't christian, he read from the bible on easter and christmas.

7. he also celebrated muslim, buddhist, and jewish feast days.

8. when asked why, he replied, " i respect and honor all four great prophets: christ, mohammed, moses, and buddha, so that i can appeal to any one of them in heaven." (marco polo always remembered this statement.)

9. from israel, the polos journeyed along the silk road, through mountains and deserts, until they reached the alph river in shangtu province, where the khan's summer palace was located.

10. the khan's empire was so huge, he established a pony express like the one america used to carry mail in the wild west during the 1800s.

11. marco polo wrote a book, *cathay,* that gave europeans their earliest information about china.

Posttest: Numbers, Abbreviations, & Acronyms

> **Underline** each abbreviation, word, or number that has been used incorrectly. Write the correction above it.

United States
1. The exploration of outer space by the U.S. is the responsibility of the National Aeronautics and Space Administration.

2. N.A.S.A. headquarters are located in Washington, DC.

3. If you ever care to correspond with NASA, send your letter to 400 Maryland Ave., Wash., D.C. 20546.

4. During last sem.'s unit on space exploration, 7 students wrote to N.A.S.A. for info.

5. After a decade of moon exploration by space probes, 2 U.S. astronauts landed on the lunar surface on July twentieth, 1969.

6. A total of six two-man crews of Amer. astronauts landed on the moon between nineteen sixty-nine and nineteen seventy-two.

7. They returned to Earth with over seven hundred ninety lbs. of moon rocks.

8. Some of the craters on the moon's surface are fifty-six miles across.

9. The moon is slightly more than 1/4 the size of Earth. (1/4 is the same as 25%.)

10. Earth has 1 moon, while Jupiter has 63 and Saturn has 33.

11. A total eclipse of the moon took place on Oct. twenty-eighth, 1985.

12. Ken needs 6 11-inch straws to complete his model of a futuristic spaceship.

13. A light-year is a unit of length equal to the distance that light travels in 1 year.

14. This distance is about five trillion eight hundred seventy-eight billion miles.

Posttest: Plurals & Spelling

> **Underline** each word spelled incorrectly. Write the correct spelling above it.

1. Turquoise has been a *valuable* valuble stone for years; many cultures and civilizations have used it.

2. The powerful Aztec, Incan, and Mayan people used turquoise as a symbol of their gods.

3. The Egyptians, the Chinese, and the Pueblo Indians were using turquoise stones in jewlery centurys before the Europeans.

4. Merchants broughth the preshus stones from the Orient to Turkey, where they became known as "turquoise" to the Europeans.

5. Major deposits of turquoise are found in Tibet and Iran, but large deposits also exhist in the southwestern United States.

6. The Navajo and others in America still use turquoise as protection against injuries, illneses, and contagous diseazes.

7. Turquoise stones range in color from yellow to gray, but sky blue and lime green are usually prefered.

8. Nowadays, turquoise can be died, treated with minneral oil, or waxxed to deepen the color.

9. The demand for turquoise remains so great that artifisial vareities of the stone are produced.

10. Any respecktible dealer will issiue a certificate stating that the stone is authentick.

11. Buyers today might become ill if they descover that their expensive peice of jewelry is actualy plastic.

Posttest: Using the Right Word

Underline each word used incorrectly below and write the correction above it.

Whether
1. <u>Weather</u> their tracking hurricanes or deciding if its going to rein, many

   Americans turn on they're televisions and watch the Whether Channel.

2. This station broadcasts 24 ours a day, 7 days a weak.

3. Whenever large storms are cited, weather station personal jump into action.

4. They monitor bits and peaces of information that seam to pore threw the

   station, especially when a hurricane forms.

5. A hurricane may go passed the East Coast and cause only miner damage.

6. However, if it turns inland, know one nos what coarse it will take or how much

   property people might loose.

7. Sometimes a hurricane causes alot of damage, and it's affects are seen for years.

8. Residents may be urged to leave and take only what they need to get bye.

9. Some people except this news and leave, but others chose to stay and face the

   storm.

10. Millions of Americans weight by their televisions to see wear the hurricane

    will go.

11. Weather Channel viewers like to check there local forecasts, sew every ate

    minutes the weather four their area appears at the bottom of the TV screen in

    bright capitol letters.

12. It is well that people can receive continuous weather reports—whether their

    tracking a storm or just planning a picnic.

Final Proofreading Posttest—Part 1

> **Write** plurals for the following words:

1. potato *potatoes*
2. box _____
3. piano _____
4. sheep _____
5. knife _____
6. studio _____

7. ABC _____
8. sister-in-law _____
9. spy _____
10. radius _____
11. ranch _____
12. key _____

> **Cross** out each lowercase letter that should be capitalized and write your correction above it.

1.   M S   G   W   J   S
   mr. smith goes to washington is a movie starring jimmy stewart.

2. senator ted kennedy represents the state of massachusetts.

3. aunt jo registered her car with the department of transportation.

4. my uncle, who works for the democratic party, is visiting us.

5. christopher columbus, an italian explorer, was financed by queen isabella of

   spain when he set out to find a new route to india.

6. the New England Patriots football team won three super bowls.

7. muslims call their supreme being *allah*.

8. we studied that in social studies 104.

9. the declaration of independence was ratified on july 4, 1776, by the continental

   congress in philadelphia, pennsylvania.

10. my mother saw the united states women's soccer team win the world cup.

11. she bought me a t-shirt that said, "play like a girl—kick it!"

Write out the following abbreviations:

1. GA *Georgia*

2. UT _____

3. dept. _____

4. lb _____

5. m _____

6. mi. _____

7. oz. _____

8. Rd. _____

9. gal. _____

10. ASAP _____

11. pd. _____

12. yd. _____

13. km _____

14. ea. _____

15. w/o _____

Write a short phrase explaining the difference between the words in each pair below.

1. principle, principal

   principle is "an idea"; principal is "a person," "a sum of money," or "primary"

2. its, it's

   _____

3. can, may

   _____

4. accept, except,

   _____

5. lay, lie

   _____

6. loose, lose

   _____

7. counsel, council

   _____

8. lend, borrow

   _____

   _____

Final Proofreading Posttest—Part 2

1 October ~~twelfth~~ 12 , 2006

2 Lana R Wendricks Ph D

3 Department of Geography, University of Illinois

4 Three hundred five Green Street

5 Urbana IL 61820

6 Dear Dr Wendricks

7   I understand you are the new manager of the University of Illinois

8 mapmaking project Would you consider using Lever Electronics GlobeNav

9 420 System I would like to offer the university a discount you can buy 3

10 GlobeNav 420s for only 999 95

11   The system is easy to use a *waypoint* shows the original position on

12 the screen and a dotted line follows the route even if a user has made a

13 U turn Hows that for technology

14   Here are 2 more features you'll enjoy a window program that groups

15 your information plus an outstanding memory capability. The system can

16 store up to seven hundred fifty positions

17   Did you happen to read the In-Fisherman magazine dated June 17

18 2005 Ive enclosed a copy. Here is a quotation from page thirty-five, in the

19 article entitled Finding Your Way

20   It gives position fixes in seconds not minutes. It will hold

21   that position whether youre a quarter mile out in the water or

22   along a high and narrow cliff or even along Interstate Five. We

23   rate this product an A plus.

24   Dr Wendricks Lever Electronics has sold almost 410000 of these units

25   in the United States and Canada We hope your university will consider

26   our product for the budget year two thousand seven to 2008. Would it be

27   possible to set up a meeting with you Dr Burrows who is the projects

28   ex manager may want to be present as well.

29   Please contact my office at 972-555-2222 any day after eight-thirty

30   a m. I would appreciate a chance not only to sell our product but also to

31   prove my claims thats how excited I am about the GlobeNav 420

32   Sincerely

Peter H. Reynolds

33   Peter H Reynolds

34   Vice President Lever Electronics Inc

Circle the correct spelling.

1. cheif, (chief)

2. krisis, crisis

3. existance, existence

4. experience, experiance

5. eighth, eigth

6. chocolate, chocalate

7. justise, justice

8. receive, recieve

9. appearence, appearance

10. sking, skiing

11. pastime, passtime

12. maintain, maintian

13. occasion, ocassion

14. tomorrow, tomarrow

Posttest: Nouns

> **Underline** all words used as nouns below. Identify the first noun in each sentence: write *P* for proper or *C* for common on the first blank; write *A* for abstract and *CN* for concrete on the second blank.

   _C_ _A_ **1.** One <u>practice</u> that seems to aid <u>patients</u> is bringing <u>animals</u> into their

                  <u>rooms</u>.

   ___ ___ **2.** Dogs and cats visit hospitals, but fish and birds may visit, too.

   ___ ___ **3.** One of St. Louis' many hospitals uses rabbits and other soft,

                  quiet animals to help depressed patients.

   ___ ___ **4.** Hospitals often have dogs on duty throughout the day.

   ___ ___ **5.** Patients pet the dogs and sometimes throw balls or socks for a game

                  of catch.

> **Underline** all words used as nouns below. For each sentence, identify only the first noun's case (write *NOM* for nominative, *POS* for possessive, and *OBJ* for objective).

   _____ **1.** Studies show that patients who see trees from their rooms recover faster

                  than those who see brick walls.

   _____ **2.** A patient's view while lying flat in bed is also important.

   _____ **3.** Now architects are designing hospitals with as many outside rooms as

                  possible.

   _____ **4.** Researchers have also found that landscape and wildlife paintings help

                  patients recover faster.

   _____ **5.** By wearing headphones and listening to soothing sounds from nature,

                  patients can reduce their anxiety.

Posttest: Pronouns

> **Underline** the personal pronoun in each sentence below. Identify the pronoun's number (*S* for singular or *P* for plural) on the first blank; identify the pronoun's case (*NOM* for nominative, *POS* for possessive, or *OBJ* for objective) on the second blank.

_S_ _NOM_ **1.** Traveling into Death Valley, I saw a sight that's hard to believe: the "sliding rocks" of Racetrack Playa.

___ _____ **2.** Racetrack Playa (a dry lake bed) is three miles long, and its north end is only three inches higher than the south end.

___ _____ **3.** The rocks in the Playa slide along the flat lake bed, but no one knows what moves them.

___ _____ **4.** A group of us went to study this mystery.

___ _____ **5.** We found that rocks fell onto the lake bed from a rock formation located on the north end.

> **Underline** the pronoun in each sentence below. Identify the pronoun's class (*PER* for personal, *REL* for relative, *IND* for indefinite, *INT* for interrogative, *DEM* for demonstrative, and *REX* for reflexive).

IND **1.** Somehow dozens of rocks, <u>some</u> weighing hundreds of pounds, end up at the south end, leaving grooves in the ground.

_____ **2.** No one has ever seen a rock in motion, yet the rocks have clearly moved.

_____ **3.** Scientists who have studied this suggest that high winds are responsible.

_____ **4.** Some geologists have convinced themselves the rocks were frozen in ice and slid along with help from the winds.

_____ **5.** Who is right?

_____ **6.** That remains a mystery.

_____ **7.** We may never know, because the Racetrack Playa is now considered a United States biosphere, and access to the site is very limited.

Posttest: Verbs

Underline all the verbs below. Include helping (auxiliary) and linking verbs. In each sentence, identify only the first verb's number on the first blank (*S* for singular or *P* for plural); then identify the first verb's tense on the second blank (present, past, future, present perfect, past perfect, future perfect).

_P_ **_present_** **1.** At the Dallas Aquarium, red-bellied piranhas <u>look</u> like harmless panfish.

___ _____ **2.** For example, yesterday when the attendant entered the tank with food, they swam to the far end and cowered.

___ _____ **3.** We do not expect this kind of behavior from fish that have such a ferocious reputation.

___ _____ **4.** I hear they can snap off a finger that is poked into the water.

___ _____ **5.** Supposedly, a school of piranhas can devour a whole cow.

___ _____ **6.** Piranhas usually eat small fish, but they do not devour their dinner whole.

___ _____ **7.** Rather, tiny, moon-shaped bites are taken from a victim's tail or fin.

___ _____ **8.** Researchers had originally thought that this behavior was like the wolf's (the wolf first cripples its prey so the kill is easier).

___ _____ **9.** More recently, scientists have discovered that the piranha only wants the fins and tails because these fish parts contain high amounts of protein.

___ _____10. Evidently if you are a piranha, you can never get enough protein!

___ _____11. Before too long—and luckily for the piranha—its victim will have grown back its fins and tail, and the whole process can begin again.

Posttest: Adjectives & Adverbs

> **Underline** the adjectives once (except the articles *a*, *an*, or *the*—do not underline those). Draw an arrow to the noun or pronoun that each adjective modifies. Underline the adverbs twice. Draw an arrow to the verb, adverb, or adjective that each adverb modifies.

1. The American game of checkers is a symbol of good-natured competition.

2. People think it is only played in quiet places by old men.

3. Players need good memories; there are 500 quintillion possible moves.

4. Checker champions are often thoughtful, patient people.

5. Players closely analyze plays to reach master status.

6. Most textbooks about checkers mainly address strategies.

7. Opening and closing moves often are given colorful names like the "Goose Walk" or the "Boomerang."

8. Bobby Fischer, the world-renowned chess master, was challenged to a game of checkers and a game of chess by George Vidlak, a top checkers player.

9. They started with the chess game, which Vidlak energetically played to a draw.

10. Fischer then childishly refused to play the checkers game.

11. An early book about the game of checkers once advised players to win without bragging and to lose without anger.

12. Bobby Fischer should have studied an etiquette book harder.

Posttest: Prepositions, Conjunctions, & Interjections

Underline each preposition once, underline each interjection twice, and circle each conjunction.

1. It is not easy to become a firefighter, (since) training academies have entrance standards that equal those <u>at</u> the best universities.

2. The top-notch program in Tucson, Arizona, accepted only 42 out of 1,500 applicants in 1999.

3. Most recruits for the Tucson program were about 30 years old, and seven of them were women.

4. Tucson's recruits are athletic people who like risky sports: flying, skiing, scuba diving, and—yikes—even rock climbing.

5. Not only do the recruits take medical courses, but also they take classes in fire science, physics, and chemistry.

6. Half of the recruits already have a college education, and the other half are continuing their education in other ways.

7. Well, the recruits obviously have to learn a lot more than how to aim a hose at the flames.

8. During training, they learn to walk a hose through 100 feet of thick mud.

9. The recruits must keep the hose pointed at a car tire while they struggle through the mud.

10. The hose does its best to snake backwards because water shoots out the front end at 95 gallons a minute.

11. The hoses both buck and kick with a wallop, and, hey, even the small fire hoses can break a recruit's arm or leg!

12. If you wish to become a firefighter, you need to study and be physically fit.

Final Parts of Speech Posttest—Part 1

> **Underline** each noun once and each verb twice. Circle all pronouns.

1. The <u>class</u> <u><u>proved</u></u> to (themselves) that everyone could pass the test.

2. Jeremy is writing his résumé; the factory where he worked closed this past week.

3. After he scribbled the orders on his pad, the waiter filled each glass with water.

4. The seal lifted its head and barked for more fish.

5. My aunt bought herself a ring, and she wears it on her pinkie.

6. The group gave Mrs. Crocutt a gift.

> **Review** the sentences above and find two words that fit each of the descriptions below.

1. Two collective nouns: _____

2. Two reflexive pronouns: _____

3. Two possessive pronouns: _____

4. Two nouns used as subjects: _____

   _____

5. Two pronouns used as a subject: _____

6. Two proper nouns: _____

7. Two nouns used as direct objects: _____

   _____

8. Two nouns used as objects of prepositions: _____

9. Two auxiliary verbs: _____

© Great Source. All rights reserved. (9)

208

Underline the adjectives once and the adverbs twice.

1. <u>old</u> tractor

2. handled <u><u>carefully</u></u>

3. worked more precisely

4. quickly cooked the rice

5. eternally grateful client

6. they were more confident

7. bad breath

8. he sang badly

9. meat was too tough

10. weekly newspaper

11. newspaper delivered weekly

12. Spanish rice

Underline the prepositions once, underline the interjections twice, and circle the conjunctions.

1. We boarded the cruise ship (and) made our way <u>to</u> our cabin, located <u>on</u> the "Aloha Deck."

2. Yikes! The room was tiny.

3. The bathroom was so small that the sink was built outside of it, and near the bed, but we didn't care.

4. I hoped that I wouldn't awake in the night and bang the sink with my elbow.

5. We didn't stay in the room long because there was so much to do elsewhere on the ship.

6. We ate, we walked, we shopped, we swam, we danced, and, oh boy, did I mention that we got lots of sunshine?

7. Not only were there three full meals scheduled throughout the day, but there were four snacks, too.

8. Besides having fun on the ship, we also explored several tropical islands and rode on donkeys and motor scooters across some beautiful terrain.

9. We had a great time both on and off the ship.

Final Parts of Speech Posttest—Part 2

> **Rewrite** the sentences below, changing passive verb phrases to active verb phrases. **Supply a subject when necessary.**

1. The fence around the compound was climbed by hordes of monkeys.

Hordes of monkeys climbed the fence around the compound.

2. A huge feast was being served in the main dining hall.

_____

3. Terry's dog was washed and brushed painstakingly to remove the skunk odor.

_____

_____

4. Fans are being blown out of their seats by the band.

_____

5. The endless piles of laundry were washed by young women.

_____

> **Underline** the verbals. Label each using *G* for gerunds, *I* for infinitives, and *P* for participles.

        G

1. <u>Jaywalking</u> across busy streets is a shortcut to broken bones.

2. I have to go running more often to stay in shape.

3. Smacking her lips in total enjoyment, the baby ate her mashed apricots.

4. To learn how to fly a plane, you must enjoy sitting still for long periods of time.

5. Watching kids jump in freshly raked leaves is an autumn tradition.

6. I took up snowboarding last winter to join my friends.

7. To snowboard well, it helps to practice skateboarding first.

Write sentences using the elements requested.

1. (Use the possessive pronoun *my* and an adjective of your choice.)

My old guitar now hangs on my wall.

2. (Use the preposition *into* and an adverb.)

_____

3. (Use the coordinating conjunction *but* and the relative pronoun *that.*)

_____

_____

4. (Use the indefinite pronoun *everyone* and an active verb.)

_____

5. (Use the indirect object *me* and the direct object *ball.*)

_____

6. (Use the collective noun *team* and the coordinating conjunction *and.*)

_____

_____

7. (Use the present tense verb *likes* and the subordinating conjunction *although.*)

_____

_____

8. (Use the past perfect tense verb *had thought.*)

_____

9. (Use the future tense verb *will sing* and a pair of correlative conjunctions.)

_____

_____

Posttest: Subjects & Predicates

> **Draw** a line between the complete subject and the complete predicate. If the subject is compound, write *CS* on the blank. If the predicate is compound, write *CP* in the blank. Then circle each simple subject and predicate.

___*CP*___ **1.** (Rube Goldberg) | (was born) in 1883 and (died) in 1970.

_____ **2.** He was a Pulitzer Prize-winning cartoonist, sculptor, and author.

_____ **3.** Rube graduated from the University of California and went to work as an engineer.

_____ **4.** His complicated drawings and funny cartoons soon drew notice.

_____ **5.** Rube quit his engineering job and moved to New York to work full-time as a cartoonist.

_____ **6.** Readers loved his cartoon "inventions"—imaginary machines that made simple tasks amazingly complex.

_____ **7.** Myriad gears, levers, cups, and balls sequentially turned, flipped, poured, and rolled—all just to perform a single task.

_____ **8.** Purdue University celebrates the creative and artistic genius of this "cartoon engineer" with its annual Rube Goldberg Machine Contest.

_____ **9.** Each contraption must complete a task in 20 or more steps, demonstrating the contestant's science and engineering skills.

_____ **10.** "Toasting Bread," "Turning on a Radio," and "Making a Cup of Coffee" are titles of past contests.

Posttest: Phrases

Identify the underlined phrases as gerund, infinitive, participial, prepositional, or appositive.

infinitive   **1.** Tonya's responsibility will be <u>to keep the bikes in good condition</u>.

_____   **2.** <u>Walking the dogs</u> was always an adventure.

_____   **3.** The man <u>running down the street</u> is my teacher.

_____   **4.** The baby crawled <u>up the steps</u> to the landing.

_____   **5.** The former president, <u>the woman in the tweed suit</u>, voted "no."

_____   **6.** Isn't that Jerry Ford, <u>the former president</u>?

_____   **7.** Hema made no friends by <u>flying off the handle</u>.

_____   **8.** <u>Waving his hand</u>, the police officer tried to stop the cars.

_____   **9.** <u>Sailing down the Nile</u> was one of Brubaker's secret dreams.

_____   **10.** I'm quite eager <u>to cruise down the Amazon</u>.

_____   **11.** They sailed the River Thames between <u>London and Hampton Court</u>.

_____   **12.** <u>To float down the river</u> in early morning is an adventure.

_____   **13.** The river, <u>swollen by rain</u>, was full of tree limbs.

_____   **14.** <u>Built by popular demand</u>, roller coasters are the primary attraction at theme parks.

_____   **15.** My father and mother, <u>Fred and Wilma Bolin</u>, are city council members.

Posttest: Clauses

> **Identify** each underlined clause below by using *N* for noun, *ADV* for adverb, or *ADJ* for adjective.

ADJ **1.** Before the 1500s, nearly all pencils were made from lead, a material that was poisonous.

_____ **2.** Later on, pencil makers began to use graphite that was nontoxic and left a darker mark.

_____ **3.** Unfortunately, graphite was so soft and brittle that it needed a casing.

_____ **4.** String, an early casing, was what was wrapped around the graphite sticks.

_____ **5.** Later, graphite was inserted into wooden holders that had been cored out by hand.

_____ **6.** When a certain pencil maker chose yellow casings as an advertising gimmick, he launched a tradition.

_____ **7.** The Chinese, who used the color yellow to represent royalty, developed high-quality graphite.

_____ **8.** Few know that 75 percent of all pencils manufactured today are yellow.

_____ **9.** What amazes me is that most of the two billion pencils used in the United States have erasers.

_____ **10.** Most pencils that are sold in Europe do not have that little pink rubber tip.

_____ **11.** Do you think that Europeans make fewer mistakes?

_____ **12.** Get out your pencil and circle the answer that you feel is correct.

Posttest: Kinds & Types of Sentences

Label each sentence by type on the first blank: declarative *(D)*, interrogative *(INT)*, imperative *(IMP)*, exclamatory *(E)*, or conditional *(CON)*. Add the correct end punctuation.

Next, label each sentence by kind on the second blank: simple *(S)*, compound *(CD)*, complex *(CX)*, or compound-complex *(CD-CX)*.

<u>CON</u>   <u>CX</u>   **1.** If you were to walk into almost any natural history museum, I'm sure you would find gigantic skeletons of prehistoric animals.

_____ _____ **2.** Have you ever seen the skeleton of a *Brachiosaurus* dinosaur

_____ _____ **3.** These creatures stood about 50 feet tall, and they weighed about 65 tons

_____ _____ **4.** They were huge

_____ _____ **5.** The *Brachiosaurus* probably had a good sense of smell, for it had very large nostrils on top of its head, and it had a powerful heart to pump blood to its brain, which was at the end of a 30-foot-long neck

_____ _____ **6.** If I had to pick my favorite dinosaur, it would be *Tyrannosaurus rex,* the "tyrant lizard king," with its large, pointed, replaceable teeth

_____ _____ **7.** *T-rex* had a huge head with well-developed jaw muscles that crushed its victims, as well as a slim, stiff-pointed tail that provided balance

_____ _____ **8.** Prehistoric creatures had to watch out for *T-rex*'s four-foot jaw, a jaw whose eight-inch-long teeth could handle 500 pounds of meat and bones in one bite

_____ _____ **9.** Some museums have life-sized replicas of dinosaurs, which sometimes scare small children until they realize the creatures are fake

_____ _____ **10.** Visit a dinosaur exhibit and see for yourself

Posttest: Subject-Verb Agreement

> **Cross** out any verb that does not agree in number with its subject. Write the correction above it.

1. Unidentified flying objects, or UFO's, ~~was~~ *were* seen long before the Wright brothers flew their first airplane.

2. Medieval writings mentions "weirde things in the skye," and European paintings and tapestries shows people gazing at discs in the heavens.

3. Until the Roswell, New Mexico, incident in 1947, most Americans wasn't particularly intrigued by "alien sightings."

4. A rancher and his hired hands found the remains of what they thought were an alien spaceship.

5. Government officials claimed the spaceship were a wayward weather balloon, not a Martian wreck.

6. There was alien corpses allegedly seen by an army nurse.

7. The army nurse reported the corpses she saw was smaller, slimmer, and more delicate than most human adults.

8. Everyone who have seen recent movies about spaceships have an idea of what the army nurse described.

9. The United States Air Force do investigate UFO sightings.

10. However, their investigative teams has published a "Project Blue Book"—a 1,465-page report—which basically say, "There seem to be nothing to report."

11. Stories like those about Roswell has inspired many television shows.

Posttest: Pronoun-Antecedent Agreement

> **Cross** out any pronoun that does not agree with its antecedent. Write the correct pronoun above it. Two sentences are correct as is.

1. Parents should not send ~~his or her~~ *their* sick children to a day-care center.

2. When Jonas Salk discovered the polio vaccine, it became a world-famous scientist.

3. Neither Mike nor Alexis needs glasses; each has 20-20 vision.

4. Both Jackie and Maria can speak for herself.

5. One of the saleswomen lost their customers because they failed to complete each sale properly.

6. One of the shoes is missing their sole.

7. Lamont's stories always lose his appeal near the end.

8. The doctors finished his or her rounds while Ms. Rue took their break.

9. Each player on the coed team gives the game their all.

10. Nadine Gordimer's and Ernest Hemingway's novels reflect her and his real-life experiences.

11. Neither of the women sang their part well.

12. If one of the doctors is still here, ask them to wait.

13. Pat is one of those people who are continually amazed at his employees' talents.

14. No one has found their shoes yet.

15. Giorgio, along with his sisters, has learned to play checkers.

16. Either Dad or grandpa will bring their razor and fishing gear.

Posttest: Combining Sentences

Rewrite the following essay combining sentences so that they are more effective.

Lou Gehrig never missed a day of elementary school. His mother encouraged him to attend college. She wanted him to be an accountant. She wanted him to be an engineer. At Columbia University, a baseball scout saw Lou play. The scout worked for the New York Yankees. The scout signed Lou.

Lou replaced Wally Pipp at first base. Lou played the next 2,130 consecutive games. Lou played the next 14 years without missing a game, despite broken fingers, fevers, and back pain. The boy never missed a day of elementary school. The man never missed a day of baseball. They called him the *Iron Horse*.

_____

_____

_____

_____

_____

_____

_____

_____

_____

_____

_____

_____

_____

Posttest: Sentence Problems 1

Correct the following essay to eliminate sentence fragments, comma splices, and run-on sentences. Insert colons and periods, delete commas and periods, capitalize sentence beginnings, and lowercase words as necessary.

1   Mohandas K. Gandhi had one mission in life: To free 350 million

2   Indian people from British rule. He wanted to do this peacefully, Gandhi

3   believed people could free themselves from tyranny. Without resorting to

4   terrorism or bloodshed.

5   When he was a boy, few guessed that the young, timid Gandhi would

6   someday become a great leader, after all, he was a member of the Vaisya

7   caste, which included mostly farmers and merchants, despite such humble

8   beginnings, Gandhi went to college and became a lawyer soon he was

9   helping people fight racial injustice with a nonaggressive resistance he

10   called *satyagraha,* which means "truth and love with firmness."

11   Mohandas Gandhi influenced many people in 1959, a young theological

12   student. By the name of Martin Luther King. Heard a lecture about this

13   great spiritual leader. King was so excited by the idea of nonaggressive

14   resistance that he bought a half dozen books about Gandhi, using

15   Gandhi's nonviolent resistance, King helped break racial barriers for

16   African Americans. Here in the United States.

Posttest: Sentence Problems 2

Correct the following problems: deadwood and wordiness; nonstandard language and double negatives; and shifts in number, tense, person, and voice. Cross out and change words as needed.

1   About 5 million young people in the United States, Puerto Rico,

2   Guam, and the Virgin Islands ~~are members of, or you might say~~ belong

3   to / 4-H clubs. Many young people join 4-H because they're fun and

4   educational and they learn new things. Club members take part in

5   educational programs that aim to, hopefully, help participants to develop

6   new and unfamiliar skills and become good citizens.

7   Each year, 4-H club members, who are very helpful, serve their

8   communities by completing one or more special projects annually. Some

9   members of 4-H clubs might plant trees or be teaching safety programs,

10   or conduct paper drives and do other environmentally related projects.

11   Other 4-H club members also might have participated in food projects and

12   learn the principles of good nutrition and nutritious meals.

13   People who join 4-H clubs try hard to strive to be responsible,

14   reliable, fruitful, and productive citizens. It is good to belong to 4-H clubs,

15   especially one that will help you become productive and fruitful. Every

16   4-H club is governed by this one particular motto. Members are expected

17   to demonstrate the values found in my motto: "To Make the Best Better."

18   If a person can't support this ideal, you probably shouldn't never join 4-H.

Final Sentence Posttest

> **Draw** a line between each complete subject and complete predicate. Label each compound subject *CS*. Label each compound predicate *CP*.

                                      CS

1. Durians, rambutans, and mangosteens | are exotic fruits found in Malaysia.

2. Durians look like spiky green footballs and smell like dead animals.

3. Some tourists have compared the odor of the durian to rotting vegetables.

4. The government discourages eating durians in public.

5. Train stations, bus stops, and airline terminals post "No Durians" signs.

6. The "No Durians" sign has a red slash like our "No Smoking" sign, but it pictures the green fruit instead of a cigarette.

7. Restaurants must install special fans so durian eaters won't offend other diners.

8. Despite their stench, durians are popular because they taste heavenly.

9. The pulp inside looks velvety and tastes like almond custard.

> **Identify** each underlined phrase as either gerund, infinitive, participial, prepositional, or appositive.

            gerund

1. <u>Hitting the baseballs</u> thrown <u>by his father</u> made Samle happy.

2. The player <u>fielding the ball</u>, <u>Jonas Jones</u>, is an all-star.

3. <u>To hit a home run</u> was the ten-year-old's dream.

4. The softball landed <u>on top of the roof</u>.

5. <u>Hit by the pitch</u>, the player limped and moaned.

6. The runner, <u>having slammed into the third baseman</u>, was booed.

7. Was that Megan who smacked the ball <u>over the fence</u> <u>into the parking lot</u>?

> **Identify** the underlined clauses by type on the first blank: noun *(N)*, adjective *(ADJ)*, or adverb *(ADV)*. Then identify each type of sentence on the second blank: declarative *(D)*, interrogative *(INT)*, imperative *(IMP)*, exclamatory *(E)*, or conditional *(C)*. Add the correct end punctuation.

_N_ _INT_ **1.** Have you ever heard <u>people talk about Stradivarius violins</u>?

_____ _____ **2.** Then you may know <u>that some sell for more than $250,000 at auctions</u>

_____ _____ **3.** During the early 1700s, Antonio Stradivari designed and built more than 1,100 musical instruments <u>that are considered "perfect" violins</u>

_____ _____ **4.** <u>Although few exist today</u>, look to see if your violin is marked "Stradivarius"

_____ _____ **5.** The label doesn't mean the instrument is genuine, <u>since many violin makers have copied his style over the years</u>

_____ _____ **6.** If a violin is a real "Strad," experts <u>who have studied hundreds of instruments</u> can identify it by its wood grain, varnish, and craftsmanship

> **Change** each verb as needed so that it agrees in number with its subject. Change each pronoun as necessary so that it agrees in number, person, and gender with its antecedent.

1. Rain or shine, Matthew walked ~~their~~ *his* dogs in the park.

2. One of the semitrailer trucks was gunning their engine at the rest area.

3. The team were on a phenomenal winning streak.

4. Neither Shelly nor Shania are working at the store this evening.

5. Half of the students was on the biology field trip.

6. A person must try to reach their full potential.

7. Each of the video games are rated for violence and language content.

8. Mathematics are like a foreign language—using it well takes practice.

Rewrite the following sentences to eliminate substandard language, double negatives, wordiness, and misplaced modifiers.

1. Rory didn't want none of the desserts.

Rory didn't want any of the desserts. (or) *Rory wanted none of the*

desserts.

2. Our golden retriever, Lefty, jumped off of the raft.

3. Bjorn should of left the original paint color on the walls.

4. Maisy wanted to curl her hair, but she couldn't curl her hair because her arm was encased in a cast all the way from the top of her shoulder all the way down to her wrist.

5. Uncle Henry held the baby smoking a big cigar.

6. I haven't hardly had a chance to do my homework.

7. Waiting for the bus, the stray dog bit our neighbor.

8. Did he go with?

Final SkillsBook Posttest

Part 1: Identifying Common Errors

> **Test** your knowledge of usage, grammar, spelling, and other common errors by answering the standardized test questions below. Each sentence below is either correct—or one of its underlined sections contains an error. (No sentence contains two errors.)
>
> **Circle** the letter corresponding to the incorrect section. If the sentence has no error, circle the *E*.

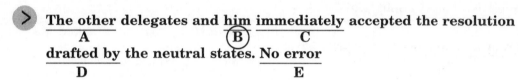

> The other delegates and <u>him</u> <u>immediately</u> accepted the resolution
>   A   (B)   C
> <u>drafted by the neutral states.</u> <u>No error</u>
>   D   E

Note: The correct answer is *B*. This pronoun is part of a compound subject. It should be in the nominative case *he*, not the objective case *him*.

1. A town <u>on the plains</u> of Colombia
           A
<u>uses solar panels</u> <u>to generate</u> most of
    B   C
<u>their electricity.</u> <u>No error</u>
   D   E

2. The people <u>from my school</u>
           A
<u>who are going</u> to the party in Bristol
    B
are Paula, Tran, and <u>me.</u> <u>No error</u>
 C   D   E

3. Cleopatra <u>who</u> was twenty years
        A
old when Julius Caesar landed in
<u>Egypt, was competing</u> with her
   B
<u>brother, Ptolemy XIII,</u> <u>for</u> power in
     C   D
Egypt. <u>No error</u>
     E

4. Glenn has seen amazing <u>tricks but</u>
                  A
he doubts that <u>anyone</u> can squeeze
    B   C
blood <u>out of turnips.</u> <u>No error</u>
    D   E

5. When we <u>finally arrived</u> at the
         A
cottage, <u>a note and a bowl</u>
        B
<u>of fresh fruit</u> <u>was waiting</u> for us.
   C   D
<u>No error</u>
 E

6. Kacy's guiding <u>principle</u> when
          A
purchasing <u>stationery</u> <u>seemed</u> to be
      B   C
finding the <u>best buy.</u> <u>No error</u>
      D   E

7. "<u>Whom</u> will attend the jazz concert
    A

at the high school just <u>south</u> of
                   B

<u>downtown?</u>" <u>wondered</u> Connor.
   C   D

<u>No error</u>
  E

8. This <u>summer</u>, Mary plans <u>to do</u> one
     A   B

of the <u>following:</u> get a job, take
      C

classes, <u>or be traveling</u> to Europe.
         D

<u>No error</u>
  E

9. If Renata <u>had known</u> the song,
        A

she <u>surely</u> <u>would have played</u> it
   B   C

<u>for us.</u> <u>No error</u>
 D   E

10. According to the <u>coach,</u> <u>Nikki</u> <u>was</u>
           A   B

the <u>better</u> soccer <u>player</u> of the three.
   C   D

<u>No error</u>
  E

11. After <u>Jamal</u> <u>reached</u> the finish line of
     A   B

the triathlon, he <u>lay</u> down and
         C

<u>fall asleep</u> within minutes. <u>No error</u>
  D   E

12. If you travel far enough <u>north</u> from
               A

anywhere on <u>Earth</u>, <u>you</u> will
       B   C

eventually reach the <u>Arctic Circle.</u>
          D

<u>No error</u>
  E

13. "Carina, can you tell me <u>who's</u>
    A   B

the author of the <u>book</u>
         C

<u>'Huckleberry Finn'?</u>" asked Ms.
     D

McLeod. <u>No error</u>
     E

14. Neither of the <u>mischievous</u>
         A

nieces <u>admit</u> to <u>receiving</u> the
    B   C

<u>foreign potatoes.</u> <u>No error</u>
  D   E

15. We all noticed <u>that the division</u> of the
          A

players into blue squads and red

squads <u>are</u> not working <u>too</u> <u>well.</u>
    B   C D

<u>No error</u>
  E

16. By the time she gets to Phoenix, <u>her</u>
                  A

friends <u>will have had</u> <u>they're</u> Gila
     B   C

monster for <u>nearly</u> a week.
       D

<u>No error</u>
  E

17. Is it true that your <u>Dad</u> met
                               A
<u>Senator Bradley</u> as the <u>senator</u> was
        B   C
walking to his office in the <u>Capitol</u>?
                              D
<u>No error</u>
   E

18. One <u>also might say</u> that she
            A
was strongly <u>effected</u> by the
             B
overwhelming <u>gratitude of</u>
             C
<u>her patients</u>. <u>No error</u>
   D   E

19. Manny <u>packed his suitcases</u>,
              A
<u>picked up his tickets</u>, and
        B
<u>arrives at the airport</u> with <u>very little</u>
        C   D
time to spare. <u>No error</u>
               E

20. The head <u>principal</u> and some of the
                 A
teachers <u>are</u> <u>laying</u> down new
         B   C
regulations <u>for student conduct</u>.
            D
<u>No error</u>
   E

21. The problem of <u>how to deal</u> with all
                       A
the <u>deer</u> in our neighborhood <u>concern</u>
    B   C
many of our <u>neighbors</u>. <u>No error</u>
            D   E

Part 2: Improving Sentences

> Laura Ingalls Wilder published her first book <u>and she was 65 years old then.</u>
>
> (A) and she was 65 years old then.
> (B) when she was 65 years old.
> (C) at age 65 years old.
> (D) upon reaching 65 years of age.
> (E) at the time when she was 65.

Note: The answer is B. The original and A are awkward, as is E. Both C and D are wordy.

1. The <u>team's failure to keep it's cool</u> led to a technical foul.
   (A) The team's failure to keep it's cool
   (B) The teams failure to keep it's cool
   (C) The teams failure to keep their cool
   (D) The team's failure to keep their cool
   (E) The team's failure to keep its cool

2. My dentist's office lies on the north side of town, <u>to the east of the water tower.</u>
   (A) to the east of the water tower.
   (B) to the water tower's east.
   (C) and the water tower is to the east.
   (D) and on water tower's east side.
   (E) by the water tower.

3. Has anyone told you <u>the identity of the person who painted the mural?</u>
   (A) the identity of the person who painted the mural?
   (B) of the painter of the mural?
   (C) as to who painted the mural?
   (D) who painted the mural?
   (E) about the mural painter's identity?

4. Why don't you serve <u>my friend and I</u> some of your famous fried squid?
   (A) my friend and I
   (B) my friend and me
   (C) I and my friend
   (D) my friend along with me
   (E) my friend along with I

5. The coach, as well as her staff, were very concerned about Felicity's injury.

   (A) The coach, as well as her staff, were
   (B) The coach, as well as her staff, was
   (C) The coach, as well as her staff, are
   (D) The coach or her staff were
   (E) The coach, as well as her staff, have been

6. Having committed his third offense, the judge gave him the most severe penalty.

   (A) the judge gave him the most severe penalty.
   (B) he was given the most severe penalty by the judge.
   (C) the most severe penalty was given by the judge.
   (D) the penalty was the most severe that the judge could give him.
   (E) the judge punished him most severely.

7. The author says that she has always written with pencil and paper; and that she always will.

   (A) has always written with pencil and paper; and that she always will.
   (B) has always and always would write with pencil and paper.
   (C) has always written with pencil and paper, and she always will.
   (D) will have always written with pencil and paper.
   (E) always has written with pencil and paper and would always.

8. The last band's music was loud, with a good beat, and easy to dance to.

   (A) with a good beat, and easy to dance to.
   (B) had a good beat, and easy to dance to.
   (C) and had a good beat, as well as being easy to dance to.
   (D) had a good beat, and was easy to dance to.
   (E) with a good beat, and you could dance to it.

9. I am irritated that he teases me every time when he sees me.

   (A) me every time when he sees me.
   (B) me every time he sees me.
   (C) me, whenever I am seen by him.
   (D) me at every time he sees me.
   (E) me, whenever he sees me.

10. Please try to understand that I am neither for your idea or against it.

    (A) for your idea or against it.
    (B) for or against your idea.
    (C) for your idea nor against it.
    (D) for your idea nor against your idea.
    (E) for your idea or am I against it.

11. Dramatically, by practicing every day, Zack's performance improved.

    (A) Dramatically, by practicing every day, Zack's performance improved.
    (B) By practicing every day, Zack's performance improved dramatically.
    (C) By practicing every day, Zack dramatically improved his performance.
    (D) Zack's performance improved dramatically by practicing every day.
    (E) Dramatically, Zack's performance improved by his practicing every day.

12. Jennifer wants to go to nursing school, become a midwife, and to deliver babies.

(A) to go to nursing school, become a midwife, and to deliver babies.

(B) to attend nursing school, become a midwife, and to deliver babies.

(C) to go to nursing school, to become a midwife, and deliver babies.

(D) to go to nursing school and to become a midwife, and to deliver babies.

(E) to go to nursing school, become a midwife, and deliver babies.

13. The sound coming from the garage was like a B-52 bomber.

(A) like a B-52 bomber.

(B) like the roar of a B-52 bomber.

(C) like that of a B-52 bomber's.

(D) the same as a B-52 bomber.

(E) a B-52 bomber.

14. Pedro has had many illnesses: colds, the measles, chicken pox, and the mumps, but he is well now.

(A) illnesses: colds, the measles, chicken pox, and the mumps, but

(B) illnesses: colds, the measles, chicken pox, the mumps, but

(C) illnesses, colds, the measles, chicken pox, and the mumps, but

(D) illnesses—colds, the measles, chicken pox, and the mumps but

(E) illnesses—colds, the measles, chicken pox, and the mumps—but

15. Did I ever tell you that I once photographed an elephant in my pajamas?

(A) I once photographed an elephant in my pajamas?

(B) I once photographed an elephant with my pajamas?

(C) an elephant was once photographed by me in my pajamas?

(D) I once photographed an elephant while I was in my pajamas?

(E) I once photographed an elephant wearing my pajamas?

16. All of the tickets were sold in less than 15 minutes on account a the group's tremendous popularity.

(A) All of the tickets were sold in less than 15 minutes on account a the group's tremendous popularity.

(B) On account of the group's tremendous popularity, all of the tickets were sold in less than 15 minutes.

(C) All of the tickets were sold in less than 15 minutes being that the group was tremendously popular.

(D) All of the tickets were sold in less than 15 minutes because of the group's tremendous popularity.

(E) All of the tickets were sold in less than 15 minutes in view of the fact that the group is tremendously popular.

Part 3: Improving Paragraphs

> **Read** the following essay—a first draft in need of editing. Do not correct the text directly. Instead, answer the questions listed after the essay to identify and fix mistakes. Circle the letter next to the answer you think is best.

(1) A few centuries ago, sailors in the tropics reported seeing mermaids, legendary creatures with the head and upper body of a woman and the tail of a fish. (2) Some people speculate that the sailors may actually have been seeing manatees. (3) These are large mammals that live their whole lives in the water. (4) The only other mammals that spend their whole lives in the water are whales.

(5) Manatees have heavy, gray bodies that are fishlike in form and end in a tail. (6) They can grow to 13 feet long and weigh over 500 pounds. (7) They are totally herbivorous; that is, they eat only plants. (8) Specifically, they eat seaweeds and sea grasses. (9) They eat up to 100 pounds of vegetation a day.

(10) There are three different types of manatees. (11) There is the Amazon manatee, the Caribbean manatee, and the African manatee. (12) Their population is diminishing. (13) Manatees are now an endangered species. (14) Manatees have no natural enemies; humans are causing their decline. (15) In many places humans are ruining their habitats. (16) They are running over them with boats, polluting the water with chemicals and other waste, and digging canals in their grazing areas.

(17) One type of manatee has already become extinct. (18) In 1741 explorers discovered the Steller's sea cow, which grew up to 30 feet long and weighed up to 4 tons. (19) Within 30 years, the Steller's sea cow had been hunted out of existence.

1. Which of the following is the best way to revise the underlined portions of sentences 10 and 11 (reproduced below) in order to combine the two sentences?

    There are three different types of manatees. There is the Amazon manatee, the Caribbean manatee, and the African manatee.

    (A) manatees, such as the
    (B) manatees: the
    (C) manatees, for example, the
    (D) manatees, the
    (E) manatees, including the

2. Assume you have just combined sentences 10 and 11. If you were to insert a new sentence just after 11, which of the following would create the best transition to sentence 12?

    (A) Manatees are close relatives of another animal called a dugong.
    (B) They all live in the Atlantic Ocean.
    (C) Although they live in different parts of the world, they all share the same danger.
    (D) How could they have spread to different parts of the world?
    (E) All of them live in shallow water.

3. In context, which of the following could best be inserted at the beginning of sentence 3?

    (A) For example,
    (B) Today,
    (C) Incidentally,
    (D) As a result,
    (E) Also called sea cows,

4. Which of the following would be the best way to combine sentences 7, 8, and 9?

(A) They are totally herbivorous, that is, they eat only plants, such as seaweeds and sea grasses, and they eat up to 100 pounds of vegetation a day.

(B) Being totally herbivorous, they eat only plants—seaweeds and sea grasses—up to 100 pounds of vegetation a day.

(C) Being totally herbivorous, they eat only plants—up to 100 pounds of seaweeds and sea grasses a day.

(D) They are totally herbivorous, they eat only plants (such as seaweeds and sea grasses), and they eat up to 100 pounds of vegetation a day.

(E) They eat up to 100 pounds of vegetation a day, such as seaweeds and sea grasses, as they are totally herbivorous, that is, they eat only plants.

5. What is the best way to revise the underlined portion of sentence 13?

(A) They
(B) In fact, manatees
(C) By the way, manatees
(D) Not coincidentally, manatees
(E) However, manatees

6. To conclude the final paragraph in the best way, which of the following sentences should be added after sentence 19?

(A) What a huge animal!
(B) Unless we take steps to save the remaining manatees, they will disappear as well.
(C) Isn't that a tragedy?
(D) What can you do to save them?
(E) They were insulated by very thick blubber.

POSTTEST
Answer key

232

Posttest: End Punctuation

> **Place** periods, question marks, and exclamation points where they are needed in the following narrative. Capitalize the first word in a sentence.

1 Have you heard of Alaska's famous dog-sledding race, the Iditarod?

2 Each sled team includes 7 to 18 dogs. Usually the dogs line up in pairs,

3 with one dog on each side of the gangline. A gangline—also called a

4 towline—is the tether or rope that links the team to the sled.

5 Sledders usually train several dogs to lead. That's because each dog

6 may have a different strength or weakness. Some lead dogs don't like to

7 face the wind, for instance. Others dislike working their way through the

8 forest. Some don't accept commands well, but they keep the gangline nice

9 and taut. Still others maintain a fast pace on straightaways, only to cause

10 tangles when they round a turn. An all-around leader—one who does

11 everything well—is a rarity.

12 Sledders, or mushers, use special terms to describe their lead dogs. Can

13 you guess what a "pacesetter" does?! It keeps the team moving fast on

14 straight portions of the trails. What do you think a "command leader" does?

15 It steers tightly on turns.

16 A lead dog becomes both the brain and the "steering wheel" of its

17 team. It must listen for the driver's special commands. Haw means "go left."

18 Gee means "go right." The lead dog must also set a good pace and keep

19 the gangline taut. If the leader fails to do this, the other dogs will have

20 trouble running in sync, and utter chaos may result. It's easy to see why

21 a good lead dog may be a sledder's most valuable asset.

(Answers to page 187)

Posttest: Commas

> Add commas where they are needed.

1. Black Elk, an Oglala Sioux from South Dakota, became one of the most respected American Indian leaders in the twentieth century.

2. In a vision, Black Elk saw the sky filled with dancing horses, a spotted eagle, a flowering tree, and a tepee with a rainbow door.

3. The symbols in Black Elk's vision—the eagle, the flowers, and the rainbow—meant humankind would one day live in peace.

4. Black Elk, who was nine years old then, did not tell anyone about his vision.

5. He was afraid no one would believe him, so he kept his vision to himself.

6. When the white men came, they said to the Oglala Sioux, "You may keep your land as long as grass shall grow and the water flow."

7. A few years later, the white men discovered gold in the Black Hills, and in their fervor to obtain it, they forgot their promise to the Indians.

8. The discovery of gold in the Black Hills of South Dakota, a beautiful, sacred place to the Indians, started a chain of events—events that led to tragedy and hardship, events that saddened Black Elk.

9. The Battle of the Little Bighorn, which occurred on June 25, 1876, was a major turning point.

10. After the Battle of the Little Bighorn, the Indians traveled from place to place, became desperate for food, and gradually succumbed to sickness.

11. In 1931, Black Elk told his life story to John G. Neihardt, a writer who published the book *Black Elk Speaks*.

12. Black Elk died in 1950 on Pine Ridge Reservation, South Dakota, saddened that humankind still was not living in peace.

(Answers to page 188)

Posttest: Semicolons & Colons

> **Add** semicolons and colons where they are needed.

1. Pluto, a cold chunk of rock and ice, is a small planet ; it measures about 1,500 miles in diameter.

2. Pluto resembles Earth in two ways : it has a moon, and its orbit is tilted.

3. If you lived on Pluto, you would never have a birthday ; it takes 248 Earth-years for this planet to revolve once around the sun!

4. Some scientists want to classify Pluto as an asteroid ; they don't feel it is large enough to be a planet.

5. Astronomers have never agreed on a single definition for the word "planet" ; however, most scientists consider celestial objects to be planets if they are round, if they directly orbit a star, and if they are large enough to shine in the night sky.

6. Pluto might be called an asteroid for three reasons : it is smaller than other planets, its gravity is very weak, and its orbit is tilted.

7. Many scientists argue that Pluto should remain a planet ; they say it has enough gravity to keep its spherical shape.

8. Scientists also point out that Pluto has a solid surface ; Jupiter, on the other hand, is just a giant ball of gas.

9. On February 3, 1999, the International Astronomical Union ended the debate this way : they declared Pluto a planet.

10. Students can still use "My Very Educated Mother Just Served Us Nine Pizzas" to remember the sequence of planets : Mercury, Venus, Earth, Mars, Jupiter, Saturn, Uranus, Neptune, and Pluto.

(Answers to page 189)

Posttest: Hyphens & Dashes

Add hyphens and dashes where they are needed.

1. We made a U-turn when we realized we had forgotten something—my brother, Zach.

2. The Humphrey-Hawkins bill passed last week.

3. At the age of five—*five*, mind you—her daughter speaks three languages.

4. Three-fourths of the student body doesn't know the school song—and doesn't care!

5. The Bobcats lost the game 24-18.

6. Was that a B-flat he just played on the violin?

7. The gas tank is three-quarters empty.

8. People are still experiencing the effects of the first H-bomb.

9. My brother-in-law loves to play pool.

10. Neighbors, friends, family—what would a wedding be without them?

11. Many of us enjoy being average, run-of-the-mill people.

12. When a person is shell-shocked, it means he or she is exhausted because of excessive stress.

13. He lived through the crash—just barely—and he'll never be the same.

14. For the rest of his life, someone else will have to fasten the buttons on his shirt sleeves, tie his shoes, and cut his fingernails—all the little things we take for granted.

15. I sometimes wonder why it's so difficult to appreciate—really appreciate—being able to walk and talk and see and hear.

Posttest: Apostrophes

> **Write** the contraction or the possessive form needed to correct the underlined words. Write *C* in the blank if the sentence is already correct.

Alice's	**1.**	Alice brother did not understand the experiment.
brother-in-law's	**2.**	My brother-in-law mother is a kind lady.
José's	**3.**	José garage is filled with spare tires.
year's	**4.**	Your prize is a year supply of crunchy dog food!
_C_	**5.**	It's time for my appointment.
don't	**6.**	I dont want to be late.
Ann/Chris's	**7.**	Ann and Chris uncle will be here tonight.
somebody else's	**8.**	The hat doesn't belong to me; it's somebody else.
Jerry/Hunter/Ali's	**9.**	Jerry, Hunter, and Ali car is parked in the driveway.
_R's_	**10.**	Are there three R in the word "referred"?
Couldn't	**11.**	Couldnt you forget about yesterday?
boss's	**12.**	Shanika is driving the boss car.
_C_	**13.**	The three waitresses are late for work.
defense's	**14.**	The secretary of defense wife hosted the party.
Ceci's/Carol's	**15.**	Ceci and Carol bicycles are here. (Each owns a bike.)
professor's	**16.**	The professor nose is chubby.
. . . Association's	**17.**	The Tucson High School Theater Association banquet is tonight.
aunt/uncle's	**18.**	My aunt and uncle house was sold last week.
king of Siam's	**19.**	The king of Siam wife was interviewed on the news.
aren't	**20.**	We arent finished yet.

(Answers to page 191)

Posttest: Quotation Marks & Italics (Underlining)

> **Add** quotation marks where they are needed. Underline words that should be in italics.

1. "I studied for that test and still didn't pass it," complained George.

2. Did she discuss Whittier's poem "The Eternal Goodness"?

3. "Age of Gold" is a phrase in Emerson's poem "Character."

4. "Who's staring at you?" he asked.

5. "Claire, Mr. Langdon said, "please concentrate on one thing at a time."

6. <u>Improvisation for the Theater</u> is a fine book written by Viola Spolin.

7. Are you planning to sail on the <u>Kansas City Clipper</u>?

8. Miss Berg asked, "Did you ever read London's short story "To Build a Fire"?

9. The only narrative poem Jerry read is "Old Christmas"; now he's reading "Sweet and Low," a lyric poem.

10. My mother subscribes to both <u>Time</u> and <u>Newsweek</u>.

11. Mr. Ryken's conversation is always sprinkled with "ah's" and "ahem's."

12. Professor Lenken used the book <u>Zen and the Art of Motorcycle Maintenance</u> in his psychology class.

13. Ms. Jensen asked whether we had studied Rölvaag's book <u>Giants in the Earth</u>.

14. In 1955, four different singers recorded the same song. Amazingly, all four versions of "It's Almost Tomorrow" made the Top Forty.

15. In the late fifties and early sixties, some of the new and unusual dance fads were named by songs: "The Stroll" (1957), "The Walk" (1958), "The Bunny Hop" (1959), and "The Twist" (1960).

(Answers to page 192)

Posttest: Punctuation

Proofread the paragraphs below. Add punctuation marks where they are needed (and capital letters at the beginnings of sentences).

1   The development of America's railroad as a dependable means of
2   transportation was a long, frustrating process. Many people helped make
3   the railroad a reality, but one man stood out: Horatio Allen.
4   As a young college graduate, Allen gazed with awe upon the strange,
5   steam-powered vehicles being tested in England's coalfields during the
6   1820s. He and others like him did their best to introduce the locomotive to
7   America. In return they faced the scorn of those who advocated horsepower,
8   mule power, sail power, waterpower, and even foot power.
9   Allen persevered; however, it was not until the 1860s and the end of
10   the Civil War that his dream—building an American railroad—was truly
11   realized. Then, as the nation's attention shifted from the South to the
12   wide-open West, the railroad suddenly became a vital means of
13   transportation. With much enthusiasm, railroad companies undertook the
14   task of satisfying the new demand for rail power. The invention of steel
15   rails in 1865 made it possible to meet this growing need, and four years
16   later, the first transcontinental railway was completed.
17   The now-famous scene depicting the driving of the golden spike in
18   Promontory Point, Utah, marked the beginning of a new era in United
19   States history. The railroad quickly became the main transportation system
20   of an expanding nation.

(Answers to page 193)

Posttest: Capitalization

> **Cross out** each lowercase letter that should be capitalized and write your correction above it.

1. Marco Polo was born in Venice, Italy, in about 1254.

2. His father, Nicolò, was a wealthy merchant who purchased goods in the Orient and resold them to European markets.

3. When Marco was about 17, he traveled with his father and his uncle to the court of the Mongol conqueror Kublai Khan in China.

4. They sailed down the Adriatic Sea, across the Mediterranean Sea, to the city of Jerusalem.

5. The Polos stopped there because the khan (*khan* is a title like *prince*) wanted holy oil from the tomb of Jesus Christ.

6. Even though the khan wasn't Christian, he read from the Bible on Easter and Christmas.

7. He also celebrated Muslim, Buddhist, and Jewish feast days.

8. When asked why, he replied, " I respect and honor all four great prophets: Christ, Mohammed, Moses, and Buddha, so that I can appeal to any one of them in heaven." (Marco Polo always remembered this statement.)

9. From Israel, the Polos journeyed along the Silk Road, through mountains and deserts, until they reached the Alph River in Shangtu Province, where the khan's summer palace was located.

10. The khan's empire was so huge, he established a pony express like the one America used to carry mail in the Wild West during the 1800s.

11. Marco Polo wrote a book, Cathay, that gave Europeans their earliest information about China.

Posttest: Numbers, Abbreviations, & Acronyms

> **Underline** each abbreviation, word, or number that has been used incorrectly. Write the correction above it.

United States
1. The exploration of outer space by the U.S. is the responsibility of the National

   Aeronautics and Space Administration.

   NASA   *D.C.*
2. N.A.S.A. headquarters are located in Washington, DC.

3. If you ever care to correspond with NASA, send your letter to 400 Maryland
Avenue Washington
   Ave., Wash., D.C. 20546.

          semester's   *seven*   *NASA*
4. During last sem.'s unit on space exploration, 7 students wrote to N.A.S.A. for
information
   info.

                                          two United States
5. After a decade of moon exploration by space probes, 2 U.S. astronauts landed on
                            20
   the lunar surface on July twentieth, 1969.

                              American
6. A total of six two-man crews of Amer. astronauts landed on the moon between
       1969   *1972*
   nineteen sixty-nine and nineteen seventy-two.

                              790   *pounds*
7. They returned to Earth with over seven hundred ninety lbs. of moon rocks.

                                    56
8. Some of the craters on the moon's surface are fifty-six miles across.

                    one-fourth   *One-fourth*   *percent*
9. The moon is slightly more than 1/4 the size of Earth. (1/4 is the same as 25%.)
        one   *sixty-three*   *thirty-three*
10. Earth has 1 moon, while Jupiter has 63 and Saturn has 33.

                              October 28
11. A total eclipse of the moon took place on Oct. twenty-eighth, 1985.
          six
12. Ken needs 6 11-inch straws to complete his model of a futuristic spaceship.

                                                            one
13. A light-year is a unit of length equal to the distance that light travels in 1 year.
          5,878,000,000,000 (or) 5 trillion 878 billion
14. This distance is about five trillion eight hundred seventy-eight billion miles.

          (Answers to page 195)

242

Posttest: Plurals & Spelling

> **Underline** each word spelled incorrectly. Write the correct spelling above it.

1. Turquoise has been a *valuable* valuble stone for years; many cultures and civilizations have used it.

2. The powerful Aztec, Incan, and Mayan people used turquoise as a *symbol* symbal of their gods.

3. The Egyptians, the Chinese, and the Pueblo Indians were using turquoise stones in *jewelry* jewlery *centuries* centurys before the Europeans.

4. Merchants *brought* broughth the *precious* preshus stones from the Orient to Turkey, where they became known as "turquoise" to the Europeans.

5. Major deposits of turquoise are found in Tibet and Iran, but large deposits also *exist* exhist in the southwestern United States.

6. The Navajo and others in America still use turquoise as protection against injuries, *illnesses* illneses, and *contagious* contagous *diseases* diseazes.

7. Turquoise stones range in color from yellow to gray, but sky blue and lime green are usually *preferred* prefered.

8. Nowadays, turquoise can be *dyed* died, treated with *mineral* minneral oil, or *waxed* waxxed to deepen the color.

9. The demand for turquoise remains so great that *artificial* artifisial *varieties* vareities of the stone are produced.

10. Any *respectable* respecktible dealer will *issue* issiue a certificate stating that the stone is *authentic* authentick.

11. Buyers today might become ill if they *discover* descover that their expensive *piece* peice of jewelry is *actually* actualy plastic.

(Answers to page 196)

Posttest: Using the Right Word

Underline each word used incorrectly below and write the correction above it.

1. *Whether* *they're*   *it's*   *rain*
   Weather their tracking hurricanes or deciding if its going to rein, many
                             their   *Weather*
   Americans turn on they're televisions and watch the Whether Channel.

2.   *hours*   *week*
   This station broadcasts 24 ours a day, 7 days a weak.

3.   *sighted*   *personnel*
   Whenever large storms are cited, weather station personal jump into action.

4.   *pieces*   *seem* *pour* *through*
   They monitor bits and peaces of information that seam to pore threw the

   station, especially when a hurricane forms.

5.   *past*   *minor*
   A hurricane may go passed the East Coast and cause only miner damage.

6.   *no*   *knows* *course*
   However, if it turns inland, know one nos what coarse it will take or how much
                        lose
   property people might loose.

7.   *a lot*   *its effects*
   Sometimes a hurricane causes alot of damage, and it's affects are seen for

   years.

8.   *by*
   Residents may be urged to leave and take only what they need to get bye.

9.   *accept*   *choose*
   Some people except this news and leave, but others chose to stay and face the

   storm.

10.   *wait*   *where*
    Millions of Americans weight by their televisions to see wear the hurricane

    will go.

11.   *their*   *so*   *eight*
    Weather Channel viewers like to check there local forecasts, sew every ate
                          for
    minutes the weather four their area appears at the bottom of the TV screen in
          capital
    bright capitol letters.
         good   *they're*
12. It is well that people can receive continuous weather reports—whether their

    tracking a storm or just planning a picnic.

(Answers to page 197)

Final Proofreading Posttest—Part 1

Write plurals for the following words:

1. potato ___*potatoes*___

2. box ___*boxes*___

3. piano ___*pianos*___

4. sheep ___*sheep*___

5. knife ___*knives*___

6. studio ___*studios*___

7. ABC ___*ABC's (or) ABCs*___

8. sister-in-law ___*sisters-in-law*___

9. spy ___*spies*___

10. radius ___*radii*___

11. ranch ___*ranches*___

12. key ___*keys*___

Cross out each lowercase letter that should be capitalized and write your correction above it.

1. mr. smith goes to washington is a movie starring jimmy stewart.
_(M S G W J S)_

2. senator ted kennedy represents the state of massachusetts.
_(S T K M)_

3. aunt jo registered her car with the department of transportation.
_(A J D T)_

4. my uncle, who works for the democratic party, is visiting us.
_(M D P)_

5. christopher columbus, an italian explorer, was financed by queen isabella of spain when he set out to find a new route to india.
_(C C I Q I S I)_

6. the denver broncos football team won a super bowl.
_(T D B S B)_

7. muslims call their supreme being allah.
_(M A)_

8. we studied that in social studies 104.
_(W S S)_

9. the declaration of independence was ratified on july 4, 1776, by the continental congress in philadelphia, pennsylvania.
_(T D I J C C P P)_

10. my mother saw the united states women's soccer team win the world cup.
_(M U S W C)_

11. she bought me a t-shirt that said, "play like a girl—kick it!"
_(S T P)_

Write out the following abbreviations:

1. GA *Georgia*
2. UT *Utah*
3. dept. *department*
4. lb *pound*
5. m *meter*

6. mi. *mile (or) mill*
7. oz. *ounce*
8. Rd. *Road*
9. gal. *gallon*
10. ASAP *as soon as possible*

11. pd. *paid*
12. yd. *yard*
13. km *kilometer*
14. ea. *each*
15. w/o *without*

Write a short phrase explaining the difference between the words in each pair below.

1. principle, principal

   principle is "an idea"; principal is "a person," "a sum of money," or "primary"

2. its, it's

   its is a possessive pronoun; it's is a contraction for "it is"

3. can, may

   can means "ability to"; may means "to ask permission"

4. accept, except,

   accept means "to believe" or "to receive"; except means "all but"

5. lay, lie

   lay means "to place"; lie means "to recline"

6. loose, lose

   loose means "free or untied"; lose means "to misplace"

7. counsel, council

   counsel means "to give advice"; council is "a group"

8. lend, borrow

   lend means "to give for temporary use"; borrow means "to receive for temporary use"

(Answers to page 199)

Final Proofreading Posttest—Part 2

> **Correct** the following letter for punctuation and number usage. When adding end punctuation, capitalize the first word in the sentence.

1 October ~~twelfth~~ *12*, 2006

2 Lana R. Wendricks, Ph.D.

3 Department of Geography, University of Illinois

4 ~~Three hundred five~~ *305* Green Street

5 Urbana, IL 61820

6 Dear Dr. Wendricks:

7   I understand you are the new manager of the University of Illinois

8 mapmaking project. Would you consider using Lever Electronics' GlobeNav

9 420 System? I would like to offer the university a discount. You can buy *three* ~~3~~

10 GlobeNav 420s for only $999.95.

11   The system is easy to use. A *waypoint* shows the original position on

12 the screen, and a dotted line follows the route even if a user has made a

13 U-turn. How's that for technology?

14   Here are *two* ~~2~~ more features you'll enjoy: a window program that groups

15 your information *(optional)*, plus an outstanding memory capability. The system can

16 store up to ~~seven hundred fifty~~ *750* positions.

17   Did you happen to read the <u>In-Fisherman</u> magazine dated June 17,

18 2005? I've enclosed a copy. Here is a quote from page ~~thirty-five,~~ *35* in the

19 article entitled "Finding Your Way." *(or)* ":

20   It gives position fixes in seconds *(or)* — not minutes. It will hold

21   that position whether you're a quarter mile out in the water or

22   along a high and narrow cliff or even along Interstate ~~Five~~ 5. We

23   rate this product an A-plus.

24   Dr. Wendricks, Lever Electronics has sold almost 410,000 of these units

25   in the United States and Canada. We hope your university will consider

26   our product for the budget year ~~two thousand seven~~ 2007 to 2008. Would it be

27   possible to set up a meeting with you? Dr. Burrows, who is the project's

28   ex-manager, may want to be present as well.

29   Please contact my office at 972-555-2222 any day after ~~eight-thirty a.m.~~ 8:30 *(or)* A.M.

30   I would appreciate a chance not only to sell our product but also to prove

31   my claims. That's how excited I am about the GlobeNav 420. *(or)* !

32   Sincerely,

Peter H. Reynolds

33   Peter H. Reynolds

34   Vice President, Lever Electronics, Inc.

Circle the correct spelling.

1. cheif, (chief)	**8.** (receive,) recieve
2. krisis, (crisis)	**9.** appearence, (appearance)
3. existance, (existence)	**10.** sking, (skiing)
4. (experience,) experiance	**11.** (pastime,) passtime
5. (eighth,) eigth	**12.** (maintain,) maintian
6. (chocolate,) chocalate	**13.** (occasion,) ocassion
7. justise, (justice)	**14.** (tomorrow,) tomarrow

(Answers to page 201)

Posttest: Nouns

> **Underline** all words used as nouns below. Identify the first noun in each sentence: write *P* for proper or *C* for common on the first blank; write *A* for abstract and *CN* for concrete on the second blank.

_C_ _A_ **1.** One <u>practice</u> that seems to aid <u>patients</u> is bringing <u>animals</u> into their

<u>rooms</u>.

_C_ _CN_ **2.** <u>Dogs</u> and <u>cats</u> visit <u>hospitals</u>, but <u>fish</u> and <u>birds</u> may visit, too.

_P_ _CN_ **3.** One of <u>St. Louis'</u> many <u>hospitals</u> uses <u>rabbits</u> and other soft,

quiet <u>animals</u> to help depressed <u>patients</u>.

_C_ _CN_ **4.** <u>Hospitals</u> often have <u>dogs</u> on <u>duty</u> throughout the <u>day</u>.

_C_ _CN_ **5.** <u>Patients</u> pet the <u>dogs</u> and sometimes throw <u>balls</u> or <u>socks</u> for a <u>game</u>

of <u>catch</u>.

> **Underline** all words used as nouns below. For each sentence, identify only the first noun's case (write *NOM* for nominative, *POS* for possessive, and *OBJ* for objective).

NOM **1.** <u>Studies</u> show that <u>patients</u> who see <u>trees</u> from their <u>rooms</u> recover faster

than those who see brick <u>walls</u>.

POS **2.** A <u>patient's</u> <u>view</u> while lying flat in <u>bed</u> is also important.

NOM **3.** Now <u>architects</u> are designing <u>hospitals</u> with as many outside <u>rooms</u> as

possible.

NOM **4.** <u>Researchers</u> have also found that landscape and wildlife <u>paintings</u> help

<u>patients</u> recover faster.

OBJ **5.** By wearing <u>headphones</u> and listening to soothing <u>sounds</u> from <u>nature</u>,

<u>patients</u> can reduce their <u>anxiety</u>.

(Answers to page 202)

Posttest: Pronouns

Underline the personal pronoun in each sentence below. Identify the pronoun's number (*S* for singular or *P* for plural) on the first blank; identify the pronoun's case (*NOM* for nominative, *POS* for possessive, or *OBJ* for objective) on the second blank.

S NOM **1.** Traveling into Death Valley, <u>I</u> saw a sight that's hard to believe: the "sliding rocks" of Racetrack Playa.

S POS **2.** Racetrack Playa (a dry lake bed) is three miles long, and <u>its</u> north end is only three inches higher than the south end.

P OBJ **3.** The rocks in the Playa slide along the flat lake bed, but no one knows what moves <u>them</u>.

P OBJ **4.** A group of <u>us</u> went to study this mystery.

P NOM **5.** <u>We</u> found that rocks fell onto the lake bed from a rock formation located on the north end.

Underline the pronoun in each sentence below. Identify the pronoun's class (*PER* for personal, *REL* for relative, *IND* for indefinite, *INT* for interrogative, *DEM* for demonstrative, and *REX* for reflexive).

IND **1.** Somehow dozens of rocks, <u>some</u> weighing hundreds of pounds, end up at the south end, leaving grooves in the ground.

IND **2.** <u>No one</u> has ever seen a rock in motion, yet the rocks have clearly moved.

REL **3.** Scientists <u>who</u> have studied this suggest that high winds are responsible.

REX **4.** Some geologists have convinced <u>themselves</u> the rocks were frozen in ice and slid along with help from the winds.

INT **5.** <u>Who</u> is right?

DEM **6.** <u>That</u> remains a mystery.

PER **7.** <u>We</u> may never know, because the Racetrack Playa is now considered a United States biosphere, and access to the site is very limited.

(Answers to page 203)

Posttest: Verbs

Underline all the verbs below. Include helping (auxiliary) and linking verbs. In each sentence, identify only the first verb's number on the first blank (*S* for singular or *P* for plural); then identify the first verb's tense on the second blank (present, past, future, present perfect, past perfect, future perfect).

_P_ _present_ **1.** At the Dallas Aquarium, red-bellied piranhas <u>look</u> like harmless panfish.

_S_ _past_ **2.** For example, yesterday when the attendant <u>entered</u> the tank with food, they <u>swam</u> to the far end and <u>cowered</u>.

_P_ _present_ **3.** We <u>do</u> not <u>expect</u> this kind of behavior from fish that <u>have</u> such a ferocious reputation.

_S_ _present_ **4.** I <u>hear</u> they <u>can snap</u> off a finger that <u>is poked</u> into the water.

_S_ _present_ **5.** Supposedly, a school of piranhas <u>can devour</u> a whole cow.

_P_ _present_ **6.** Piranhas usually <u>eat</u> small fish, but they <u>do</u> not <u>devour</u> their dinner whole.

_P_ _present_ **7.** Rather, tiny, moon-shaped bites <u>are taken</u> from a victim's tail or fin.

_P_ _past perfect_ **8.** Researchers <u>had</u> originally <u>thought</u> that this behavior <u>was</u> like the wolf's (the wolf first <u>cripples</u> its prey so the kill <u>is</u> easier).

_P_ _present perfect_ **9.** More recently, scientists <u>have discovered</u> that the piranha only <u>wants</u> the fins and tails because these fish parts <u>contain</u> high amounts of protein.

_S_ _present_ **10.** Evidently if you <u>are</u> a piranha, you <u>can</u> never <u>get</u> enough protein!

_S_ _future perfect_ **11.** Before too long—and luckily for the piranha—its victim <u>will have grown</u> back its fins and tail, and the whole process <u>can begin</u> again.

Posttest: Adjectives & Adverbs

> **Underline** the adjectives once (except the articles *a*, *an*, or *the*—do not underline those). Draw an arrow to the noun or pronoun that each adjective modifies. Underline the adverbs twice. Draw an arrow to the verb, adverb, or adjective that each adverb modifies.

1. The American game of checkers is a symbol of good-natured competition.

2. People think it is only played in quiet places by old men.

3. Players need good memories; there are 500 quintillion possible moves.

4. Checker champions are often thoughtful, patient people.

5. Players closely analyze plays to reach master status.

6. Most textbooks about checkers mainly address strategies.

7. Opening and closing moves often are given colorful names like the "Goose Walk" or the "Boomerang."

8. Bobby Fischer, the world-renowned chess master, was challenged to a game of checkers and a game of chess by George Vidlak, a top checkers player.

9. They started with the chess game, which Vidlak energetically played to a draw.

10. Fischer then childishly refused to play the checkers game.

11. An early book about the game of checkers once advised players to win without bragging and to lose without anger.

12. Bobby Fischer should have studied an etiquette book harder.

(Answers to page 205)

Posttest: Prepositions, Conjunctions, & Interjections

> **Underline** each preposition once, underline each interjection twice, and circle each conjunction.

1. It is not easy to become a firefighter, (since) training academies have entrance standards that equal those <u>at</u> the best universities.

2. The top-notch program <u>in</u> Tucson, Arizona, accepted only 42 <u>out of</u> 1,500 applicants <u>in</u> 1999.

3. Most recruits <u>for</u> the Tucson program were about 30 years old, (and) seven <u>of</u> them were women.

4. Tucson's recruits are athletic people who like risky sports: flying, skiing, scuba diving, (and) <u><u>yikes</u></u>—even rock climbing.

5. (Not only) do the recruits take medical courses, (but also) they take classes <u>in</u> fire science, physics, (and) chemistry.

6. Half <u>of</u> the recruits already have a college education, (and) the other half are continuing their education <u>in</u> other ways.

7. <u><u>Well</u></u>, the recruits obviously have to learn a lot more than how to aim a hose <u>at</u> the flames.

8. <u>During</u> training, they learn to walk a hose <u>through</u> 100 feet <u>of</u> thick mud.

9. The recruits must keep the hose pointed <u>at</u> a car tire (while) they struggle <u>through</u> the mud.

10. The hose does its best to snake backwards (because) water shoots <u>out</u> the front end <u>at</u> 95 gallons a minute.

11. The hoses (both) buck (and) kick <u>with</u> a wallop, (and,) <u><u>hey</u></u>, even the small fire hoses can break a recruit's arm (or) leg!

12. (If) you wish to become a firefighter, you need to study (and) be physically fit.

Final Parts of Speech Posttest—Part 1

> **Underline** each noun once and each verb twice. Circle all pronouns.

1. The class proved to (themselves) that (everyone) could pass the test.

2. Jeremy is writing (his) résumé; the factory where (he) worked closed this past week.

3. After (he) scribbled the orders on (his) pad, the waiter filled each glass with water.

4. The seal lifted (its) head and barked for more fish.

5. (My) aunt bought (herself) a ring, and (she) wears (it) on (her) pinkie.

6. The group gave Mrs. Crocutt a gift.

> **Review** the sentences above and find two words that fit each of the descriptions below.

1. Two collective nouns: _class, group_

2. Two reflexive pronouns: _themselves, herself_

3. Two possessive pronouns: _his, its, my, her_

4. Two nouns used as subjects: _class, group, Jeremy, factory, waiter, seal, aunt_

5. Two pronouns used as a subject: _everyone, he, she_

6. Two proper nouns: _Jeremy, Mrs. Crocutt_

7. Two nouns used as direct objects: _test, résumé, orders, glass, head, ring, gift_

8. Two nouns used as objects of prepositions: _pad, water, fish, pinkie_

9. Two auxiliary verbs: _could, is_

(Answers to page 207)

Underline the adjectives once and the adverbs twice.

1. <u>old</u> tractor
2. handled <u>carefully</u>
3. worked <u>more precisely</u>
4. <u>quickly</u> cooked the rice
5. <u>eternally</u> <u>grateful</u> client
6. they were <u>more</u> <u>confident</u>

7. <u>bad</u> breath
8. he sang <u>badly</u>
9. meat was <u>too</u> <u>tough</u>
10. <u>weekly</u> newspaper
11. newspaper delivered <u>weekly</u>
12. <u>Spanish</u> rice

Underline the prepositions once, underline the interjections twice, and circle the conjunctions.

1. We boarded the cruise ship (and) made our way <u>to</u> our cabin, located <u>on</u> the "Aloha Deck."

2. <u><u>Yikes!</u></u> The room was tiny.

3. The bathroom was so small (that) the sink was built <u>outside of</u> it, (and) <u>near</u> the bed, (but) we didn't care.

4. I hoped (that) I wouldn't awake <u>in</u> the night (and) bang the sink <u>with</u> my elbow.

5. We didn't stay <u>in</u> the room long (because) there was so much to do elsewhere <u>on</u> the ship.

6. We ate, we walked, we shopped, we swam, we danced, (and) <u><u>oh boy</u></u>, did I mention (that) we got lots <u>of</u> sunshine?

7. (Not only) were there three full meals scheduled <u>throughout</u> the day, (but) there were four snacks, too.

8. <u>Besides</u> having fun <u>on</u> the ship, we also explored several tropical islands (and) rode <u>on</u> donkeys (and) motor scooters <u>across</u> some beautiful terrain.

9. We had a great time (both) <u>on</u> (and) <u>off</u> the ship.

Final Parts of Speech Posttest—Part 2

> **Rewrite** the sentences below, changing passive verb phrases to active verb phrases. Supply a subject when necessary.

1. The fence around the compound was climbed by hordes of monkeys.

   Hordes of monkeys climbed the fence around the compound.

2. A huge feast was being served in the main dining hall.

   Waiters were serving a huge feast in the main dining hall.

3. Terry's dog was washed and brushed painstakingly to remove the skunk odor.

   Terry painstakingly washed and brushed his dog to remove the

   skunk odor.

4. Fans are being blown out of their seats by the band.

   The band is blowing the fans out of their seats.

5. The endless piles of laundry were washed by young women.

   Young women washed the endless piles of laundry.

> **Underline** the verbals. Label each using *G* for gerunds, *I* for infinitives, and *P* for participles.

1. <u>Jaywalking</u> across busy streets is a shortcut to <u>broken</u> bones.
          G   *P*

2. I have <u>to go</u> <u>running</u> more often <u>to stay</u> in shape.
               I   *G*   *I*

3. <u>Smacking</u> her lips in total enjoyment, the baby ate her <u>mashed</u> apricots.
        P   *P*

4. <u>To learn</u> how <u>to fly</u> a plane, you must enjoy <u>sitting</u> still for long periods of time.
        I   *I*   *G*

5. <u>Watching</u> kids jump in freshly <u>raked</u> leaves is an autumn tradition.
        G   *P*

6. I took up <u>snowboarding</u> last winter <u>to join</u> my friends.
                    G   *I*

7. <u>To snowboard</u> well, it helps <u>to practice</u> <u>skateboarding</u> first.
        I   *I*   *G*

(Answers to page 209)

> **Write sentences using the elements requested.**

1. (Use the possessive pronoun *my* and an adjective of your choice.)

My old guitar now hangs on my wall.

2. (Use the preposition *into* and an adverb.)

The child quickly jumped into the pool.

3. (Use the coordinating conjunction *but* and the relative pronoun *that*.)

The flowers that I planted didn't come up, but thousands of

dandelions did.

4. (Use the indefinite pronoun *everyone* and an active verb.)

Everyone booed loudly at the missed call.

5. (Use the indirect object *me* and the direct object *ball*.)

Throw me the ball.

6. (Use the collective noun *team* and the coordinating conjunction *and*.)

The team and their coach had a winning season.

7. (Use the present tense verb *likes* and the subordinating conjunction *although*.)

Although Yoshio likes to fish, he hates to clean his catch.

8. (Use the past perfect tense verb *had thought*.)

June Cleaver had thought that "Theodore" was such a nice name.

9. (Use the future tense verb *will sing* and a pair of correlative conjunctions.)

Both Mom and Dad will sing at the banquet.

Posttest: Subjects & Predicates

> **Draw** a line between the complete subject and the complete predicate. If the subject is compound, write *CS* on the blank. If the predicate is compound, write *CP* in the blank. Then circle each simple subject and predicate.

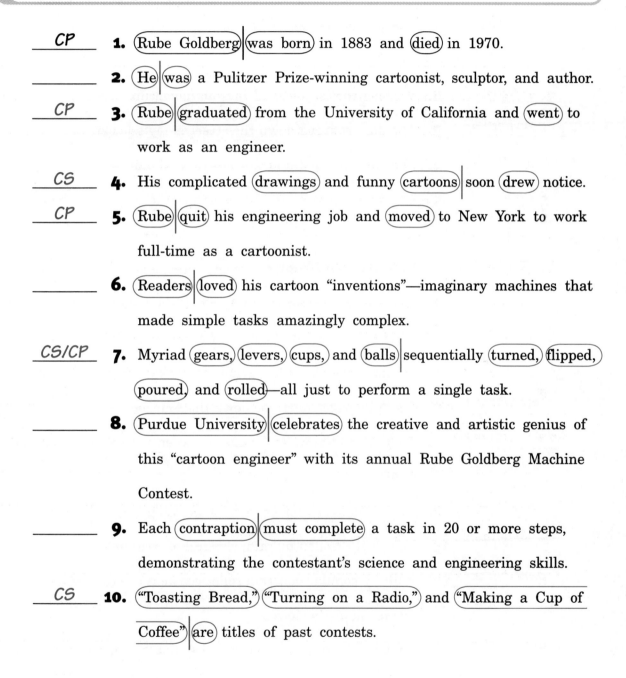

_**CP**_   **1.** (Rube Goldberg) (was born) in 1883 and (died) in 1970.

_____   **2.** (He) (was) a Pulitzer Prize-winning cartoonist, sculptor, and author.

_**CP**_   **3.** (Rube) (graduated) from the University of California and (went) to work as an engineer.

_**CS**_   **4.** His complicated (drawings) and funny (cartoons) soon (drew) notice.

_**CP**_   **5.** (Rube) (quit) his engineering job and (moved) to New York to work full-time as a cartoonist.

_____   **6.** (Readers) (loved) his cartoon "inventions"—imaginary machines that made simple tasks amazingly complex.

_**CS/CP**_   **7.** Myriad (gears,) (levers,) (cups,) and (balls) sequentially (turned,) (flipped,) (poured,) and (rolled)—all just to perform a single task.

_____   **8.** (Purdue University) (celebrates) the creative and artistic genius of this "cartoon engineer" with its annual Rube Goldberg Machine Contest.

_____   **9.** Each (contraption) (must complete) a task in 20 or more steps, demonstrating the contestant's science and engineering skills.

_**CS**_   **10.** ("Toasting Bread,") ("Turning on a Radio,") and ("Making a Cup of Coffee") (are) titles of past contests.

(Answers to page 211)

Posttest: Phrases

> **Identify** the underlined phrases as gerund, infinitive, participial, prepositional, or appositive.

infinitive **1.** Tonya's responsibility will be <u>to keep the bikes in good condition</u>.

gerund **2.** <u>Walking the dogs</u> was always an adventure.

participial **3.** The man <u>running down the street</u> is my teacher.

prepositional **4.** The baby crawled <u>up the steps</u> to the landing.

appositive **5.** The former president, <u>the woman in the tweed suit</u>, voted "no."

appositive **6.** Isn't that Jerry Ford, <u>the former president</u>?

gerund **7.** Hema made no friends by <u>flying off the handle</u>.

participial **8.** <u>Waving his hand</u>, the police officer tried to stop the cars.

gerund **9.** <u>Sailing down the Nile</u> was one of Brubaker's secret dreams.

infinitive **10.** I'm quite eager <u>to cruise down the Amazon</u>.

prepositional **11.** They sailed the River Thames <u>between London and Hampton Court</u>.

infinitive **12.** <u>To float down the river</u> in early morning is an adventure.

participial **13.** The river, <u>swollen by rain</u>, was full of tree limbs.

participial **14.** <u>Built by popular demand</u>, roller coasters are the primary attraction at theme parks.

appositive **15.** My father and mother, <u>Fred and Wilma Bolin</u>, are city council members.

(Answers to page 212)

Posttest: Clauses

> **Identify** each underlined clause below by using *N* for noun, *ADV* for adverb, or *ADJ* for adjective.

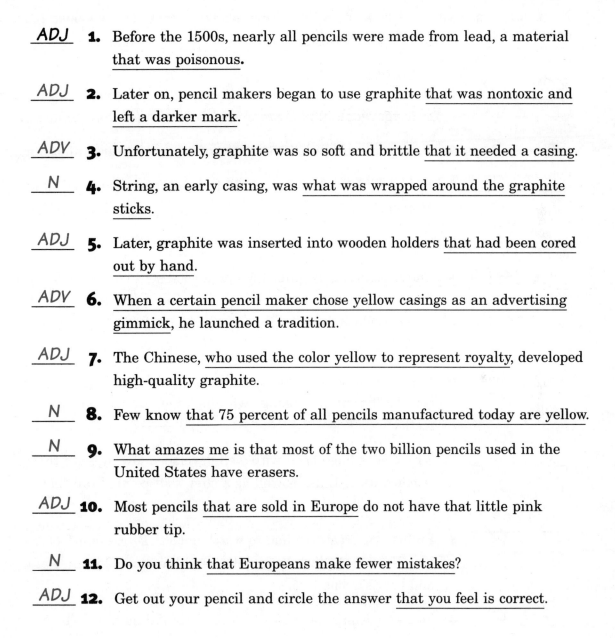

ADJ **1.** Before the 1500s, nearly all pencils were made from lead, a material that was poisonous.

ADJ **2.** Later on, pencil makers began to use graphite that was nontoxic and left a darker mark.

ADV **3.** Unfortunately, graphite was so soft and brittle that it needed a casing.

N **4.** String, an early casing, was what was wrapped around the graphite sticks.

ADJ **5.** Later, graphite was inserted into wooden holders that had been cored out by hand.

ADV **6.** When a certain pencil maker chose yellow casings as an advertising gimmick, he launched a tradition.

ADJ **7.** The Chinese, who used the color yellow to represent royalty, developed high-quality graphite.

N **8.** Few know that 75 percent of all pencils manufactured today are yellow.

N **9.** What amazes me is that most of the two billion pencils used in the United States have erasers.

ADJ **10.** Most pencils that are sold in Europe do not have that little pink rubber tip.

N **11.** Do you think that Europeans make fewer mistakes?

ADJ **12.** Get out your pencil and circle the answer that you feel is correct.

(Answers to page 213)

Posttest: Kinds & Types of Sentences

> **Label** each sentence by type on the first blank: declarative *(D)*, interrogative *(INT)*, imperative *(IMP)*, exclamatory *(E)*, or conditional *(CON)*. Add the correct end punctuation.
>
> **Next,** label each sentence by kind on the second blank: simple *(S)*, compound *(CD)*, complex *(CX)*, or compound-complex *(CD-CX)*.

CON **CX**   **1.** If you were to walk into almost any natural history museum, I'm sure you would find gigantic skeletons of prehistoric animals.

INT **S**   **2.** Have you ever seen the skeleton of a *Brachiosaurus* dinosaur?

D **CD**   **3.** These creatures stood about 50 feet tall, and they weighed about 65 tons.

E **S**   **4.** They were huge!

D **CD-CX**   **5.** The *Brachiosaurus* probably had a good sense of smell, for it had very large nostrils on top of its head, and it had a powerful heart to pump blood to its brain, which was at the end of a 30-foot-long neck.

CON **CX**   **6.** If I had to pick my favorite dinosaur, it would be *Tyrannosaurus rex,* the "tyrant lizard king," with its large, pointed, replaceable teeth.

D **CX**   **7.** *T-rex* had a huge head with well-developed jaw muscles that crushed its victims, as well as a slim, stiff-pointed tail that provided balance.

D **CX**   **8.** Prehistoric creatures had to watch out for *T-rex*'s four-foot jaw, a jaw whose eight-inch-long teeth could handle 500 pounds of meat and bones in one bite.

D **CX**   **9.** Some museums have life-sized replicas of dinosaurs, which sometimes scare small children until they realize the creatures are fake.

IMP **S**   **10.** Visit a dinosaur exhibit and see for yourself.

(Answers to page 214)

Posttest: Subject-Verb Agreement

> **Cross out** any verb that does not agree in number with its subject. Write the correction above it.

1. Unidentified flying objects, or UFO's, ~~was~~ *were* seen long before the Wright brothers flew their first airplane.

2. Medieval writings ~~mentions~~ *mention* "weirde things in the skye," and European paintings and tapestries ~~shows~~ *show* people gazing at discs in the heavens.

3. Until the Roswell, New Mexico, incident in 1947, most Americans ~~wasn't~~ *weren't* particularly intrigued by "alien sightings."

4. A rancher and his hired hands found the remains of what they thought ~~were~~ *was* an alien spaceship.

5. Government officials claimed the spaceship ~~were~~ *was* a wayward weather balloon, not a Martian wreck.

6. There ~~was~~ *were* alien corpses allegedly seen by an army nurse.

7. The army nurse reported the corpses she saw ~~was~~ *were* smaller, slimmer, and more delicate than most human adults.

8. Everyone who ~~have~~ *has* seen recent movies about spaceships ~~have~~ *has* an idea of what the army nurse described.

9. The United States Air Force ~~do~~ *does* investigate UFO sightings.

10. However, their investigative teams ~~has~~ *have* published a "Project Blue Book"—a 1,465-page report—which basically ~~say~~ *says*, "There ~~seem~~ *seems* to be nothing to report."

11. Stories like those about Roswell ~~has~~ *have* inspired many television shows.

(Answers to page 215)

Posttest: Pronoun-Antecedent Agreement

Cross out any pronoun that does not agree with its antecedent. Write the correct pronoun above it. One sentence is correct as is.

1. Parents should not send ~~his or her~~ *their* sick children to a day-care center.

2. When Jonas Salk discovered the polio vaccine, ~~it~~ *he* became a world-famous scientist.

3. Neither Mike nor Alexis needs glasses; each has 20-20 vision.

4. Both Jackie and Maria can speak for ~~herself~~ *themselves*.

5. One of the saleswomen lost ~~their~~ *her* customers because ~~they~~ *she* failed to complete each sale properly.

6. One of the shoes is missing ~~their~~ *its* sole.

7. Lamont's stories always lose ~~his~~ *their* appeal near the end.

8. The doctors finished ~~his or her~~ *their* rounds while Ms. Rue took ~~their~~ *her* break.

9. Each player on the coed team gives the game ~~their~~ *his or her* all.

10. Nadine Gordimer's and Ernest Hemingway's novels reflect ~~her and his~~ *their* real-life experiences.

11. Neither of the women sang ~~their~~ *her* part well.

12. If one of the doctors is still here, ask ~~them~~ *him or her* to wait.

13. Pat is one of those people who are continually amazed at ~~his~~ *their* employees' talents.

14. No one has found ~~their~~ *her or his* shoes yet.

15. Giorgio, along with his sisters, has learned to play checkers.

16. Either Dad or grandpa will bring ~~their~~ *his* razor and fishing gear.

Posttest: Combining Sentences

> **Rewrite** the following essay combining sentences so that they are more effective.

Lou Gehrig never missed a day of elementary school. His mother encouraged him to attend college. She wanted him to be an accountant. She wanted him to be an engineer. At Columbia University, a baseball scout saw Lou play. The scout worked for the New York Yankees. The scout signed Lou.

Lou replaced Wally Pipp at first base. Lou played the next 2,130 consecutive games. Lou played the next 14 years without missing a game, despite broken fingers, fevers, and back pain. The boy never missed a day of elementary school. The man never missed a day of baseball. They called him the *Iron Horse*.

Answers will vary.

Lou Gehrig never missed a day of elementary school. His mother, who wanted him to be either an accountant or an engineer, encouraged him to attend college. He enrolled at Columbia University, where he played baseball. When a New York Yankee baseball scout saw Lou play there, he signed him to replace Wally Pipp at first base. Despite broken fingers, fevers, and back pain, Lou played 2,130 consecutive games over the next 14 years. The boy never missed a day of elementary school; the man—called the <u>Iron Horse</u>—never missed a day of baseball.

(Answers to page 217)

Posttest: Sentence Problems 1

> **Correct** the following essay to eliminate sentence fragments, comma splices, and run-on sentences. Insert colons and periods, delete commas and periods, capitalize sentence beginnings, and lowercase words as necessary.

1 Mohandas K. Gandhi had one mission in life: To free 350 million

2 Indian people from British rule. He wanted to do this peacefully. Gandhi

3 believed people could free themselves from tyranny Without resorting to

4 terrorism or bloodshed.

5 When he was a boy, few guessed that the young, timid Gandhi would

6 someday become a great leader. After all, he was a member of the Vaisya

7 caste, which included mostly farmers and merchants. Despite such humble

8 beginnings, Gandhi went to college and became a lawyer. Soon he was

9 helping people fight racial injustice with a nonaggressive resistance he

10 called *satyagraha,* which means "truth and love with firmness."

11 Mohandas Gandhi influenced many people. In 1959, a young theological

12 student By the name of Martin Luther King Heard a lecture about this

13 great spiritual leader. King was so excited by the idea of nonaggressive

14 resistance that he bought a half dozen books about Gandhi. Using Gandhi's

15 nonviolent resistance, King helped break racial barriers for African

16 Americans here in the United States.

(Answers to page 218)

© Great Source. All rights reserved. (9)

Posttest: Sentence Problems 2

> **Correct** the following problems: deadwood and wordiness; nonstandard language and double negatives; and shifts in number, tense, person, and voice. Cross out and change words as needed.

Answers will vary.

1   About 5 million young people in the United States, Puerto Rico,

2   Guam, and the Virgin Islands ~~are members of, or you might say~~ belong

3   to/ 4-H clubs. Many ~~young people~~ join 4-H because ~~they're~~ *it's* fun and

4   educational. ~~and they learn new things.~~ Club members take part in

5   ~~educational~~ programs that aim to/ ~~hopefully~~/ help participants to develop

6   new and unfamiliar skills and become good citizens.

7   Each year, 4-H club members/ ~~who are very helpful~~/ serve their

8   communities by completing one or more special projects. ~~annually.~~ Some

9   members ~~of 4-H clubs might~~ plant trees or ~~be~~ teaching safety programs,

10   or conduct paper drives and do other environmentall~~y~~ ~~related~~ projects.

11   Other ~~4-H club~~ members ~~also might have~~ participated in food projects and

12   learn the principles of good nutrition. ~~and nutritious meals.~~

13   People who join 4-H clubs ~~try hard to~~ strive to be responsible,

14   ~~reliable~~/ fruitful, and productive citizens. ~~It is good to belong to 4-H clubs,~~

15   ~~especially one that will help you become productive and fruitful. Every~~

16   ~~4-H club is governed by this one particular motto.~~ Members are expected

17   to demonstrate the values found in ~~my~~ *their* motto: "To Make the Best Better."

18   If a person can't support this ideal, ~~you~~ *he or she* probably shouldn't ~~never~~ join 4-H.

     (Answers to page 219)

Final Sentence Posttest

> **Draw** a line between each complete subject and complete predicate. Label each compound subject *CS*. Label each compound predicate *CP*.

                                 CS

1. Durians, rambutans, and mangosteens | are weird, exotic fruits found in Malaysia.

                                          CP

2. Durians | look like spiky green footballs and smell like dead animals.

3. Some tourists | have compared the odor of the durian to rotting vegetables and public restrooms.

4. The government | discourages eating durians in public.

                                 CS

5. Train stations, bus stops, and airline terminals | post "No Durians" signs.

6. The "No Durians" sign | has a red slash like our "No Smoking" sign, but it | pictures the green fruit instead of a cigarette.

7. Restaurants | must install special fans so durian eaters won't offend other diners.

8. Despite their stench, durians | are popular because they taste heavenly.

                                  CP

9. The pulp inside | looks velvety and tastes like almond custard.

> **Identify** each underlined phrase as either gerund, infinitive, participial, prepositional, or appositive.

        gerund   *prepositional*

1. <u>Hitting the baseballs</u> thrown <u>by his father</u> made Samle happy.

        participial   *appositive*

2. The player <u>fielding the ball</u>, <u>Jonas Jones</u>, is an all-star.

      infinitive

3. <u>To hit a home run</u> was the ten-year-old's dream.

              prepositional

4. The softball landed <u>on top of the roof</u>.

      participial

5. <u>Hit by the pitch</u>, the player limped and moaned.

             participial

6. The runner, <u>having slammed into the third baseman</u>, was booed.

                  prepositional *prepositional*

7. Was that Megan who smacked the ball <u>over the fence</u> <u>into the parking lot</u>?

(Answers to page 220)

> **Identify** the underlined clauses by type on the first blank: noun *(N)*, adjective *(ADJ)*, or adverb *(ADV)*. Then identify each type of sentence on the second blank: declarative *(D)*, interrogative *(INT)*, imperative *(IMP)*, exclamatory *(E)*, or conditional *(C)*. Add the correct end punctuation.

<u>_N_</u> <u>_INT_</u> **1.** Have you ever heard <u>people talk about Stradivarius violins</u>?

<u>_N_</u> <u>_E(or)D_</u> **2.** Then you may know <u>that some sell for more than $250,000 at auctions</u>! (or) .

<u>_ADJ_</u> <u>_D_</u> **3.** During the early 1700s, Antonio Stradivari designed and built more than 1,100 musical instruments <u>that are considered "perfect" violins.</u>

<u>_ADV_</u> <u>_IMP_</u> **4.** <u>Although few exist today,</u> look to see if your violin is marked "Stradivarius."

<u>_ADV_</u> <u>_D_</u> **5.** The label doesn't mean the instrument is genuine, <u>since many violin makers have copied his style over the years.</u>

<u>_ADJ_</u> <u>_C_</u> **6.** If a violin is a real "Strad," experts <u>who have studied hundreds of instruments</u> can identify it by its wood grain, varnish, and craftsmanship.

> **Change** each verb as needed so that it agrees in number with its subject. Change each pronoun as necessary so that it agrees in number, person, and gender with its antecedent.

1. Rain or shine, Matthew walked ~~their~~ *his* dogs in the park.

2. One of the semitrailer trucks was gunning ~~their~~ *its* engine at the rest area.

3. The team ~~were~~ *was* on a phenomenal winning streak.

4. Neither Shelly nor Shania ~~are~~ *is* working at the store this evening.

5. Half of the students ~~was~~ *were* on the biology field trip.

6. A person must try to reach ~~their~~ *his or her* full potential.

7. Each of the video games ~~are~~ *is* rated for violence and language content.

8. Mathematics ~~are~~ *is* like a foreign language—using it well takes practice.

(Answers to page 221)

> **Rewrite** the following sentences to eliminate substandard language, double negatives, wordiness, and misplaced modifiers.

1. Rory didn't want none of the desserts.

Rory didn't want any of the desserts. (or) Rory wanted none of the desserts.

2. Our golden retriever, Lefty, jumped off of the raft.

Our golden retriever, Lefty, jumped off the raft.

3. Bjorn should of left the original paint color on the walls.

Bjorn should have left the original paint on the walls.

4. Maisy wanted to curl her hair, but she couldn't curl her hair because her arm was encased in a cast all the way from the top of her shoulder all the way down to her wrist.

Maisy wanted to curl her hair, but she couldn't because her entire arm was in a cast.

5. Uncle Henry held the baby smoking a big cigar.

Smoking a big cigar, Uncle Henry held the baby.

6. I haven't hardly had a chance to do my homework.

I haven't [(or) have hardly] had a chance to do my homework.

7. Waiting for the bus, the stray dog bit our neighbor.

The stray dog bit our neighbor who was waiting for the bus.

8. Did he go with?

Did he go? (or) Did he go with them?

(Answers to page 222)

Final SkillsBook Posttest

Part 1: Identifying Common Errors

> **Test** your knowledge of usage, grammar, spelling, and other common errors by answering the standardized test questions below. Each sentence below is either correct—or one of its underlined sections contains an error. (No sentence contains two errors.)
>
> **Circle** the letter corresponding to the incorrect section. If the sentence has no error, circle the *E*.

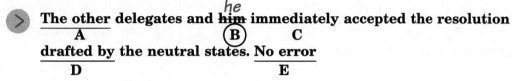

> *he*
> The other delegates and ~~him~~ immediately accepted the resolution
>   A   (B)   C
> drafted by the neutral states. No error
>   D   E

Note: The correct answer is *B*. This pronoun is part of a compound subject. It should be in the nominative case *he,* not the objective case *him.*

1. A town <u>on the plains</u> of Colombia
                A
uses solar panels <u>to generate</u> most of
        B   C
its
~~their~~ electricity. <u>No error</u>
 (D)   E

2. The people <u>from my school</u>
                        A
<u>who are going</u> to the party in Bristol
        B
are Paula, Tran, and <u>me.</u> <u>No error</u>
 C   (D)   E
                          I

3. Cleopatra who was twenty years
         (A) ,
<u>old when</u> Julius Caesar landed in
old when Julius Caesar landed in
Egypt, <u>was competing</u> with her
            B
brother, <u>Ptolemy XIII,</u> <u>for power</u> in
              C   D
Egypt. <u>No error</u>
           E

4. Glenn has seen amazing <u>tricks but</u>
                                    (A)
he doubts that <u>anyone</u> <u>can squeeze</u>
                    B   C
blood <u>out of</u> turnips. <u>No error</u>
          D   E

5. When we <u>finally arrived</u> at the
                    A
cottage, <u>a note</u> and a bowl
              B
                    were
of fresh fruit <u>~~was~~</u> waiting for us.
        C   (D)
<u>No error</u>
    E

6. Kacy's guiding <u>principle</u> when
                        A
purchasing <u>stationery</u> <u>seemed</u> to be
                B   C
finding the <u>best buy.</u> <u>No error</u>
                D   (E)

(Answers to page 223)

7. "~~Whom~~ *Who* will attend the jazz concert
         (A)
at the high school just <u>south</u> of
                          B
<u>downtown?"</u> <u>wondered</u> Connor.
   C   D
<u>No error</u>
   E

8. This <u>summer,</u> Mary plans <u>to do</u> one
        A   B
of the <u>following:</u> get a job, take
        C
classes, ~~or be traveling~~ *travel* to Europe.
            (D)
<u>No error</u>
   E

9. If Renata <u>had known</u> the song,
              A
she surely <u>would have played</u> it
        B   C
<u>for us.</u> No error
   D   (E)

10. According to the <u>coach,</u> Nikki <u>was</u>
                        A   B
the ~~better~~ *best* <u>soccer player</u> of the three.
     (C)   D
<u>No error</u>
   E

11. After Jamal <u>reached</u> the finish line of
        A   B
the triathlon, he <u>lay</u> down and
                    C
~~fall~~ *fell* asleep within minutes. <u>No error</u>
  (D)   E

12. If you travel far enough <u>north</u> from
                               A
anywhere on <u>Earth,</u> <u>you</u> will
             B   C
eventually reach the <u>Arctic Circle.</u>
                        D
<u>No error</u>
   (E)

13. "Carina, can you tell me <u>who's</u>
              A   B
the author of the <u>book</u>
                    C
/<u>Huckleberry Finn</u>/?" asked Ms.
        (D)
McLeod. <u>No error</u>
          E

14. Neither of the <u>mischievous</u>
                       A
nieces ~~admit~~ *admits* to <u>receiving</u> the
        (B)   C
<u>foreign potatoes.</u> <u>No error</u>
   D   E

15. We all noticed <u>that the division</u> of the
                      A
players into blue squads and red
squads ~~are~~ *is* not working <u>too</u> <u>well.</u>
        (B)   C   D
<u>No error</u>
   E

16. By the time she gets to Phoenix, <u>her</u>
                                       A
friends <u>will have had</u> ~~they're~~ *their* Gila
          B   (C)
monster for <u>nearly</u> a week.
             D
<u>No error</u>
   E

17. Is it true that your ~~Dad~~ *dad* met
$\overset{\text{A}}{\text{(A)}}$
Senator Bradley as the senator was
$\underset{\text{B}}{\quad}$ $\underset{\text{C}}{\quad}$
walking to his office in the Capitol?
$\underset{\text{D}}{\quad}$
No error
$\underset{\text{E}}{\quad}$

18. One also might say that she
$\underset{\text{A}}{\quad}$
was strongly ~~effected~~ *affected* by the
(B)
overwhelming gratitude of
$\underset{\text{C}}{\quad}$
her patients. No error
$\underset{\text{D}}{\quad}$ $\underset{\text{E}}{\quad}$

19. Manny packed his suitcases,
$\underset{\text{A}}{\quad}$
picked up his tickets, and
$\underset{\text{B}}{\quad}$
arrived ~~arrives~~ at the airport with very little
(C) $\underset{\text{D}}{\quad}$
time to spare. No error
$\underset{\text{E}}{\quad}$

20. The head principal and some of the
$\underset{\text{A}}{\quad}$
teachers are laying down new
$\underset{\text{B}}{\quad}$ $\underset{\text{C}}{\quad}$
regulations for student conduct.
$\underset{\text{D}}{\quad}$
No error
(E)

21. The problem of how to deal with all
$\underset{\text{A}}{\quad}$
the deer in our neighborhood ~~concern~~ *concerns*
$\underset{\text{B}}{\quad}$ (C)
many of our neighbors. No error
$\underset{\text{D}}{\quad}$ $\underset{\text{E}}{\quad}$

(Answers to page 225)

Part 2: Improving Sentences

> **Read** the following sentences, paying careful attention to the underlined sections. Beneath each sentence you will find five ways of phrasing the underlined part. Choice A repeats the original; the other four are each different.
>
> **Circle** the answer that best expresses the meaning of the original sentence. If you think the original is best, circle A. Your selection should produce the most effective sentence—clear and precise, without awkwardness, ambiguity, or errors.

 Laura Ingalls Wilder published her first book <u>and she was 65 years old then.</u>

    (A) and she was 65 years old then.
    (B) when she was 65 years old.
    (C) at age 65 years old.
    (D) upon reaching 65 years of age.
    (E) at the time when she was 65.

Note: The answer is *B*. The original and *A* are awkward, as is *E*. Both *C* and *D* are wordy.

1. The <u>team's failure to keep it's cool</u> led to a technical foul.

    (A) The team's failure to keep it's cool
    (B) The teams failure to keep it's cool
    (C) The teams failure to keep their cool
    (D) The team's failure to keep their cool
    (E) The team's failure to keep its cool

2. My dentist's office lies on the north side of town, <u>to the east of the water tower.</u>

    (A) to the east of the water tower.
    (B) to the water tower's east.
    (C) and the water tower is to the east.
    (D) and on water tower's east side.
    (E) by the water tower.

3. Has anyone told you <u>the identity of the person who painted the mural?</u>

    (A) the identity of the person who painted the mural?
    (B) of the painter of the mural?
    (C) as to who painted the mural?
    (D) who painted the mural?
    (E) about the mural painter's identity?

4. Why don't you serve <u>my friend and I</u> some of your famous <u>fried squid?</u>

    (A) my friend and I
    (B) my friend and me
    (C) I and my friend
    (D) my friend along with me
    (E) my friend along with I

(Answers to page 226)

5. The coach, as well as her staff, were very concerned about Felicity's injury.

(A) The coach, as well as her staff, were

(B) The coach, as well as her staff, was

(C) The coach, as well as her staff, are

(D) The coach or her staff were

(E) The coach, as well as her staff, have been

6. Having committed his third offense, the judge gave him the most severe penalty.

(A) the judge gave him the most severe penalty.

(B) he was given the most severe penalty by the judge.

(C) the most severe penalty was given by the judge.

(D) the penalty was the most severe that the judge could give him.

(E) the judge punished him most severely.

7. The author says that she has always written with pencil and paper; and that she always will.

(A) has always written with pencil and paper; and that she always will.

(B) has always and always would write with pencil and paper.

(C) has always written with pencil and paper, and she always will.

(D) will have always written with pencil and paper.

(E) always has written with pencil and paper and would always.

8. The last band's music was loud, with a good beat, and easy to dance to.

(A) with a good beat, and easy to dance to.

(B) had a good beat, and easy to dance to.

(C) and had a good beat, as well as being easy to dance to.

(D) had a good beat, and was easy to dance to.

(E) with a good beat, and you could dance to it.

9. I am irritated that he teases me every time when he sees me.

(A) me every time when he sees me.

(B) me every time he sees me.

(C) me, whenever I am seen by him.

(D) me at every time he sees me.

(E) me, whenever he sees me.

10. Please try to understand that I am neither for your idea or against it.

(A) for your idea or against it.

(B) for or against your idea.

(C) for your idea nor against it.

(D) for your idea nor against your idea.

(E) for your idea or am I against it.

11. Dramatically, by practicing every day, Zack's performance improved.

(A) Dramatically, by practicing every day, Zack's performance improved.

(B) By practicing every day, Zack's performance improved dramatically.

(C) By practicing every day, Zack dramatically improved his performance.

(D) Zack's performance improved dramatically by practicing every day.

(E) Dramatically, Zack's performance improved by his practicing every day.

(Answers to page 227)

12. Jennifer wants <u>to go to nursing school, become a midwife, and to deliver babies.</u>

   (A) to go to nursing school, become a midwife, and to deliver babies.

   (B) to attend nursing school, become a midwife, and to deliver babies.

   (C) to go to nursing school, to become a midwife, and deliver babies.

   (D) to go to nursing school and to become a midwife, and to deliver babies.

   (E) to go to nursing school, become a midwife, and deliver babies.

13. The sound coming from the garage was <u>like a B-52 bomber.</u>

   (A) like a B-52 bomber.

   (B) like the roar of a B-52 bomber.

   (C) like that of a B-52 bomber's.

   (D) the same as a B-52 bomber.

   (E) a B-52 bomber.

14. Pedro has had many <u>illnesses: colds, the measles, chicken pox, and the mumps, but</u> he is well now.

   (A) illnesses: colds, the measles, chicken pox, and the mumps, but

   (B) illnesses: colds, the measles, chicken pox, the mumps, but

   (C) illnesses, colds, the measles, chicken pox, and the mumps, but

   (D) illnesses—colds, the measles, chicken pox, and the mumps but

   (E) illnesses—colds, the measles, chicken pox, and the mumps—but

15. Did I ever tell you that <u>I once photographed an elephant in my pajamas?</u>

   (A) I once photographed an elephant in my pajamas?

   (B) I once photographed an elephant with my pajamas?

   (C) an elephant was once photographed by me in my pajamas?

   (D) I once photographed an elephant while I was in my pajamas?

   (E) I once photographed an elephant wearing my pajamas?

16. <u>All of the tickets were sold in less than 15 minutes on account a the group's tremendous popularity.</u>

   (A) All of the tickets were sold in less than 15 minutes on account a the group's tremendous popularity.

   (B) On account of the group's tremendous popularity, all of the tickets were sold in less than 15 minutes.

   (C) All of the tickets were sold in less than 15 minutes being that the group was tremendously popular.

   (D) All of the tickets were sold in less than 15 minutes because of the group's tremendous popularity.

   (E) All of the tickets were sold in less than 15 minutes in view of the fact that the group is tremendously popular.

(Answers to page 228)

Part 3: Improving Paragraphs

> **Read** the following essay—a first draft in need of editing. Do not correct the text directly. Instead, answer the questions listed after the essay to identify and fix mistakes. Circle the letter next to the answer you think is best.

(1) A few centuries ago, sailors in the tropics reported seeing mermaids, legendary creatures with the head and upper body of a woman and the tail of a fish. (2) Some people speculate that the sailors may actually have been seeing manatees. (3) These are large mammals that live their whole lives in the water. (4) The only other mammals that spend their whole lives in the water are whales.

(5) Manatees have heavy, gray bodies that are fishlike in form and end in a tail. (6) They can grow to 13 feet long and weigh over 500 pounds. (7) They are totally herbivorous; that is, they eat only plants. (8) Specifically, they eat seaweeds and sea grasses. (9) They eat up to 100 pounds of vegetation a day.

(10) There are three different types of manatees. (11) There is the Amazon manatee, the Caribbean manatee, and the African manatee. (12) Their population is diminishing. (13) Manatees are now an endangered species. (14) Manatees have no natural enemies; humans are causing their decline. (15) In many places humans are ruining their habitats. (16) They are running over them with boats, polluting the water with chemicals and other waste, and digging canals in their grazing areas.

(17) One type of manatee has already become extinct. (18) In 1741 explorers discovered the Steller's sea cow, which grew up to 30 feet long and weighed up to 4 tons. (19) Within 30 years, the Steller's sea cow had been hunted out of existence.

1. Which of the following is the best way to revise the underlined portions of sentences 10 and 11 (reproduced below) in order to combine the two sentences?

   There are three different types of manatees. There is the Amazon manatee, the Caribbean manatee, and the African manatee.

   (A) manatees, such as the
   (B) manatees: the
   (C) manatees, for example, the
   (D) manatees, the
   (E) manatees, including the

2. Assume you have just combined sentences 10 and 11. If you were to insert a new sentence just after 11, which of the following would create the best transition to sentence 12?

   (A) Manatees are close relatives of another animal called a dugong.
   (B) They all live in the Atlantic Ocean.
   (C) Although they live in different parts of the world, they all share the same danger.
   (D) How could they have spread to different parts of the world?
   (E) All of them live in shallow water.

3. In context, which of the following could best be inserted at the beginning of sentence 3?

   (A) For example,
   (B) Today,
   (C) Incidentally,
   (D) As a result,
   (E) Also called sea cows,

                    (Answers to page 229)

4. Which of the following would be the best way to combine sentences 7, 8, and 9?

(A) They are totally herbivorous, that is, they eat only plants, such as seaweeds and sea grasses, and they eat up to 100 pounds of vegetation a day.

(B) Being totally herbivorous, they eat only plants—seaweeds and sea grasses—up to 100 pounds of vegetation a day.

(C) Being totally herbivorous, they eat only plants—up to 100 pounds of seaweeds and sea grasses a day.

(D) They are totally herbivorous, they eat only plants (such as seaweeds and sea grasses), and they eat up to 100 pounds of vegetation a day.

(E) They eat up to 100 pounds of vegetation a day, such as seaweeds and sea grasses, as they are totally herbivorous, that is, they eat only plants.

5. What is the best way to revise the underlined portion of sentence 13?

(A) They
(B) In fact, manatees
(C) By the way, manatees
(D) Not coincidentally, manatees
(E) However, manatees

6. To conclude the final paragraph in the best way, which of the following sentences should be added after sentence 19?

(A) What a huge animal!
(B) Unless we take steps to save the remaining manatees, they will disappear as well.
(C) Isn't that a tragedy?
(D) What can you do to save them?
(E) They were insulated by very thick blubber.

(Answers to page 230)